THE BLACK SIDE

REV. E. R. CARTER.

THE BLACK SIDE

By

Rev. Edward R. Carter

The Black Heritage Library Collection

BOOKS FOR LIBRARIES PRESS
FREEPORT, NEW YORK
1971

First Published 1894
Reprinted 1971

F294
A8C17

Reprinted from a copy in the
Fisk University Library Negro Collection

INTERNATIONAL STANDARD BOOK NUMBER:
0-8369-8882-5

LIBRARY OF CONGRESS CATALOG CARD NUMBER:
78-170692

PRINTED IN THE UNITED STATES OF AMERICA

THE

BLACK SIDE.

A PARTIAL HISTORY OF THE BUSINESS, RELIGIOUS
AND EDUCATIONAL SIDE OF THE NEGRO
IN ATLANTA, GA.

BY

REV. E. R. CARTER,

*Author of " Our Pulpit Illustrated," " Descriptive
Scenes of Europe and the Orient."*

———

ATLANTA, GA.
1894.

PREFACE.

This Book comes to the public from one who has the care of a large pastorate, busy studying and praying in order to find how he may best serve his flock; it comes to a people who are not all prepared to appreciate a work of this kind from one of their own race.

The Negro, it seems to the author, is not yet ready to encourage its men of a historical and literary turn of mind—not even those who are in advance of the common people. I have often thought if I was anything else but of the race I am, I might, perhaps, be something and be able to do and also make somebody else something, but as it is, I am doubtful. Yet I feel encouraged enough not to despair, but to push forward under God's help with hope to become something and to yet make my people something. It is universally conceded that my people have accomplished what no other race in the world ever accomplished in so short a time, and notwithstanding I am not so flushed with what we have accomplished to forget the fact that we have not as yet more than got our foot on the bottom round of the ladder, whose top leads to all that a race must possess to be classed with the races who passed through centuries to lay their hands on the top round.

Generations must come and go before this can be done. It took five hundred years to make a Jew in the days of Abraham, eight hundred years to make a Roman in Cicero's time, and one thousand years to make an Englishman. We have done well for the time we have had, but not well enough. To stop and take time to argue about what we have done, is like a little boy boasting of his manly acts before he has hardly commenced in life, so we may by so doing spoil all we have done. Yet we may, as we go, on speak of what we have done for our own encouragement and inspiration of those who are to follow in our footprints.

The Black Side will be one of the factors in solving the great Negro problem.

These beautiful, cultured faces, either in the school of experience or letters, will do much in advancing a step farther in finding the answer in the great problem.

This book represents men, young and old, who have come to the front in life with everything to discourage them, no lucrative position to inspire them, nothing to encourage save the natural ability being an impetus to their successful business tact which the God of Nature has abundantly crowned the Negro with.

It is hoped that this book will do much when it is read to give a great impetus to the younger ones.

This wish is the inmost throbbing of the Author's life.

INTRODUCTORY.

BY BISHOP H. M. TURNER, D.D., LL.D.

" To everything there is a season and a time to every purpose under the heaven," says the wise King of Israel. He further says: " I have seen the travail, which God hath given to the sons of men to be exercised in it." Recognizing the truth of these divine declarations, this is evidently the time and the season for so much of the Hamitic races as includes the Negro, to take their place among the literary men of the present age, and rapidly are they doing so. Year after year additions to our libraries are made by the productions of this cold-shouldered and undervalued race.

A few years ago it was argued by the contemners of the Negro that he was not only degraded, non-intellectual, but created an inferior race by that God who is no respecter of persons, and as such was destitute of a knowledge of governmental institutions, and could not comprehend the subtilties of any system of philosophy. Another charge that has repeatedly been alleged, was that he either had no history or had been too incompetent to preserve it. This allegation is false and ever has been, as all ancient history abounds with the genius, skill, bravery, adventure and enterprise of the Hamitic races; and the same has been preserved, not only in recorded annals, but in granite shafts and heaven-towering spires. The man, or men, who make such assertions, advertise their ignorance of history upon the one hand, or proclaim their disregard of truth upon the other.

Who built the pyramids of Egypt ? Who embalmed the dead heroes that have defied the tooth of time for four thousand years ? Who founded and organized the first civil governments ? Who built the first floating crafts and spread their sails to the breeze ? Who first carved wood and chiseled stone ? What people instituted military protection, and marshalled men by thousands to the defense of their country ? Who first designed the hieroglyphics and made them the symbols of thought and expression ? Who gave Greece that alphabet which enabled Homer to write his world-famed Iliad ? Echo answers, Who ?

Read the historic lore of ages, and the footprints and finger-marks of the sons of Ham will tell the inquiring student who. But let us admit that the Negro was a degraded being during the days of our enthrallment and forced dehumanized condition. Is it any marvel ? Was not every form of our environment degraded ? Were we not brought up under a degraded people ? Were not the whites, to whom we belonged, equally degraded, and did they not close the doors of every avenue that looked toward our elevation ? But why pause to discuss that phase of this doleful subject ? Thank God, the Negro has outlived them all, and our duty now is to look to the future. While we may not entirely forget the past, we may remember it only as an incentive to achieve grander results in the progressive hereafter.

That other falsehood also, that the Negro can only attain to certain limited conditions, is equally defunct. He can, and will, do what any other people can.

Hinton R. Helper, of South Carolina, says, in his works on " Negroism," that only from the fair Caucasian race can statesmen, orators, poets, philosophers, historians, lawyers, physicians, merchants and editors be obtained, to say nothing of great authors, logical ministers of the gospel, manufacturers, adventurers, etc. Let us, however, see. From Mr. Helper's own State we have the world-renowned Bishop D. A. Payne, D.D., LL.D.; the celebrated Robert Smalls ; the learned F. L. Cardoza; the mathematical professor, J. W. Morris, A.M., LL.B., the national famed Robert B. Elliott, and eloquent Richard H. Cain, both of whom held the United States Congress spellbound; the fluent yet learned Rev. Frank J. Grimkee, D.D.; the massive-brained Elder A. T. Carr, whose granite shaft in Charleston's cemetery vies with John C. Calhoun's; and the universally-known and ever to be lamented W. J. Simmons, D.D., LL.D., and the able physician, J. J. Durham, A.M., M.D.

This catalogue takes in but a small number of the black celebrities of South Carolina, but it suffices to controvert his own position, whether set forth ignorantly or intentionally. And, if we will step ontside of the little State above mentioned, and glance over a few pages representing the present and the past, what an array of Negro talent confronts us! Will any one dare to say that Toussaint L'Overture, in point of actual generalship, was not the peer of Bonaparte, Wellington or Washington, and with the same resources to draw from would not have been more famous than any one of them ?

Shall we pause to recount the mathematical prodigies of Benjamin Banneker, who brought President Jefferson to his feet, or Phillis Wheatley, whose poetic genius won the admiration of the cultured men and women of America and Europe ? May we not well lift our hats at the name-shrine of Dr. Garnett, Samuel Ward, Dr. McCune Smith, the elder Downing, Dr. Bias, Lewis Woodson, Rev. Andrew Marshall, who lived to the age of a hundred and four years, Major Martin R. Delaney, Captain Small, to say nothing of Douglass, Wears and a long list of living lights, whose splendor-blaze eclipses the flicker ing lights of our race beraters and would-be contemners? But still they come; slowly, yet surely, the years are giving us a retinue of lights, whose effulgence enters into our homes and is bidding our ignorance, vice and immorality disappear. This is a glorious age in some respects, in which the Negro is living, notwithstanding the reign of barbarism that has been inaugurated by white mobs, lynchers and incarnate fiends, who are putting to death from a thousand to fifteen hundred of us without judge or jury, here in the midst of schools and churches, every year. But the God of the Negro still lives and holds the store of his vengeance, and will mete out retribution sooner or later if he will only be true to himself and stand guiltless before the bar of an enlightened conscience. The time is ripe for the Negro to fight his own battles, seek his own fame, achieve his own greatness and immortalize his own name. Let the young men, who may read these pages, remember that their fathers are growing old, and the mothers of the young ladies are doing the same, and prepare to supply their places and radiate a moral luster that will redound to the good of our race.

Greatness has no color; learning is neither white nor black. There is no such thing as colored intelligence, white intelligence or black intelligence. There is no such being as a white God; God is neither white nor black. There is no such place as a white heaven, where every angel, cherub and seraph is white. If there were, it would be a dull, monotonous place. Heaven, with its population, is as variegated in its color as the flowers of the forest, or as the stars in the sky.

The one great want of the Negro race is men learned in all the sciences, philosophies and professions of civilization and an unadulterated Christianity. We need great poets to write hymns in harmony with our color, and not

RESIDENCE OF ALFRED NASH.

cherish the idea that God must pull off our black skin before we can pass through the pearly gates into the New Jerusalem.

Rev. E. R. Carter, the author of the book to which this is an introduction, is grandly contributing his part in the promotion and general advancement of our race. As a preacher of the gospel, he has few equals; as a temperance lecturer, he has no superior; as a traveler and explorer, he has been to the summit of Calvary, where the Son of God expiated for the sin of the world. He has inspected the Egyptian pyramid with his own keen and observant eye, as well as rolled in the saliferous waters of the Dead Sea. He has given the public a book of near three hundred pages entitled *Our Pulpit Illustrated*, in which can be found the profile, not only of a large number of eminent colored divines and gentlemen of his own colored denomination, but of Methodists, Presbyterians and others of worth and merit. No young minister in the State of Georgia is more industrious, more venturesome, more popular, more forethoughted and more studious than he. While largely self-made, he will, in a few years, if he continues in his noble work, wear every title of distinction which the college can confer, and go down to his grave beloved, honored and wept for. I bespeak for this inimitable production a wide sale, thorough and profitable reading, not only by the members of our race on this side of the broad Atlantic, but on the fertile plains and golden sands of the sunlit landscape of Africa, where in the fullness of time, the sons and daughters of our race will achieve wonders in every department of civilization and Christianity that will be spoken of from pole to pole. Africa, the future home of her goaded and oppressed children, where they shall stand out in the grandeur of their individuality, and men like Brother Carter will have their names woven in prose and song.

THE BLACK SIDE.

CHAPTER I.

THE HISTORY OF THE BLACK SIDE OF ATLANTA.

In beginning the history of the Black Side, or the Afro-American, in this the beautiful, enterprising city of Atlanta, because of the unfriendly relations existing between most of the whites and blacks, and because of the continual effort to debar and prevent the Brother in Black from entering into any lucrative business, I am inclined to use the words of the Apostle Paul: "For here we have no continued city, but seek one to come."

This condition of affairs causes a feeling of unrest and everlasting perturbation, which unsettles all permanent thought and action, and we wonder what will be the result or outcome of such a state of affairs?

Notwithstanding the effort to close every avenue which leads to trade-learning against the negro, the Black Side of this city has surmounted obstacles, leaped over impediments, gone ahead, purchased the soil, erected houses of business and reared dwellings, which show architectural skill and taste, and, as Mr. Crumbly says, if given a white man's chance and let alone, will accomplish what any other race has accomplished or can accomplish. By the above assertions we would not have our readers believe that we think ourselves utterly friendless in our sojourn here, for there are among us white brothers who will do us any favor or show us unlimited courtesy; yet Southern custom and public sentiment clasp these in fetters so binding that they are hindered from carrying to any great extent these higher feelings, however hard they may strive to do so. In giving the history of the Black Side in this city, which will include also some prominent features of the Black Side out of the city, I am obliged to go out into this field as did Ruth into the field of Boaz, with the little handful which I have gleaned from the acts and doings of that small number of the colored people, which helped to form this now great city in its infancy. It has been said that diligence and accuracy are the only merits which a historic writer may ascribe to himself. I have spared neither care or pains to secure the facts as to the Black Side of this city.

I would not say that the work is without error; to assert such would be the grossest egotism. In presenting to the public the facts as to the history of the negroes here, I give in connection herewith a brief sketch of the oldest living Afro-American in this city, viz: Andrew Montgomery. Allow me to add that he it is who furnishes the information concerning the history of the early days of Atlanta.

Like many others of his race, he lived during the dark days of slavery, and bore the cruel treatment characteristic of those days, and having lived his four score years and more, he is still here to relate to the younger generation the history of the early days of Atlanta.

Andrew Montgomery was born at Buck Creek, Jackson county, Georgia, in the year of our Lord, 1808. He passed through all the vicissitudes of slavery life, had several owners, from whom he received both kind and cruel treatment. When quite young he became converted, and ever afterward lived a devout Christian.

At quite an early age he came to this city, then called Terminus. At this time there were not more than fifty colored persons here, and of that number only two were not slaves. These were Mary Combs and Ransom Montgomery.

Mary Combs was the first colored person to own property in this city. Her property occupied the place where Wheat street meets Peachtree street. This property she sold, and with the proceeds purchased her husband.

Ransom Montgomery, who was a brother to Andrew Montgomery, was the second person of color who possessed a share in Atlanta's soil. He obtained his freedom by a noble act of his life. This act was the saving of the lives of more than one hundred passengers during the burning of the bridge over the Chattahoochee river while a passenger train was crossing it. By this act the State of Georgia unloosed the chains of slavery which bound Ransom, made him a free man, and gave him all that land lying near and around the Macon round-house and along where the Milner spring used to be.

There were others here who owned property. Bob Webster, better known as Bob Yancy, Dougherty Hutchins and Jacob Nelson. Several others, of whom we shall speak farther on, and who became prominent in the legislature of Georgia, came after the above named persons in having a share of Terminus. Every age has its great men, and these, of whom we have just spoken, were considered as such, esteemed and held in high respect by their own race, as well as by members of the white race. Although not able in those early days to exhibit patriotism for their brothers in black, when the days of slavery were no more these rendered great service to their people and became their leaders.

CHAPTER II.

MARTHASVILLE.

The population of Terminus increased gradually until 1843, when it was able to boast of about ten white families. Now it was that the inhabitants became ambitious for a corporate name and charter. Application was made to the legislature for a charter which was granted, and the village was christened under the name of Marthasville, in honor of the daughter of ex-Governor Wilson Lumpkin, who at that time held the reins of State power in his hands.

At this time the Hamitic population of Marthasville was quite small, for not all of the ten white families were able to hold slaves, and very minute was the number of free men among the sons of Ham. Nothing noteworthy concerning them transpired to mark their existence in the village of Marthasville till the establishing of the first colored church. That came about in this way. During the days of Terminus the whites and blacks worshipped in the same house, the whites using it on mornings and allowing the negroes to use it in the afternoons, requiring them to use portions of scriptures as refer to passages like, servants obey your masters, etc. Or, to use Father Montgomery's words, "The negroes had to consider themselves the shoe soles and the whites the upper leather." But finally, there chanced to pass by one who proclaimed the Word as found in Christ Jesus, regardless of one's feelings. This enraged the whites, who refused the negroes privilege to hold services in their church house again. So Father Montgomery, of whom we have already spoken, called together a number of the brethren to devise means by which to establish a place of worship. This number consisted of Nelus

Murphy, Henry Strickland, Vine Ware, Sam Fisher and Father Montgomery himself. These constituted the Board of Trustees whose business it was to obtain ground on which to erect a house of worship. The smallest sum for which land could then be purchased was seventy dollars and on to one hundred.

Father Montgomery called upon Colonel L. P. Grant who gave him a portion of land. Major Terry selected a suitable site, on what is now Jenkins Street, for the building which was soon erected thereupon. This house stood till destroyed by the Federals.

The land was then taken from the Negroes but by order of Colonel Grant was returned to them, He then gave deeds for the same, and finally this site was sold and a more desirable one on Wheat Street was purchased, and upon it was erected another house of worship. To this was given the name, Old Bethel, and from it the present church derived its name, Bethel Church. Thus was established the first colored church in Marthasville, and it was Methodist.

The chief events of this period were namely, the appearance of the *Luminary*, the first newspaper, and the completion of the entire line of the Georgia Railroad, the first train running through from Augusta to Marthasville September 15, 1845, arriving about dark.

In 1846 Marthasville could boast of another railroad. This was the Macon and Western Railroad, which had just been completed.

After the entering of the railroad things in Marthasville took a turn. The villagers were buoyed up by these events, and feeling themselves " too great " for a village incorporation, made an effort to obtain a charter for a city. The first attempt failed, but the second was a success.

Thus after a life of five years the village gave up the title of Marthasville and received instead that of Atlanta.

CHAPTER III.

ATLANTA.

The name, Atlanta was suggested, through a letter to Mr. Richard Peters, by Mr. Edgar Thompson, as a more suitable one for the terminus of the Western and Atlantic Railroad. Thus, in 1847 the Legislature of Georgia legalized the name and change, so that, as Marthasville, Atlanta existed.

Now in the year 1848, Atlanta numbered about five hundred souls. This population consisted chiefly of working men employed by the various railroads. There were continual new developments in the city of Atlanta, but as nothing of importance concerning the Black Side occurred, we pass on to Atlanta during the war.

This period cannot be truly described, except by him who had the opportunity to witness the scenes thereof himself.

The writer was a small slave who then lived at Athens, Ga., but not so far away that he could not hear the continual report of cannon and gun, the sounds of which, echoing and reverberating, traversed the distance from this city, where a mighty struggle was going on, to the place of his abode; and often in the still hours of night could be heard those terrific roarings as of muttering thunder.

Under the flying shells which sent down torrents of fire, as in the days of Sodom, houses were consumed, and the inmates were forced to take refuge in holes or caves and flee to the woods for protection. Many, in fleeing, were seriously injured, while others, from the strokes of shells, lay bleeding and dying. This was a sad picture, a pitiable scene! The loss on the white side was great.

REV. JAMES TATE.

SAMUEL FREEMAN.

Only a few blacks suffered loss of property, for not as yet were their possessions much in real estate.

In fact, this struggle was more of gain than loss to the black side; for the shells of General Sherman were the strokes of the hammer of liberty, unfastening the fetters of the accursed and inhuman institution of slavery!

These strokes were joy to the "Brother in Black." Yes, they rejoiced when they saw the Confederate flag fall like Lucifer and trail in the dust, and in its stead the Union flag floating in the breeze, publishing to the nations that the diabolical temple of traffic in human blood had been overthrown and buried in everlasting oblivion, and the temple of the Goddess of Liberty had arisen.

> Yes, they cried for joy;
> It from the slave's eye did beam;
> His heart o'erflowed with ecstasy
> That was not all a dream!
> The cries of the long enslaved,
> We are free, we are free!

CHAPTER IV.

ATLANTA AFTER THE WAR.

In 1867, by order of General Pope, the Constitutional Convention met in the city of Atlanta for the purpose of revising the Constitution of the State of Georgia, and reconstructing the political affairs concerning the government generally. And be it said to the honor of the Black Side, that the majority who composed that Convention were some of the noblest and most patriotic of the sons of Ham. This meeting brought about fiery, bitter speeches from both sides, which made this period almost as dangerous as any preceding it. This is a chapter in the history of the metropolis of the South equally as difficult to narrate, especially when referring to the feeling which existed between the two races.

It was, however, the year of jubilee for the Black Side. Nearly all public affairs were under their control, or that of the party to which they belonged. In the same year of the reconstruction, Rufus B. Bullock was elected Governor of Georgia. Hence, the Governor, Speaker of the House and Representatives were all supporters of the principles and party of the Black Side.

All over the State, as well as at Atlanta, began the organization of leagues, which were for the purpose of inspiring and encouraging the Republican party in this State.

This league trumpet could have been heard from the mountains to the seaboard. The reinforcement of their energies and power was the backbone and the life-giving power of the Republican party. In Atlanta could be seen the sable sons of Ham, who a few days previous, handled a plow, saw, shovel or pick, crowding into the Legislature and Senate Hall, for the purpose of making laws for the government of their former owners. In nearly every seat in the old capitol hall were seated the ebony-faced men, once slaves, now free men and statesmen. There sat H. M. Turner, now D.D., LL.D., U. L. Houston, Madison Davis, Romulus Moore, Alfred Richardson, the martyr of the Republican party, James Simm, Jacob Fuller, Campbell and Bradley, and a number of others whom we cannot mention at this point. There sat they beneath the capitol dome, while the stars and stripes played peacefully in the breeze, assuring them of protection and security.

Those were times worthy of appreciation and recognition.

Every child should be told of the hands which aided in the reconstruction of the government of this grand

old Empire State of the South, should be told of the
honors conferred upon their fathers, and the high positions
to which they were chosen, notwithstanding their insuffi-
ciency in many instances.   It is the history of the race,
and is therefore worthy of repetition.   Those were trying
times ; they called forth all that there was in our fathers.
Though the emblem of peace waved over them, yet they
walked the streets in jeopardy.   However, they were
not molested to any injurious extent.   This was pre-
vented through the wise counsel of the better class of
the brothers in white ; and from the fear of worse happen-
ings than those through which the country had but recently passed.   What was true concerning the state of
affairs in Atlanta, was equally true of the State of
Georgia.   While the brothers in black were rejoicing in
their sleeves over their freedom, they were at the same
time trembling in their boots, from fear of losing their
life, so great was the hostility between the two races.
Jehovah be praised! Most of this hostility is over. The
white man is glad that the black man is free and the
black man is glad that the white man is free. The struggle is now in another line.   Education, wealth, suprem-
acy are what the races are now fighting to gain.

The first two powers the Black Side is bound to have ;
yes, determined to possess. The third never enters his
brains ; he cares nothing for it.   All he asks is a citizen's
privilege, the rights of a tax-payer and free access to
the public positions of the city, which he is compelled to
support, and whose laws he so eagerly strives to protect.
I doubt whether there are people living by the side of
another people who pay as much taxes as the Negro in
this city for the support of its government, and who
share so little recognition in the government of the city.

CHAPTER V.

THE PROGRESS OF THE BLACK SIDE OF TO-DAY.

After the Southern Cause had been lost and the country became quiet, the Negro then realized that he must act for himself. Standing alone, possessing nothing, he closed his eyes to the past to open them to the dawn of a new day.

The many hardships and privations which he had so long and patiently borne, energized him to strive to make a brighter future for himself and children ; accordingly, James Tate, who is now one of the most successful wholesale and retail merchants of the Black Side, or the average business man of the White Side, in the year 1866 commenced a grocery business on Walton street, near the First Baptist Church (white). His total stock at that time amounted to $6.00 (six dollars). He now carries a stock of more than $6,000 (six thousand dollars), in a neat, two-story brick building on Decatur street, where he has resided since 1867. This man was the first to open and teach a school in this city. He might rightly be called the father of the beginning of business and enterprise, as well as of the intellectual source. The first of the Black Side of this now thriving city to open a store, the first to open a school, the first to teach a school! From him no doubt came the inspiration for the many who have come after him. Business houses among the Black Side are now established all over this wonderful vestibule of the South ; businesses of every class and kind, from the junk to the dry-goods store.

The next event of importance in the history of the Black Side of Atlanta was the establishment of the Atlanta University. "This institution was chartered in

1867, soon after the shackles of slavery had been removed, and civil and religious liberty had been declared
the natural heritage of the colored race by the great
benefactor and patriot of modern times, Abraham
Lincoln." Though chartered in 1867, the University
was not properly opened until 1869. This inestimable
source of knowledge and instruction to the Black Side
was organized and established under the auspices of the
broad-hearted, Godly-minded Professor Edmund Asa
Ware, who, through conflicting opinions of the North
and South, came to this city to open a channel of learning for the children of Ham. Upon one of the many
hills which surround the city of Atlanta, where battles
were fought to keep the negro in bondage and ignorance,
sets this grand institution, a lasting monument to the good
man who raised it ; sending forth yearly, men and women,
boys and girls, to wage battles against ignorance, crime
and vice.

In the year 1868, under the leadership of Rev. Frank
Quarles, the First Colored Baptist Church was organized. This body consisted of about twenty-five members, among whom were John Carter, Levi Allen, Jake
Whittaker, James Tate, Orange Davis, Betsy Rucker,
Mary Whitehead and others. They first held religious
services in a car-box, in the northeastern part of the
city, on Walton street. Here they worshipped. for a
considerable time. The next place of worship was
somewhere on Luckie street, where they also held meetings quite a while. Finally a lot on corner of Haynes
and Markham streets was purchased, and a small
wooden building was put up. The membership had by
this time increased considerably, and wishing a still more
desirable site, the present lot on corner of Mitchell and
Haynes streets was, through the recommendation of
John Carter, purchased, and upon this a more commo-

dious structure of brick was erected. As the wheel of time moves onward and developments in progress are made, a new day dawns. While in the past there were none or only a few places of mercantile or intellectual resources, now Atlanta for the Black Side abounds in such innumerable places of business and of intellectual and industrial training, occupying some of the best streets and dotting the hills and borders of this fair city.

All around her borders tower, like the mighty hosts of Zion, some of the finest colleges, universities and seminaries for the Black Side, in all this Southland, regardless of class or kind! There are attached departments where youths of any age who have the power of speech can, by simple operations, be taught to read, spell and cipher, and given a practical insight into geometry without having a book placed in their hands. This form of instruction comes through the Kindergarten system, which is among the wonderful inventions of the age. In fact, Atlanta, for the Black Side, is the classic city.

On some of the most beautiful avenues and streets of this basin city are grand structures erected as altars to Jehovah, from which minarets, domes and steeples lift their heads to the azure sky. Along these same streets are many structures of brick, where various kinds of businesses are carried on.

Some of these structures are: Odd Fellows Hall, pointing upward four stories in height, on Piedmont avenue; Good Samaritan building, ascending four stories, on Ivy street; the Schell Opera House and Hall, of three stories in height, on West Mitchell street. On Marietta street, the erections of Rivers, McHenry and McKinley stand with neat brick fronts. The storehouses of Tate and Murphy occupy conspicuous places on Decatur street, while on West Mitchell street, near their beauti-

ful residences, are to be seen the two-story structures of
N. Holmes and W. H. Landrum, used as storehouses;
and, in proximity to the same, on West Hunter street, is
the handsome storehouse, with residence above, of M.
V. James. The neat storehouse and dwelling of P.
Escridge, on Wheat street, deserves special mention, for
the owner and proprietor is a man of acute business
talent. Going in another direction, we arrive at the
storehouse and dwelling of I. P. Moyer, on Peters street.
Here he carries on a flourishing business. Also on
same street are the storehouses and dwellings of King
and R. N. Davis. Such are some of the brick buildings
owned by the Black Side of Atlanta.

Returning to Wheat street, we come to the large
fancy grocery of F. H. Crumbly, where he does business
on an extensive scale. Above this place of business are
his handsomely arranged apartments. On same street
are the business houses of Pace, and C. C. Cater; the
storehouse and residence of T. M. Gooseby & Son;
the bookstore of Hagler & Co. Next in line is the
pharmacy of Drs. Slater, Butler & Co. Then, on
Fraser and Martin streets are the storehouses, near
which are the dwellings also, of Watts, Graham,
Emery, and Epps & Jones. There are other prominent grocers in the city whose names and places
of business we should be glad to mention would the
scope of this paper permit.

Briefly we mention some other enterprises carried on
by the Black Side of our business-like city of Atlanta.
Among the most prominent is that of J. McKinley,
which consists in rock-quarrying and dealing in sand and
brick. In this enterprise he employs at times more than
one hundred and fifty laborers, white and colored. Another, the Coöperative South View Cemetery Co. The
Georgia Real Estate Loan and Trust Co., of which the

Hon. H. A. Rucker is President. Atlanta Loan and Trust Co., of which W. C. Redding is President.

These enterprises show the marked ability of the Black Side in controlling and managing the most intri-cate forms of business, and is a firm denial of the asser-tion that the negro is non-progressive. It also demon-strates to the world what the negro will do if given a chance and let alone.

Just here may also be mentioned the professional pur-suits. As lawyers we have the erudite Robert Davis and the cunning, shrewd M. E. Loftin. In dentistry the famous pedestrian, Robert Badger, and the sons of the late, much lamented Roderick Badger. Let us add that there are others of our sons pursuing this profession, who will soon begin practice in this and other cities.

As we take a retrospective view of the Negro, then see him as he now is, engaged in the many enterprises, pursuits, professions and occupations, we can but exclaim like the poet :

"O, what a glorious hope is ours,
    While in this land we stay;
We *more* than taste immortal joys,
    And antedate that day."

But let us proceed. There is the firm of Drs. Asbury, Taylor & Co., known as the Friendship Drug-store. Then, that of Drs. Strong & Lockhart. All of these are skillful physicians and have an extensive practice among our people.

Those in the educational line, who are capable of fill-ing chairs of languages and sciences at the colleges of to-day are : the scholarly, linguistic Professor Wm. E. Holmes, of the A. B. S.; Professor Wm. H. Crogman, who is considered by all whose pleasure it has been to meet him, as a deep thinker, an able instructor and eloquent speaker; Professor St. George Richardson, the learned Principal of the Morris Brown College.

ALLEN'S TEMPLE.

LOYD STREET M. E. CHURCH.

GOOD SAMARITAN BUILDING.

In the public schools we have as principals: the refined, cultured, gentlemanly instructor, W. B. Matthews, of the Houston street school; the business-like and oratorical E. L. Chew, of the Gray street school; the eloquent "Boy royal of the times," F. Grant Snelson, of the Mitchell street school; and the witty, deep-thinking, progressive, self-made, Carl Walter Hill, of the Martin street school. As lady principal, there is the inestimable, Christian worker, well informed Mrs. Allie D. Carey, of the Roach street school; and of her it is truly said that nowhere is there a more intelligent, better read or better informed person in all the languages than she.

Having spoken of those who work with the mind, we now mention those whose lot it is to deal with the body. Our successful tailors are: the polite, artistic G. M. Howell; the venerable Wm. Finch, the successful Rufus Cooper, A. W. Finch, who does a flourishing business, and B. B. Brightwell, the steady. These are scarcely more than half of our successful tailors ; but this number serves to show what the Negro is doing in this line. We also have several artistic and fashionable dressmakers in our midst, and the gentle, obliging Mrs. Pennemone as milliner and hatter. Verily, the sons and daughters of Ham are applying themselves to the useful arts and professions of life.

THE GOOD SAMARITAN ORDER.

The order of the Independent Order of Good Samaritans and Daughters of Samaria was introduced into the State by the organization of Crystal Fount Lodge, No. 1, in Atlanta, Ga., on Friday night, July 9, 1875, by Rev. W. G. Strong, of Mobile, Ala., under the jurisdiction of the R. W. E. D., Grand Lodge, No. 1, of Brooklyn, N. Y.

The following officers were installed on that night :

H. R. Rakestraw, W. P. C.; Sarah Mangum, W. P. P. D.; Samuel B. Bailey, W. C.; Julia Dillard, W. P. D.; Wm. Holmes, W. V. C.; Eliza Holmes, D. of Ft.; John Davis, W. P.; Amanda Bradbury, D. of L.; S. W. Easley, Jr., W. R. S.; Beele Burkes, D. of R.; C. J. Dickerson, W. F. S.; Mary A. Snyder (King), D. of F.; Alfred Peck, W. T.; Betsy Jackson, D. of T.; James Dozier, W. Con.; Lucy Watkins, D. C.; J. H. Oliver, I. S.; Rachael Oliver, D. of K.; Peter McMurray, A. S.; Jane Scott, D. of P..

The lodge was organized with about seventy-five persons, composed of the very best people in Atlanta, among whom may be noted Mitchell Cargil, Hiram Brooks, Joseph McCants, Anderson Phelps, Rev. J. C. Riggin, Ed. Hill, Andrew Hill, Sam'l Jackson, Jackson Gates, Allen Brown, Thomas J. Henry, Mrs. J. P. McMurray, Mrs. Lizzie Lewis, Mrs. Clora Garner, Mrs. Mollie Golden, Mrs. Sully Alexander, Mrs. Amanda Hill, Mrs. Viola King, Miss Mary Garrett, Mrs. Nancy Wilson, Mrs. Lizzie Ford and others.

The list of honorary members is also brilliantly illustrated by such noted prelates as Right Rev. W. J. Gaines, D.D., Rev. S. H. Robertson, D.D., Rev. Richard Graham, and others of like note.

Crystal Fount Lodge has also furnished to the Grand Lodge of Georgia three Grand Chiefs, two Grand Presiding Daughters, viz.: J. M. Marshall, S. W. Easley, Jr., Peter McMurray, Mrs. Matilda Simmons, and Mrs J. P. McMurray, and other Grand Lodge officers, as well as National Grand Lodge officers.

The lodge since its organization has initiated into mem-

bership over three hundred persons, and has a membership to-day in good standing of about four hundred.

The secret of the marvelous financial and numeri-
cal success of this lodge is due to the fact that its treas-
ury has always been open to all charitable objects, suffering humanity, and the poor inebriate. It contributed
to the yellow fever sufferers in Savannah, Ga., in 1876,
to the afflicted in Memphis, Tenn., 1875, during the great
cholera epidemic that carried off so many souls; in this
and other ways caring for the poor, sick, afflicted, dead,
the lodge has disbursed upwards of $26,000. It has
a fine four-story brick building on Ivy street in the heart
of the city, valued as $30,000, and several shares in the
South View Cemetery of Atlanta, Ga. It was the first
of the secret orders in Atlanta to purchase real estate,
though by several years younger in the city than any of
the secret orders. In fact it has been the pioneer in every
movement looking to the advancement of "the Black
Side of Atlanta." In religion, morals, industrial, intellectual and financial progress Crystal Fount Lodge has
blazed the pathway, that others may "go and do thou
likewise."

The order is a Christian-temperance order, and its
members the world over are found in honorable stations
in life, from queens, princesses, kings, noblemen, lords,
congressmen, governors, bishops, ministers, lawyers,
doctors, laymen, professors, authors, orators, nurses,
cooks, seamstresses, laborers, and toilers after honest gain,
for the sustenance of life. Such an order as the Good
Samaritans is a power in the land and country, and is a
God-send and a blessing to mankind generally. Long
may it live and prosper.

SPELMAN SEMINARY, 1881-1893.

It is not my purpose to bring before the public the full and interesting history of the faculty of this grand and God-established institution, but rather I wish to have you know of the work which it has done, which it is doing, and which it is destined to do.

In April, 1881, there came to the city of Atlanta two consecrated Christian women from Boston, Mass., to engage in work for the women and girls of the South.

Little did Miss Sophia B. Packard and Miss Harriet E. Giles know when they entered Friendship Baptist Church and rapped at the door of the study of Rev. Frank Quarles, that they had come in answer to his prayers, and even to the prayer which he was then offering. Priscilla and Aquila had come.

After conversing with these ladies, and finding out their object, with a heart overflowing with joy and gratitude, Rev. Quarles gladly opened his church door, and on April 11, 1881, in the basement of Friendship Baptist Church, these noble-hearted and self-sacrificing women laid the foundation of the grandest work ever done for the women of the South.

The first term of work lasted only three months. Though the Southern climate was very severe, and many comforts were naturally denied these white ladies who had come to work among the colored people, these Christians felt it their duty to spend their first vacations in Atlanta, that they might learn more of the people, and that the people might learn of them and of the object in view.

During this summer they visited the homes, the Sunday-schools, gave Bible readings, organized a mission band and an educational society.

The ensuing October the second term of school opened with an increased number of sixty-nine.

The exceeding dark prospects had begun to get bright, the foundation had been laid, and, as the Lord said to Zerubbabel, he said to them: "Yet now be strong . . . for I am with you, saith the Lord of hosts."

The school had grown large enough to demand the service of another teacher, and more room was imperative.

The American Baptist Home Mission Society of the North had agreed to take charge of the work, but it questioned the wisdom of maintaining a separate school for girls. The decision was reached—the school was ever to be a school for women and girls.

The necessity for a boarding department was clearly seen, so Rev. Frank Quarles, whose sympathy was in the work from the beginning, after getting a few donations from the colored people, went North to raise money to build a boarding department. The inclemency of a New England November was too great a strain upon his Southern constitution, and he sickened and died, thus giving his life for the education of the women of his race.

In February, 1883, the old barracks, with nine acres and five frame buildings, upon a height in one of the loveliest parts of the city, was purchased. The school was moved from the basement, and the boarding department was immediately opened.

The real growth of the school was more and more plainly manifested. The "unseen hand" was constantly at work.

The third teacher, who came in December, 1882, was now to open another department—a model school—where girls could be trained to be efficient teachers in the day schools, to which most were likely to be called. The industrial feature became prominent. The students were taught sewing, cooking, house-cleaning and laundering.

This school, unlike the other schools of the kind in Atlanta, was the first to see the value of putting *mental*,
moral and *manual* training side by side, believing that the
rise of a race depends as much upon nicely kept homes
as it does upon its ability to handle Cæsar or to challenge
Euclid.

The annual progress of this school has been beyond
human conception. In 1884 the name of the school was
changed from Atlanta Baptist Female Seminary to Spelman Seminary, in honor of John D. Rockefeller's father-
in-law. Mr. Rockefeller gave the largest donation toward the purchasing of the property; he also was the
largest donor toward the erection of the first brick building, which bears his name. The chapel, office, reading
room and eleven recitation rooms are in this building.

In 1886, Union Hall, in which was the old chapel and
recitation rooms, was burned. At the time of burning it
contained the dining hall, the model school and the music
rooms. The burning of this building necessitated the
immediate erection of the second brick building, which
was named Packard Hall, in honor of the Senior Principal,
Miss S. B. Packard.

Spelman Seminary has a Preparatory Course, an Academic Course, a Collegiate Course, an Industrial Course,
a Nurse Training Course, a Missionary Training Course,
a Normal and Training Course.

THE PREPARATORY COURSE includes primary, inter-
mediate and grammar school studies. Those finishing
this course often teach in the public schools of the South.

Those completing the ACADEMIC COURSE have taken
all of the sciences commonly taught in any English course.
Some graduating from this course have held and are
holding high positions in some of the colleges which are
maintained by the Baptist Home Mission Society. The
majority finishing this course are engaged in teaching.

Others have married. From these the *model home* of the rising and future generations is hoped to come.

It is desirable that those graduating from the Academic Course will return and complete the COLLEGIATE COURSE, which is four years. This course, comprising the languages and higher sciences, was added this year.

In the INDUSTRIAL COURSE the girls are taught plain sewing, dress-cutting, cooking, house-cleaning and laundering. Much attention is given to this course, owing to the fact that while all cannot be teachers, none are exempt from properly performing the duties of our every-day home life. Certificates are awarded those who creditably complete this course.

Every woman more or less is called upon to care for the sick. To meet this demand a NURSE TRAINING COURSE was added to the Seminary in 1886. Nine-tenths of the daily deaths occur from the want of proper nursing. In this course the students are taught physiology and practical hygiene. There is a hospital, the Evarts ward, on the campus, where the nurses have the practice in nursing under the eye of a professor. There is a surgical room connected with the ward, in which cases are sometimes brought in and operated upon in the presence of the nurses.

It is well for every teacher to have some knowledge of caring for the sick. What teacher has not met with an opportunity, possibly to save life, if she had only known some of the most simple remedies which are learned in this course. A few of the students have chosen nursing as a life-work, and are earning ten or more dollars a week, working under some of the best doctors, both white and colored.

THE MISSIONARY TRAINING COURSE was added to Spelman Seminary in 1892. This course prepares those who have finished the Academic or its equivalent, to do *missionary work* in the families, churches, Sunday-schools, in this or foreign lands. This course takes in two terms of eleven months each, six months in school and five months on the field doing practical work under the direction of a teacher. The time of two teachers is given to this work. Lectures to the class from different professional men are given almost weekly. The great necessity of this work is plainly seen. It is the longing desire that all pastors will take hold and encourage the work. The Bible is the only text-book used. Expenses of this course are borne by the friends of the North.

To give the older women an opportunity of gaining an education, an Elective Course has been added specially for them. One has graduated from this course, and is doing a grand Christian work among the women of her race.

The Normal and Training Course, the last but not the least addition to Spelman Seminary, prepares graduates for teachers after the plan of the best normal schools North. Miss Griffin, from Potsdam, N. Y., is the superintendent of this course. She is ably assisted by six teachers, together with nine pupil teachers. The pupil teachers teach under the immediate eye of a regular teacher. It is hoped that ere long only teachers receiving this special training will get employment. Those who creditably take this course are awarded certificates. This course will soon occupy an immense four story brick building which is near its completion. In this building, aside from the twenty-four recitation rooms for the Normal and Training Department, there are eighteen dormitories and three recitation rooms for the Missionary Training Department, also a Chemical Laboratory and Science lecture room.

Those students wishing to become printers and whom the principals think prepared, are taught printing, which

ROCKEFELLER HALL.

GILES' HALL.

PACKARD HALL.

will enable them to get employment in many of the printing offices.

Vocal music is given twice a week without extra charge. Instrumental music, two lessons a week and a daily practice hour, is given by paying extra. You have your choice of taking on either piano or organ.

Spelman Seminary is founded upon the teachings of the Bible, therefore the Bible is taught daily to every scholar. As the result of this, two students, Miss Nora A. Gordon and Miss Clara A. Howard, were taught to hear the gracious call, replying: "Here am I, send me." They are now missionaries in Africa.

The student who does not leave this school to work for Christ and the good of all who come under her influence, has failed to carry out her instruction. The motto of Spelman Seminary, " Our whole school for Christ, "is expected to be verified in every girl who has been a member of that school.

" In 1888 a Board of Trustees was formed, and Spelman Seminary was incorporated by the State of Georgia."

The school has a nice library in which there are many valuable books, which have been donated by different friends of the North.

There is a museum in which some beautiful collections have been gathered—stuffed birds, valuable stones, and many relics from the East.

Aside from the regular courses, persons wishing to become professional dressmakers, or elocutionists, may enter and pursue said studies belonging to the profession.

There are six associations and societies belonging to this institution—Young Women's Christian Association, Congo Mission Circle, Students' Volunteer Society, Social Purity, Christian Endeavor societies, and the Lyceum. The teachers and students take an active part in the promotion of each of these organizations.

The expenses of this institution are within reach of almost every woman or girl who is desirous of an education.

Each girl has the choice of doing her own washing. There is a comfortably arranged brick laundry with all of the modern facilities. There is a regular laundress in charge, with several assistants.

Aside from the donations given by the colored churches, Sunday-schools and associations of Georgia, amounting to two per cent. of the total donations, Spelman Seminary is run by the American Baptist Home Mission Society, the Women's American Baptist Home Mission Society of New England supporting a large number of the teachers by the Slater fund, and by individuals, Hon. John D. Rockefeller being the largest individual donor. Many of the faculty, now numbering thirty-seven, whom the Lord has prospered in this world's goods, have given and are giving, their services.

Sixty-six young ladies have satisfactorily finished the academic course and are doing work in every Southern State. Two are missionaries in Africa; Miss Rubie B. Jones is a member of the faculty of the Spelman Seminary; Miss Selena M. Sloan is preceptress of the State Normal School of Florida; Miss Alice E. McEwen is an editress in Alabama; Mrs. Morgan (Ida B. Carswell) is principal of a city public school in Columbus, Ga.; Miss Essie M. Atkinson is teacher in the Gray St. School, Atlanta. Many, whose location I cannot get, are holding good positions.

There have come into this work, as have come into all others, discouragements and dark shadows, but the presence of the Lord has always been felt. The death angel has visited the institution and taken five of his consecrated ones to their reward. Each coming seemed to have been sadly realized, but none was so heart-breaking as was the calling home of the beloved and honored senior principal, Miss Sophia B. Packard, who was one of the first two who planted the mustard seed which has so rapidly grown into a great spreading tree. This sad stroke came in June, 1891. Do the women of Georgia realize their loss, is the question to be answered.

Miss Harriet E. Giles, Miss Packard's associate principal and coworker succeeded Miss Packard as principal of Spelman Seminary, with Miss Lucy H. Upton as associate principal. Under these two ladies nearly two terms have been successfully taught.

MRS. CARRIE STEELE LOGAN,

FOUNDER OF THE COLORED ORPHANAGE OF ATLANTA, GEORGIA.

This noble, Christian woman is a native of Georgia, and in this State was reared. She was a slave till, through divine providence, that great benefactor, Abraham Lincoln, set her free. While a slave she learned to read and write, the acquisition of which she has always found indispensable to her. For more than twenty years she has been in public work, and her contact with the world has been a complete education of itself. Being, for a long while, a stewardess at the depot in this city, this good woman had daily experiences of the sufferings and wants of her people.

Daily she saw hungry, half-clad, ignorant children wandering about the streets, being tossed hither and thither by the rude winds of adversity; waifs drifting down the stream of destruction! Children barefooted and crying for bread, seeking, in vain, places to lay their tired heads!

These sad sights touched the heart of Mrs. Steele, and moved to pity, she resolved to do something for the children of her race. By her industry and economy she had some time previously purchased a valuable lot on Wheat street, and upon it built a handsome cottage. She now began to think how she could better the condition of the children of her people. A divine inspiration came to her, and she grasped it eagerly; it was that she might erect a place of retreat for these little ones.

She began this arduous work by writing a short account of her life, which she placed before the public for sale. Her little book took well, and she realized an acceptable profit from it. This was the first step in the great undertaking of her life.

She then solicited aid in other ways, and to her requests many kind hearts of both races responded, and she was soon able to begin the erection of the Orphanage, which now stands a lasting monument of the great work done by this good woman.

This building is three stories in height, built of brick with a stone foundation, and well adapted to its usages. Within its walls Mrs. Logan has gathered around her fifty heretofore friendless and homeless little ones, who, at the time of their coming, were mostly ignorant and uncouth, but now are tidy, trained and being taught to read, etc.

These are taught, first of all, to pray. The older ones are being taught domestic work in all its parts, and fancy work. The boys do farm work. All attend school, which is provided for them at the Home.

They have Sunday-school every Sunday, and even the little ones of four years can repeat chapters in the Bible.

The campus is spacious and most beautiful.

The Orphanage was erected at a cost of five thousand dollars, all of which was raised through the efforts of Mrs. Logan.

She is deeply interested and wrapped up in her work, which she claims is the greatest joy of her life.

Since this noble woman has done so much for humanity, all should lend a helping hand to push forward the grand and glorious work.

Mrs. Logan has done a work which will tell in years to come.   She has placed the stepping-stones for the betterment of the race, by striving to save the boys and girls. They are the ones to be shielded from dangers and temptations.   Save, O, save the children!   God's choicest blessings rest upon him who works to this end.

Just after resigning her place at the depot, she married Mr. Logan, of New York, a Christian gentleman, a man of sterling worth.   Their ideas are mutual, both having at heart the elevation of the race; both laboring to the same end.   In Mrs. Logan he possesses a treasure rare; in him she finds all which could be desired in any one.

This Home is non-denominational; it is free to all homeless, friendless children of the city of Atlanta.   It was dedicated June 20, 1892.

Long after the founder shall have gone to her final rest this structure will still tower heavenward, and may the good work done within its limits make her memory imperishable, her name immortal.

REV. N. J. JONES,

FOUNDER OF THE COLORED MEN'S PROTECTIVE
ASSOCIATION—ABLE BAPTIST MINISTER.

Rev. N. J. Jones the subject of this sketch was born in Nashville, Nash county, North Carolina, in the year 1844, and when six years of age was brought to Pike county, Georgia, at which time he was the property of a Mr. Milton Riggins.   In 1862, when but eighteen years old, he was, for his thrift, aptness and integrity, appointed driver and foreman over a large and prosperous planta- tion, which was managed chiefly through his directions.

He also worked at the blacksmith trade, and was con- sidered a skilled and first-class workman in that line. When emancipation was declared, he was still the prop- erty of the same man, and when all of the slaves had gone, he remained with his former owner, Mr. Riggins. Mr. Jones was a great favorite with him, and until this day he highly respects him.

He came to Atlanta in the year 1866, and the follow- ing year was converted and joined the Friendship Bap- tist Church, under the venerable Rev. Frank Quarles. He has ever since labored for and devoted his Christain zeal to this church, and is a most important factor in it. He assisted largely in making the church what it is now, one of the leading Baptist churches in the State.

He was at one time employed by the firm of Messrs. Hoke, Miller & Company, and, because of his faithfulness industry and efficiency, was greatly esteemed by those gentlemen.

He is identified with many of the leading enterprises, and has enlisted his heart and hands in every commenda- ble effort which promises to promote the prosperity of his race.   In the capacity of a workman he aided in the erection of the old capitol building on Marietta street, and later served Mr. A. Landsburg, an extensive lumber dealer, whose place of business occupied the site where the Markham hotel now stands. He was made foreman over the entire business, and manager of the yard hands, and the accuracy with which he managed the business of measuring and selling lumber was commendable in no small degree. He remained with this gentleman, and after leaving him, went into the grocery business on a small scale, but by prompt attention to business, honesty and sobriety, he has built up a business surpassed by none in the city in its line. He has a large and well supplied stock of staple and fancy groceries.

In addition to his energy and arduous labors among his people, he retains the highest confidence and esteem of all good citizens of both races, who know him.

Concerning the orders and organizations of the city, he holds in some of these the highest offices in their gift. Was chosen president of a benevolent society, which office he filled with trust and ability, and from which much good has been derived.

On another occasion he was unanimously elected president of a Smallpox Society, during the time when that terrible epidemic infested our city. Through his enduring efforts, a large sum of money was collected and deposited in the James' Bank for the relief of those who might fall victims to the dreaded plague. As a worker in the Sunday-school, Rev. Jones has no peer, as there is no more useful, earnest and faithful laborer to be found. He nas been an active teacher in the Friendship Baptist church for the past twenty years, and many are the young men who have graduated from the A. B. S., who received valuable instruction in the Sunday-school class taught by Rev. Jones. It can truly be said, that no one has labored more zealously for the Sunday-school cause than

this man. Because of his activity and Christian zeal for
the cause of Christ, the church granted him license and
permission to preach the truth "as found in Christ Jesus."
He possesses a superior knowledge of the scriptures, and
his manner of expressing it is eloquent and forcible. As
a divine he stands and ranks with the leading clergy of
the State.

Along with the other noteworthy events of his life, might
be mentioned the formation of the Colored Men's Protective Association, an organization which is known far
and near, and is looked upon as being one of the best societies among the race. This large and flourishing institution was projected and founded by this good man in
the year 1886. After careful study and consideration of the
poor class of the race, he devised a means to bring them
in closer connection with that class which was more able to
help them. Thus he called a council of good men to whom
he stated his object; which was, that he desired to establish
an order or union which would take care of and help those
who were unable to help themselves. Accordingly, he,
with the council, set to work, and soon the good results
of their hard toil manifested themselves. Of course they
did not have smooth sailing. There was much opposition; but the harder seemed the struggle, the more vig-
orous grew these combatants, for they felt they were fighting for the good of humanity. Rev. Jones finally succeeded in gathering together a large mass of people from
different points in the State, and with the committee of
the following gentlemen, himself being chosen chairman
of said committee, applied to the superior court of Fulton
county for a charter. Committee, N. J. Jones, Chairman;
A. Blalock, A. Payne, H. C. Davis, A. B. H. Lowry.

December 17, 1886, the charter was received for a
term of twenty years. During the same year Rev.
Jones was elected President of the Association. During

MRS. CARRIE STEELE LOGAN.

THE CARRIE STEELE ORPHANS HOME.

REV. J. J. JONES.

the year 1887 the order had increased in number to one
thousand, and soon after to eighteen hundred.

Great and good have been the results of this order,
and all due to the noble-hearted, unselfish Rev. N. J.
Jones. Sick members receive the best attention, the
poor are cared for and the dead decently buried. This
good work is not confined to Atlanta, the society has
State rights, and, as a consequence, several branch
lodges have been established from the one of this city.
These lodges are doing creditable work, and be it said to
the honor and credit of Rev. N. J. Jones, that under his
leadership the prosperity of the lodge has been great
and rapid. As expression of the confidence placed in
him, he has been made president every year since its organization, and this without opposition. He is the acknowledged leader and chief commander, and is backed
by a number of intelligent citizens. It is an established
fact that the Colored Men's Protective Association of
Atlanta has done more to lift up fallen humanity than
any other organization in the city.

Its doors are open to all with no respect to persons;
the rich, the poor, the cast down, may enter and receive
protection, all that is needed being a reformation on the
part of those who have been or are cast down.

Those who are received must take most solemnly the
pledge which strictly requires good morals, decency
and uprightness of character, and so soon as one violates
this pledge he is excommunicated. So rapid has been
the growth of this order that the wise president saw the
need of enlarging its borders, thus giving access to a
broader field of labor. Accordingly, he called a convention to meet at Atlanta, October, 1890. In that grand
assembly were many distinguished business men from
many cities of the State. In addition to widening the

field of work and establishing better laws, the president's object was to organize a grand lodge for the State.

It is needless to say that this convention was a success under his wise jurisdiction, for he rules but wisely. The work was substantial and agreeable, the session lasting three days.

During the session the delegates from the various places united in one voice in electing Rev. Jones Supreme Grand President. Thus he stands supreme over all of the C. M. P. A. lodges.

After giving a grand banquet in honor of the president, the Convention adjourned to meet at Columbus, Ga., the following year. The Association has a large amount of capital deposited in one of the prominent banks of the city, and pays out to its sick annually from eight to nine hundred dollars. Since its organization has paid out to its members more than five thousand four hundred dollars, besides other expenses.

During the recent heavy snow Rev. Jones busied himself in looking after the poor and needy. With wagon and driver, through the snow, he was seen going from place to place issuing out provisions to those who were in need ; and by his timely aid relieved many from acute suffering.

In this fragment of a chapter, this mere outline, it is not possible to give all the good deeds performed by this godly man. He is a Christian man, affectionate in his home, pleasant and polite in his manner, with a smiling countenance for all he meets.

Rev. Jones will long live in the hearts of his people as a devoted Christian, and a leader of his people.

WEST ATLANTA W. C. T. U.

ORGANIZED MARCH 10, 1887, AT FRIENDSHIP BAPTIST
CHURCH, UNDER THE SUPERVISION OF MISS LIZZIE
STEPHENSON.

The following officers were chosen: Mrs. Ella M. Pitts, President; Mrs. E. R. Carter, Vice-President, and Mrs. M. A. Ford, Secretary.

The object of the Union is to promote the cause of temperance and morality, especially in the western part of the city. The departments of work chosen by the Union were these: Prison and Railroad Work, Press Work, Juvenile Work, Social Purity, Department of Literature.

The Union did very little during the first years of its organization except hold prayer-meetings, study temperance literature and visit the sick in the neighborhood. In 1890, with Mrs. M. A. Ford, President, regular active work began at the close of the year. The reports brought in were as follows:

Report of Mrs. M. A. Mason McCurdy, Superintendent of Prison and Railroad Work—Chain-gang visited three times; 39 books, 11 Testaments and 19 different kinds of papers distributed among prisoners; reports of W. C. T. U. sent to five different papers.

Report from Miss M. F. Pullen, Superintendent of Juvenile Work—Twenty-three talks on purity to the girls of the W. C. T. U. of the Atlanta University, and 28 talks to the Unions in the city on the following subjects: Engagements, What They Are; Engagements, What They Should Be; Care of Body, Baths, etc.; Mother's Influence; Marriage; Motherhood; Unfermented Wine; Character Building. Talks given privately to 63 persons; 23 young women took White Cross pledge.

Reports in the year closing March, 1891, were these:

Superintendent of Social Purity reported 127 pledges taken for social purity.

Superintendent of Juvenile Work, two Bands of Hope organized.

Superintendent of Work among the Girls, Miss Eunice D. Coles, reported that her class of girls had made clothing for an orphan baby; also had pieced a quilt for an orphan home in Covington, Ga. This class of girls met once a week, and sewed while some one read an interesting book to them.

At the close of the year ending March, 1892, with Mrs. E. R. Carter, President, these reports were brought in:

Superintendent of Evangelistic Work reported 21 visits made poor and sick of the neighborhood.

Superintendent of Social Purity, 23 pledges distributed, — visits made to four families, 3 public talks on purity 6 mothers' meetings.

A committee was sent to pastors of different churches to urge them to use unfermented wine on the communion table. Two surprises were given to poor families.

Through the influence of the Union enough money was raised for the burial of a poor man.

Miss M. F. Shattuck, an honorary member of the Union, gave to it $12 with which to purchase a bookcase for a library to be located in the western part of the city. A good number of books have been given by Mrs. C. C. Tucker and other friends from the A. U.

For the year ending March, 1893, the following program was sent out by our State President, Mrs. G. W. King, to be used in each Union:

On the first Monday in each month, business meeting; second Monday, science meeting; third Monday, social purity and mothers' meeting; fourth Monday, Bible reading, consecration and prayer-meeting.

During this year a number of visits were made by members of the Union to the poor and sick. Two quilts quilted for an orphan home. A room rented in which to open a library. A bookcase purchased and books marked and arranged in the case. On the opening of the library an ice-cream and strawberry festival was given, which was preceded by literary exercises.

It is the aim of the West Atlanta W. C. T. U. to continue the work begun until its influence for good can be felt from the Atlantic to the Pacific, from the lakes on the north to the gulf on the south. We shall not stop here, but continue to pray, hope and work until the whole world shall be made better for the West Atlanta Women's Christian Temperance Union having been organized.

MRS. M. A. FORD, President.

M. F. PULLEN, Secretary.

MORRIS BROWN COLLEGE.

In pursuance of the policy of the African Methodist Episcopal Church the ministers of this denomination in the State of Georgia, in 1880, resolved to build a college for the education of the young men and women.

Accordingly in 1881, under the general superintendence of Rt. Rev. W. J. Gaines, D.D., the beautiful site, overlooking the City of Atlanta, was purchased at a cost of $3,500, and thereon, in 1885, was erected the north wing of the proposed college. This portion of the building was completed and dedicated to the memory of Rt. Rev. Morris Brown, the second bishop of the A. M. E. Church. Hence the name, " Morris Brown College."

In October, 1885, Morris Brown College first opened
its doors for the admission of students eager for education.   During that year 107 were enrolled.   Since then,
many improvements have been made.   A large sum of
money has been expended in furnishing the school with
the best school furniture, as desks, seats, maps, black-
boards, clocks, globes and other necessary supplies.
The north wing was erected at a cost of about $10,000,
and last year the south wing, a building the same as the
north wing, was put up at about the same cost, thereby
making a total expenditure of about $25,000 on the two
buildings.   This amount was raised by Negroes, from
among Negroes, for Negroes of the State of Georgia.

During the first period of the history of the school it
was under the principalship of Mrs. A. D. Cary, who
was succeeded by Rev. E. W. Lee, A.M.   These principals were each zealous in promoting the welfare of the
school and, in increasing its usefulness.

In 1888 Professor A. St. Geo. Richardson was appointed
Principal of Morris Brown College, which position he still
holds with much credit.   Under his management the
school has steadily progressed from year to year.   Both
the staff of teachers and the number of pupils have been
doubled.   In 1888 there were four teachers ; now the
corps of teachers numbers eight.   The enrollment of
pupils for 1888 was 252; and at the date of writing the
enrollment for the present year is 430.

The course of instruction embraces four departments,
viz: 1st, the English Department; 2d, the Normal Department ; 3d, the Academic Department; 4th, the Industrial Department.

The English Department comprises eight classes,
taught by competent, experienced teachers, who have the
work at heart, and are interested in the moral and spiritual welfare of the pupils, as well as the development of

the intellect.   The instruction given in this, as also in the other departments, is systematic and thorough.

The Normal Department aims at giving full and sound instruction in those branches of study which are calculated best to prepare and fit the student not only for the profession of teaching, but, at the end, for the active duties of life.

In the Academic Course, the student is prepared for the higher studies embraced in the college course, and also for entering the field of business and commerce.

Although the Industrial Department is not yet fully established, it is expected to have manual training in operation and actively engaged in by the students after the opening of the next fall term in 1893.

The curriculum of studies is so arranged that on the completion of any one course the student will have acquired a good foundation for the pursuance of any higher course, or for active service in the business world should he then discontinue his studies at school.   The system of instruction is uniform throughout, and is arranged so that all the several courses are but different links in the one great educational chain that binds together the several parts of the whole system.

Music is taught to all the pupils, who are drilled in the elementary exercises of the first and second music readers.   The pupils are taught to sing with feeling and expression.   Instrumental music will be one of the new departments in the next academic year.

Drills and calisthenics form a part of the instruction to pupils in the English Department.   The various extension movements with wands, bar-bells, etc., are the ones generally practiced.

Fridays of each week are devoted to a review of the week's work done by the pupils.   Exercises, such as essays, declamations, recitations, etc., are presented by the several classes. The last hour of this day is devoted to Bible-reading and students' prayer-meeting, in which the students take a most active part, and by their interest and enthusiasm, together with the assistance of the teachers, many souls have been converted to Christ.

Upon the opening of the new building next fall arrangements will be made to accommodate, with board and lodging, students from abroad, who are now compelled to board in private families in the vicinity of the college.

In the new building it is expected to have established the Theological Department for the special training of young men about to enter the ministry.

The Academic Faculty is composed of the following efficient and experienced teachers:

A. St. Geo. Richardson, B.A., Principal, Professor of Classics and Mental Science.

Miss Carrie J. Thomas, Assistant Principal, Instructor in Science and Literature.

Miss Florence H. Martin, Instructor in History and Mathematics.

Mrs. Alice M. Hoyt, Teacher of English Branches

Miss Annie B. Thomas, Teacher of English, and secretary of Faculty.

Mrs. Ella M. Landrum, Teacher of English Branches

Mrs. I. E. Upshaw, Preceptress of Primary Department.

Miss Julia T. Allen, Assistant Primary Teacher.

In addition to the above staff of teachers Rev. S. H. Robertson, D.D., is the General Superintendent and Treasurer. The President of the Board of Trustees is Rt. Rev. Abram Grant, Presiding Bishop of the Sixth Episcopal District. Of the Executive Board Rev. E. P. Holmes is Chairman, Rev. A. W. Lowe, Secretary.

Bishop W. J. Gaines, ex-President of the Board of

BIG BETHEL.

PRINCIPAL'S RESIDENCE.   SPELLMAN SEMINARY.   DORMITORIES.

MORRIS-BROWN COLLEGE.

Trustees, has labored strenuously to place this school on
a good, sure foundation, so that its future success may
be assured and its purposes realized.

During the past five years Professor Richardson, with
his able corps of teachers, has put forth every effort to
bring this school to the front rank, so that now it stands
forth as the coming school of the Negroes in the State
of Georgia. This school is a monument to the enterprise and energy of the Negroes of Georgia.

On all their public exhibitions and concerts the students
have always acquitted themselves well, and have received
many favorable comments from both pulpit and press.
The commencement exercises reflect much credit on the
school and its energetic Principal.

Morris Brown College has graduated three young
ladies from its Normal Department. In 1890, Miss
Laurean Chandler, now teacher in Summer Hill Public
School, Atlanta; in 1892, Miss Georgia Allen, Principal
Grant Institute, McIntosh, Ga., and Miss Julia T. Allen,
teacher at Morris Brown College.

The work that is now being done is principally preparatory and normal, but in process of time the higher
courses will be fully established as the school grows
older.

Our great need is *money* sufficient to complete the entire structure of the building and equip the school with
all necessary apparatus. An endowment of about $25,000
or $30,000 would be a lasting monument to the gen-
erosity of any one who has the work of education at
heart. Should any person be thus inclined to help a
school that has thus far been helping itself without the
aid of any endowment of any sort, he would confer a
lasting benefit on the negroes of Georgia and immortalize
his name by making a bequest to this school, Morris
Brown College.

I. O. OF O. F. ST. JAMES LODGE NO. 1455.

In the year 1870, January 20, Mr. Augustus Thompson met upon the streets of Atlanta one Mr. James Lowndes, of Louisville, Ky., who had only a day previous come to Atlanta. Mr. Thompson was recognized by Mr. Lowndes by the likeness he bore to his brother who resided at Louisville, and who was a friend and acquaintance of Mr. Lowndes. A conversation arose, during which Mr. Lowndes asked Mr. Thompson if the people of Atlanta had an Odd Fellows Lodge here. Receiving a reply in the negative, he said to him that he (Mr. L.) could tell him how to organize such. The proposition was accepted, and they proceeded forthwith to discuss matters relative to it. The Lodge could be organized with twenty-five good men. Accordingly Mr. Thomson set about in search of this number. He first succeeded in gathering together six or seven good men, and on the following Sunday they met in a basement on corner Pulliam and Rawson streets, belonging to E. E. Rawson. After arranging preliminary matters they dispersed, each promising to bring some one to the next meeting. The following week they organized with the desired number—twenty-five—among which number were some of the best citizens, such as Revs. J. A. Wood, J. A. Carey and Brothers J. D. Render, A. Thompson, and others. Their next action was to write to Philadelphia to Mr. James Netum, General Secretary of Committee of Management, who forwarded the application to England. The charter was delayed for twelve months, thus it was some time before the body could be fully organized. But during this time the members cared for their sick and buried their dead, while waiting for their charter.

Finally a letter from them fell into the hands of D. B. Bowser, who had been installed as General Secretary of Committee of Management in the place of the deceased Mr. James Netum.   He wrote the body telling them so soon as their charter arrived from England he would so inform them.

In the meantime, after they had been started a period of about ten months, Rev. F. J. Peck, hearing of the movement on foot and being an ex-member from Boston, Mass., also started up a lodge and named it the Star of the South.   January, 1871, the charter and books arrived, and immediate arrangements were perfected for D. B. Bowser, of Philadelphia, to come to Atlanta to set up the lodge.   He came by the members paying him $3.00 per day, from the time he left Philadelphia till his return to that city, and also his traveling expenses, board and one gallon of beer per day.   March 5, 1871, he reached Atlanta, and during the same day set up the St. James Lodge No. 1455, one hundred members strong.

The St. James agreed to let Mr. Bowser set up the Star of the South Lodge if it would agree to pay half of the expenses, which they did.

The officers installed in St. James Lodge No. 1455 were as follows : Augustus Thompson, Noble Father; James Lowndes, Noble Grand; Rev. J. A. Wood, Vice-Grand; L. S. Smith, P. S.

The Star of South No. 1456, with sixty members and Vine Ware (now deceased) as Noble Father, was also set up.

Under the St. James Lodge a lodge was organized at Marietta, Ga., with thirty-four members.   Also one at Dalton, Ga., with forty or more members.   Then one at Augusta, Ga.

Thus it is seen from the start, the St. James No. 1455 began to work, and is still burying her dead, caring for her sick, and at this time, taking care of an old brother who has been blind for ten years; all of this time giving him from $10 to $12 per month. This Lodge has done great work. It has a lot which cost the members $3,350, and a four-story brick building costing over $11,000, making a total of $14,356. The Lodge is still growing and has a very large membership. The following brethren have done much good as Board of Directors and as Building Committee:

W. H. Landrum, M. P. V. P; W. A. Harris, Perry Calhoun, Henry Pleasant, A Dixon, Professor C. W. Hill, L. H. Cargile, Martin Alexander, Wesley Redding, Lucius Lester, Treasurer; E. B. Gibson, P. S.; Lafayette Landrum.   AUGUSTUS THOMPSON,

M. P. V. P.

HISTORICAL SKETCH OF THE ATLANTA BAPTIST SEMINARY.

THE ATLANTA BAPTIST SEMINARY, under the name of *The Augusta Institute*, was founded at Augusta, Ga., in May, 1867. It was conducted under the auspices of the National Theological Institute, by Rev. J. W. Parker, D.D.

No permanent location having been secured for it thus early in its history, it was taught at night in Springfield Baptist Church.

When Dr. Parker had been in charge but three months feeble health compelled him temporarily to suspend his labors and return North. During his absence, at his request, Rev. J. Mason Rice took the principalship and continued it until the following fall, when Dr. Parker returned to his post of duty.

Instruction was given by lectures to such ministers and deacons as found it convenient to attend, while two assistants taught females.

In November of the same year, Dr. Parker having resigned, Rev. Charles H. Corey and wife were appointed to fill the vacancy. They retained Mr. Rice, and taught with success until July 13, 1868, when Mr. Corey was transferred to the Richmond Institute, Richmond, Va.

Early in the following winter, Rev. Lucien C. Hayden, D.D., succeeded Mr. Corey in the management of the Seminary, but as the United States Educational Bureau was then establishing schools for the colored people, it was thought best to blend the efforts of the Seminary with those of the Bureau.

Dr. Hayden took charge of these schools in January, 1869. Thus, with the exception of an occasional lecture, ministerial training during that year was discontinued.

November 15, 1869, under appointment of the American Baptist Home Mission Society, Rev. W. D. Seigfried came South as the president of the Seminary. The school being still without quarters of its own, it was urged by friends that it was essential to its success that the Society should purchase a site for that purpose. Accordingly, April 21, 1870, a beautiful lot in the city of Augusta, Ga., 180 by 180 feet, centrally located on Telfair street, was bought for cash at $5,700.

Dr. Seigfried at once removed to the premises, where he had an unusually large attendance.

In the summer he went North to solicit subscriptions to reimburse the Society for the outlay in the purchase of this property. He returned early in the following autumn; but in the course of a few months he severed his connection with the institution, whose operations were a second time suspended (until August 1, 1871), when Rev. Jos. T. Robert, LL.D., was appointed to its

presidency.   A Southern gentleman of high culture and
liberal views, Dr. Robert succeeded in carrying forward
the work as none of his predecessors had been able to
do.   He conducted the school four years without an assistant.   In addition to raising funds for its maintenance,
he heard recitations five hours a day, and delivered two
lectures a week on biblical and scientific subjects.

The fifth year he had two of his advanced students aid
him in hearing classes.   In the sixth year of his connection with the Seminary Professor Sterling Gardner, an
accomplished colored gentleman, a graduate of Madison
University, Hamilton, New York, was transferred from
the Richmond Institute to assist Dr. Robert at Augusta.

Professor Gardner was eminently fitted for the work,
and did effective service, but in less than a year, after a
protracted illness, he died.   During his sickness, and after
his decease, two of his pupils, Collins H. Lyons and
William E. Holmes, aided Dr. Robert in his work.

After the death of Professor Gardner, Rev. David
Shaver, D.D., was associated with Dr. Robert as his
principal assistant, from the beginning of the session
1878-79 to the close of that of 1880–81.   A man possessed of large general information, and deeply learned in
theology and philosophy, Dr. Robert found in him a
colaborer admirably adapted to the work he loved so
well.

In the fall of 1879 the Seminary was removed to
Atlanta, Ga., and given its present name, THE AT-
LANTA BAPTIST SEMINARY.   An eligible lot of four
acres was purchased, and a commodious brick building
was erected for its use at the corner of Elliott and West
Hunter streets.

Dr. Robert continued with the school until his death,
which occurred March 5, 1884.

After the death of Dr. Robert, his first assistant, Rev.

David F. Estes, A.M., was commissioned acting president. In this capacity he served with acceptance until
May 27, 1886, when Rev. Samuel Graves, D.D., of
Grand Rapids, Michigan, was appointed to succeed Dr.
Robert. Dr. Graves is unusually well qualified to discharge the delicate and difficult duties of his position,
having had large experience as a pastor and educator.

Under him the Seminary has gone steadily forward;
its standard has been raised, its attendance increased,
and its influence widened.

As the result of Dr. Graves's efforts, the American
Baptist Home Mission Society has been enabled to secure
a lot of fourteen acres, "beautiful for situation," high
and healthful, in the western part of the city, for the sum
of $7,500, on which a building, convenient in all its ap-
pointments, 140 feet front and four stories high, has been
erected. The corner stone of this structure was laid in
May, and the Missionary Baptist Convention of Georgia,
which was then in session here, took part in the exercises
on that occasion. This building was ready for occu-
pancy December 1, 1889.

In view of the steady and substantial progress which
the Seminary has made during the twenty years of its
existence, we have reason to "thank God and take
courage."

THE COLORED PROTECTIVE ASSOCIATION,

No. 3.

In this thrifty, rushing nineteenth century, when in-
vention and enterprise are lending much in aiding the
human family in rising to the high mark of that civilization which characterizes all thorough-going, industrious
people, the negro has not shown in the least that he is

wanting on any of these lines. He has organized banking systems, building and loan associations, institutions of learning, and corporations of such nature as do aid the people in acquiring wealth in many ways which enable them to have some income outside of their daily labor.

The Colored Men's Protective Association, which is the subject of this sketch, is one of those enterprises which render many a poor man, washerwoman and mechanic's condition in time of sickness or disability less burdensome than it otherwise would have been without the existence of such an enterprise.

This benevolent enterprise was organized in Shiloh African Methodist Episcopal Church, Atlanta, Ga., August 24, 1888, by Lodge No. 1, with Robert Farmer as its President and Robert Collier as Secretary, having at the time of the organization forty-two members. Since the date of its organization the membership has grown to be 1,068. They have as a financial basis $1,633.25. They have paid out as sick benefits $842.75, and for burying the dead of the Association $275.00; for other expenses and charitable purposes $40.90. The object of this enterprise is not simply to administer to the wants of their members and to protect them in the many disadvantages that they may be called to undergo in these lines, but to stand by their fellow-men at all times and in any case of emergency or danger; and, further, to help their fellow-citizen of the "Black Side" in building up business establishments, to induce the people of the race to patronize the men of their race that are in business; and, further, to aid the unfortunate in obtaining his legal rights at this time.

The Colored Men's Protective Association has been instrumental in doing grand service to its race. Since their organization they have held their meetings in buildings owned by colored men; first, for some time in the

ODD FELLOW'S HALL.

ATLANTA BAPTIST SEMINARY.

Shiloh African Methodist Episcopal Church; then in the River's Hall, and now in the Shell Opera House, a splendid three-story building.

In the sick-room they employ the doctors of their own race, and thus build up the practice of colored physicians. Among the colored physicians Drs. I. W.. Hays and Taylor are the practicing physicians.

The Hon. Robert Farmer, who is at the head of this enterprise, is a man of wonderful natural executive power; he governs his people with the skill of a Napolean. This able man was born in the dark days of *ante bellum* times, when negroes were not allowed to learn their letters, in the county of Franklin, Ga., July 30, 1842. He is a very devout Christian minister, a straight-forward business man, a finished mechanic, a lover of his race, a man of honors and virtues that would adorn any race.

THE Mt. ZION BAPTIST CHURCH, OF ATLANTA, GA.

This is the second Baptist Church of this city. It was organized April 5, 1868, by the Revs. Dock Philip, Owen George, George Hines, M. Mitchell, Deacons Samuel Gordon, Anthony White and Milner.

The above composed the council, with the following members: Brethren James Thornton, Henry Gates, John Mackey, David Hines; Sisters Charity Owens and others, thirteen in all, and Rev. Dock Philip as pastor. This church edifice was located on Luckie Hill, where services were held for a considerable length of time.

In 1869 the church changed pastors, calling Rev.

Owen George from Griffin, Ga. He accepted the charge. During the five years of their stay on Luckie Hill many were added to the church.

In 1882 the members, becoming dissatisfied with their place of worship, agreed to move to the corner of Baker and Calhoun streets. This site was located by Rev. Owen George the pastor, and his composed trustees. They purchased a piece of land at the above named place, from Wallace & Fowler, for three hundred and fifty dollars. They erected a house of worship at a cost of $1,000, facing East Baker street. Here they worshipped till the disease of their venerable and loving pastor. After his death the church called Rev. A. W. Watson who served them two years, when for some unknown cause there came about great dissatisfaction, which resulted in the burning of their house of worship. This caused much confusion among the members and they no longer kept Rev. Watson as pastor, but called Rev. W. R. Clemons, from Greene county, Ga. This was in 1880. Having no house of worship, they went to an old box-factory and worshipped there until they could build, which they did in a short time. They marched their members from the old factory and settled them in their new house of worship, in the same spot of the first one. Their new house cost three hundred and fifty dollars. They used this house for five years, when they again became discontented, and Rev. Clemons split the church, carried out fifty-eight members and with them built a church known as Mt. Olive Church. The Mt. Zion Church being without a pastor, could not remain so, and immediately called Rev. W. L. Jones, of Roswell Junction. This was in the year 1886. He accepted the call, and soon under his wise guidance the darkness dispersed, light shone into each heart, and the prospects for advancement were bright. They moved on gradually, and

555555555

through prayer and supplication many new souls were added to their number.

The church wanted their pastor fully equipped for his high calling, so it sent him to the A. B. S. that he might gain the needed knowledge. His salary was seventy-five dollars per month, besides they giving him a comfortable home on Angier avenue.

This saying of the Saviour was a prophecy: "He that soppeth in the dish with me, has lifted his heels against me. As a proof, in 1888 Rev. Jones split this grand old church again and carried out about sixty-five members. This wounded the hearts of many. They, however, would not give up the struggle, but with Jesus as their leader, struggled on in prayer, and in 1890 called Rev. S. A. McNeal. He served them one year, when his resignation was solicited. He resigned, whereupon Rev. W. H. Tilman, from Tennessee, was chosen as pastor. He remained until June, 1892, when, without the knowledge of the members, he left them without a pastor. They heard of the good works of the oratorical W. H. Tuggle, a young pulpit divine, who was then laboring in Morgan, Putnam, Green and Rockdale counties. He was known from reputation as a preacher, praying man and a singer. He had already four churches in charge, consisting of one thousand, one hundred and eighty-six members, and found it hard to leave this field; but trusting in God, he accepted the call of the Mt. Zion Church, and was installed October, 1892. Since his acceptance very flattering are the prospects of success. Through this noble young man the church has made rapid strides toward advancement, and many wayward ones have been brought into the fold of Christ. The church edifice is among the largest of the city, and very often standing-room cannot be procured, so large is the audience.

This church is the root of more branch churches than any other in the State, six having gone out from it, being located in this city.

Surely "The Lord loveth Zion more than all the dwellings of Judea."

FLOYD H. CRUMBLY,

SOLDIER, LEADING MERCHANT, ENTERPRISING CITIZEN.

Among the prosperous men of Georgia, is Floyd H. Crumbly, of Atlanta. Of those of this city who have made the mercantile line a success, he ranks head. He has prospered and grown with the prosperity and growth of the city, and to-day is the leading young colored merchant of the town.

In commencing this business, Mr. Crumbly started at the lowest round of the ladder, but his ascent has been steady and sure. His firm resolution and strong will suffered him not to think of failure. Persevere and succeed ! were his watchwords, and these kept in view landed him safely in the harbor of success.

In the "City of Hills," May 10, 1859, the hero of our narrative first opened his eyes to the light of this world. His father was a slave, the chattel of a Methodist minister.

The elder Crumbly was a preacher to his fellow-bondsmen, in the days of servitude, and after the war he engaged in politics for a time, being a member of the Constitutional Convention of 1866, and of several successive legislatures.

The mother of the subject of this sketch was a free woman, who, just before the war, was separated from her

husband. Then, taking her son with her, she went to
Nashville, Tenn. The wife never saw the husband
again as she died in 1869. After the mother's death,
young Crumbly was brought to Atlanta and given to his
grandparents.

In the meantime, his father having learned his where-
abouts came for him, taking him under his own protection. The first teacher of young Crumbly was the Rev.
George Standing, an English minister of the M. E.
Church, a man full of good work and of the Holy Spirit.
It is not to be doubted that the principles and goodly ex-
amples of this devoted man did much to shape and
mould the character of Mr. Crumbly.

In 1876, Floyd was eighteen years old and living in
Atlanta. A recruiting officer of the United States Army
was seeking recruits for the military service, and young
Crumbly enlisted for a period of five years.

From Atlanta he was carried to St. Louis, thence to
San Antonio, where he received instruction in military
tactics, and then was assigned to Company I, Tenth
United States Cavalry, commanded by Capt. T. A. Bald-
win, stationed at Fort Richardson, Texas. Upon arrival, he was appointed lance corporal, which position he
held six months ; when he was commissioned as corporal.

At the expiration of two years he was promoted to
the rank of sergeant. This was at Fort Sill, I. T. He
was then appointed clerk of his company. In 1880, while
stationed at Fort Stockton, Texas, he was appointed Sergeant Major of white and colored troops, commanded by
Lieutenant-Colonel J. F. Wade, now Colonel of the
Fourth Cavalry. Mr. Crumbly was in the Victory Campaign of 1880, which lasted six months, commanded by
Generals Grierson and Hatch. He was discharged at
Fort Stockton after having served his country five years
of honorable and acceptable service.

During Mr. Crumbly's term of enlistment, he applied himself to study and acquired a first-rate business education. At the same time he kept up a correspondence with Miss Lula Goldsmith, whom he afterwards married.

Soon after his return from the army, Mr. Crumbly was employed by Mr. Charles H. Morgan, who was at that time a prosperous grocer, to clerk in his store at a salary of five dollars a week. He remained in the employ of Mr. Morgan for some years, and then resolved to go into business for himself. This was a bold resolve, and to many it seemed rash.

He was altogether without resources. His good name and sober habits secured for him $300 worth of goods on credit. With only ten dollars, with which he paid the first month's rent for the building in which he placed the goods above mentioned, he entered into the business of a grocer. His earnestness, honest business integrity and energy soon drew to him a good line of customers. Business prospered, and at the end of six months Mr. Crumbly began to buy the place he had been renting.

In eighteen months he had finished paying for the place, and began to buy the place next door. These places are on Wheat street, one of the principal thoroughfares of the city. On one of these lots he has erected a handsome two-story building. His trade has grown rapidly, and his stock of goods has increased in proportion, until now he has a stock of $1,500, or $2,000. Mr. Crumbly ascribes no small part of his success to the economy, devotion and sacrifice of his wife, who never failed to rejoice with him in his prosperity, and to sympathize and counsel with him in his struggle. With his wife he spent time happily and pleasantly, till the messenger Death claimed her for his own, and left him in sorrow and sadness.

The death of Mrs. Crumbly occurred October 1, 1892,

and was as an electric shock to her large circle of friends, who feel deeply her absence from their midst. In 1890 he associated himself with Messrs. H. A. Rucker, J. T. Schell, J. N. Blackshear and Alex. Hamilton in the organization of the Georgia Real Estate Loan and Trust Company, of which H. A. Rucker is President, and Mr. Crumbly is Secretary. Under these able men, this company has prospered and controls more than twenty-five thousand dollars worth of Atlanta's valuable soil. Subsequently at the session of the Grand Lodge of Freemasons of Georgia, held at Augusta, he proposed the very successful plan of a relief association for the benefit of the poor widows and orphans of deceased brethren of the order. He also has been Secretary of the Grand Lodge for more than eight years, and aided in the adoption of its present code of laws. In 1892, the Penny Savings Bank of Chattanooga, Tenn., in selecting its directors, could decide upon no better choice from this city, than Mr. Crumbly : and he was chosen one of the directors. This banking house is prosperous and reflects credit upon the Negro's financial ability. Later he was appointed by the Governor of the State of Georgia, Adjutant of Lieutenent-Colonel Thomas Grants' Staff. He possesses great military ability, and as such a man is acknowledged by all as having no equal. Mr. Crumbly is Secretary of the Board of Directors of the Carrie Steele Logan Orphanage of this city, and the founder of the Negro Historical Society of Atlanta, which body has charge of the Emancipation exercises etc., etc. Well might North Geogia be proud of such a son.

Mr. Crumbly has acquired considerable real estate and as a business man he cannot be surpassed. He is gentlemanly and courteous, pleasant and affable. The "Gate City" of the South should be grateful to her sister "City of Hills," for giving to her one so worthy of esteem, so charitable and so honorable as Floyd H. Crumbly.

J. ROBERT DAVIS,

ATTORNEY AT LAW.

J. Robert Davis, the subject of this sketch, was born at Lagrange, Troupe county, Ga., A. D. 1867. His parents came to Atlanta in 1871, bringing with them their son Robert, who was then in his fourth year. So soon as Robert arrived at a sufficient age, he was placed in the Storrs School, which was then under the unequalled *règime* of Miss Amy Williams, of Rochester, N. Y. After completing the course of study at Storrs, Robert was admitted into the junior preparatory class of the Atlanta University. By this time his young mind began to appreciate the meaning and value of study, and, he entered upon the study of the higher branches with zest ; so forcibly was he impressed with the importance of knowledge, that he eclipsed all his classmates by passing from the junior preparatory class to the senior preparatory, thus gaining a whole year by skipping the middle preparatory class.

At the age of seventeen he was fitted for college. Desiring the benefit of travel, he decided to go North, to complete his college education. He went to Lincoln University, Chester County, Penn., October, 1884.

Arriving at Lincoln, he was examined, after which he entered the junior college class. Having come from the senior preparatory class of a Southern school, his admission to the junior college class of a Northern institution, nonplused him, and not desiring to be an A.B. at so early an age, he left Lincoln University after spending about three months there, for a college with a higher curriculum, selecting Howard University at Washington, D. C.

ROBERT FARMER.

COL. F. H. CRUMBLY.

J. S. RIVERS' HOUSE.

In January, 1885, he registered in the freshman class of Howard University, college department.

He passed through the college department to within five months of completing the senior year, when there arose, between the class and the faculty, some discrepancy in which he would not yield.   So rather than sacrifice his individuality by yielding to the faculty's demands, he left his class and went to Fernandina, Fla., where he took charge of the public school of that city.

In the autumn of '89 he matriculated in the Law Department of the University of Michigan.   Here he began to prepare himself for actual warfare in this race of life.

In June, 1891, he received the degree, LL. D.   Immediately on receiving his diploma, he turned his head southward as the only field for his success in his profession.

In September, 1891, he applied for admission to the bar of Atlanta.   After passing a rigid examination before the Hon. Marshall J. Clarke, the court ordered that his license be given him.

Mr. Davis has, for a young man of his age, travelled extensively, having visited every State and Territory in the Union.   He has also visited the British Isles and the continent of Europe, and has set foot upon the soil of France, Belgium, Holland, Germany, Switzerland and Western Austria.

This young man of whom I now write is intelligent and able, besides full of energy and pluck.

He is destined to make his mark in this life among his people.

5

MISS HATTIE M. STURDIVANT,

SCHOOL-TEACHER.

In Walton county, Ga., in the little town of Monroe, March 7, 1872, was born to Eli and Martha Sturdivant their only daughter, Hattie. With her childish prattle and winsome ways, she was the joy of the household, as well as the pet of the neighbors. So soon as she was old enough she was sent to school.

Hattie made rapid progress in her studies, and her parents, desiring to give her better educational advantages than their little town afforded, moved to Atlanta, in the year 1880.

In this city, whose educational facilities are unsurpassed, they could educate their two children, their son and daughter Hattie, as they desired. Hattie was sent to a school taught in the basement of Bethel A. M. E. Church, while her brother attended another. Being diligent in study, she was soon promoted to higher classes. Her teacher then was the gentle, and amiable, and competent instructor, Miss Elizabeth Easley (Holmes).

During the summer of '82 a building was erected on W. Mitchell street. This was the Mitchell Street School, and in September of the same year, Hattie entered this school where for four years she received instruction. While a pupil there, she took the examination for county schools and secured second grade license. Now it was that her father's health began to fail rapidly, but through the inflexible zeal of the mother the children were kept in school.

In the fall of '86 Miss Hattie became a student of the Atlanta University, where she continued her studies till May, 1892, when she graduated with high honors.

While an inmate of the Atlanta University she accepted Christ as her Saviour and helper and friend ; and she now lives the true, pure life of a Christian.

She says that since she has given herself to the Lord her work seems easier, her life is happier: and you who have experienced the love of Christ can but acquiesce, for "He maketh the crooked ways straight," and " withholdeth no good things from them that walk uprightly."

Miss Hattie first began teaching by assisting Mr. B. F. Smith. She has since conducted with success her schools alone.

She united with the Friendship Baptist Church, was baptized by the Rev. E. R. Carter, and is an ardent worker in the Sunday-school.

Miss Hattie is a lady of an amiable disposition, gentle, refined and modest.

REV. ROBERT L. DARDEN,

ABLE MINISTER OF THE GOSPEL.

Among the young divines of this day who have battled with many hardships, overcome many obstacles and are now doing great and good service in the Master's vineyard, no one of them is more prominent than he of whom these words are written. His parents were formerly slaves, and at the time of his advent into this life, were in very poor circumstances; but owing to perseverance and will-power contrived to send young Robert to school during a small portion of the year. Thus his first years were spent on the farm and in the village school. Early in life there could be discovered in him signs of speech-making and oratory, which signs developed as he advanced in years, until they have reached a point which now determines our subject to be an influential pulpit orator. He encountered many difficulties, and because of his father's limited means more than once was the fond hope of one day attending a better school destroyed and scattered as the wind does the chaff. However, the time finally came, when he was given the privilege to make his own way through life; and, knowing that without education for a guide and helper, he could not be prepared for life's battles, made his way first to that grand old camp where religion and knowledge go hand in hand, the Atlanta Baptist Seminary.

At the time of his entering his worldly effects may be summed up thus. One suit of clothing, one pair of shoes, one hat, and six dollars in cash. After being in school about three months, finding himself financially embarrassed, he left and began the work of teaching, by which he was enabled to re-enter school at the opening of the next term.

So, by teaching during the vacation months, he remained in school till he completed his course of study. In 1888, realizing that he was called to the ministry, and deeming it unwise to enter so great a field without more biblical instruction, he re-entered the Seminary and took a thorough course of theology, under the efficient president of the institution, Dr. Graves. In 1890 he finished this study, and after his ordination, became the pastor of a church at Fairburn, Ga. The people of this place were not slow to find out that they had a good leader in the person of Rev. Darden, and soon the membership, as well as the congregation, increased rapidly.

Rev. Darden's next charge was the First Baptist Church, of Marietta, Ga. When he first accepted this work the church edifice was unfinished, as it had been for quite a number of years. More experienced ministers than he had left the work incomplete, and the mem-

bers to suffer. Deacons had become impatient, and all
was at a standstill till he took charge of the work. By
his labor and wise judgment the work was pushed forward to completion, and to-day the edifice, completed at
the cost of three thousand dollars, stands as a monument
to Rev. Darden's untiring zeal. It is the oldest Baptist
church in North Georgia, and has a membership and congregation of which any pastor might well be proud. He
has delivered able sermons before the different Associations in the State, but he proved himself equal to any
pulpit emergency when he delivered the conventional
sermon before the Sunday-school Baptist Convention,
held at Macon, Ga., 1892, which sermon was ordered
by the Convention to be published in all the colored journals of the State. He married Miss Daphne P. Knox,
ex-student of Atlanta University, who is refined and
gentle, and who teaches in the public schools of Marietta.
Rev. Darden is a member of the Executive Board of the
State Baptist Convention and a life-member of the Foreign Mission Convention of the United States. He has
a beautiful home in the city of Atlanta, and also a productive farm in Meriwether county, Ga. He is a
worthy young man, an advocate and defender of the
denomination with which he is identified. He is the second son of Noah and Lucy Darden, and was born in
Meriwether county, Ga., February 2d, in the year of
our Lord 1865.

MR. WILLIAM C. ROSETTE,

REAL ESTATE AND RENTING AGENT.

The young man whose name adorns this sketch is one of Atlanta's thrifty, enterprising, adopted sons. He is of a bright intellect and keen business perception. Few men would prove more serviceable, to the Black Side, in this line of business of which the undaunted spirit of this young man will make a success.

The Negroes, in the days of slavery, used to pray that the time would come when they would have men of their own race prepared to lead, conduct and foster lines of business for themselves. Providence, by the use of human agency, has answered those prayers, and we now have the men. But sometimes, because of the lack of confidence and trust imposed in them, by the very ones who prayed, I am made to wonder if these men be not in advance of those prayers. The men are here, prepared and ready, but it is a sad fact that the race is not supporting them as it should. The co-operation of the race is essential to the success of the members of that race. The success of the business into which this young man has entered depends upon the people, and that success is only gained in this way, viz.: Those among us who have houses to rent, lands to sell, should put them into the hands of our own agents, that the percentage which would make the men of other races independent might make the men of our own race equally so. Mr. Rosette was born in the classic city of Athens, Ga., 1865. His early days were spent in a private school. Later, he attended the Knox Institute of that city. His first manner of making a living was school-teaching, which he pursued several years; after which he engaged in grocery-keeping. Desiring to see some-

thing of nature before settling and taking unto himself a
wife, he sought and obtained employment over one of the
prominent railroads, and, selling his property all but two
very desirable lots, traveled for three years through many
of the States of the Union.

After having this taste of nature, he returned to his
home, where he was married to Miss Emma Eva Carey,
a former belle of Atlanta.

Soon after their marriage, by request of his wife, they
moved to Atlanta, in which city Mr. Rosette is engaged in
the aforesaid business; and, it is hoped, that the Black
Side of this city will give him the patronage which a
struggling son deserves. He is pleasant in manner, congenial and affable, and with the combined efforts of the
Negroes of this city Mr. Rosette will prove an honor to
the race.

AUGUSTUS THOMPSON, F. L. T. AND M. V. P.,

MASTER BLACKSMITH.

The subject of this sketch was born in Jackson, Miss.,
on July 8, 1837. His mother was a slave, but his father
was a freeman. His mother, Minerva Lee, with four
children, including himself, were willed to a Mr. Julius
Sappho, of Madison, Ga. So in 1840 they were moved
to Madison, The father, being a freeman, could not ac-
company his wife and children, because the removal of
a freeman to another State caused him to be enslaved.
Thus the mother and children were separated from the
father.

The early life of our subject was quietly spent. Education was denied slaves, and his chances to gain knowledge were poor indeed. However, he had a good chance

to develop his muscles. In 1855 he was apprenticed to the blacksmith trade, which he served faithfully during his apprenticeship of six years, when he was considered as a master of his profession.

His first work was at Lexington, Ga., as a journeyman, after which he was employed at Athens by the Confederate Gun Factory Company, where he made guns for the Confederacy. These guns were used in the late war. He was under Major Ferdinand Cook.

In 1863 he was detailed under Colonel Raines, and sent to Augusta, Ga., to iron off gun carriages of artillery in the Augusta Machine Works. Here he was employed until emancipated through the influence of the noble Abraham Lincoln.

In 1865 he worked as blacksmith for the Augusta Cotton Factory, and the following year married a Miss Lorie Ann Jones, who proved a true and devoted wife, and with whom he lived happily till her death, which occurred 1888. During their union there were no children given them.

From 1866 to 1870 Mr. Thompson worked incessantly for the Georgia Railroad in one or more places. At one time worked in Augusta under Colonel Frost and Mr. McDuffie as car-builder, ironing off passenger coaches. He next removed to Union Point, Ga., where he was blacksmith of that entire line of railroad.

In 1870, desiring to better his condition, he came to Atlanta, and soon obtained work in the State road shops as a boiler manufacturer, where he remained during the Messrs. Bullock and Blodgett management of that road. When the road was leased to Jos. E. Brown he was suspended.

Not being satisfied without employment, Mr. Thompson began a business for himself, which he has ever since pursued both profitably and creditably to himself. By

REV. ROBERT L. DARDEN.

AUGUSTUS THOMPSON.

REV. W. M. FINCH.

hard work and temperate habits he has realized a snug
little fortune, and is well prepared for rainy days. He
does business on South Pryor street, rear of No. 69.

Being thoroughly acquainted with his trade, and rendering satisfaction to all patronizers, he is never without
a pretty good supply of work. May he continue in the
path of success.

In the latter part of the year 1870 Mr. Thompson met
a Mr. James Lowndes of Louisville, Ky., who was a
member of the order of Odd Fellows, and who had a
"general law" governing the order of the G. U. O. of
O. F. They conversed together concerning Odd Fellow-
ism. Mr. Thompson became deeply interested in it.
Ideas were exchanged, plans were arranged, and the or-
ganizing, through the efforts of Mr. Thompson, of the
first colored lodge of Odd Fellows in the Empire State
of the South was the result. He next organized a lodge
at Marietta, then one at Dalton, Ga., and from these have
sprung many other lodges.

It is with pride and pleasure that Mr. Thompson re-
calls those days, and now looks upon the result of his
work. Ah, verily we reap what we sow. These grand
institutions have done much toward helping and uplifting
the Negro race. He is still a member and trustee of the
oldest lodge in this State.

The enterprising spirit of this man would not permit
him to be satisfied with a mere organization. He desired more—a home for this organization—so he brought
the matter before the Assembly, which discussed it fully,
finally deciding in favor of Mr. Thompson's plans for a
home, and now, through his influence, stands a fine four-
story brick building, which should reflect credit on any
race, and is an ornament to any city. To show their appreciation of the founder, this lodge has made him an

honorary member, and this but extends to him the deserved merit.

Mr. Thompson is a man who deals squarely and honestly with and by his fellow-men, and commands the respect of both races.

In 1889 he was happily wedded to Miss Katie McClendon, in whom he finds a helpmate true, and who shares his cares and happiness with him.

In September, 1892, he was converted and united with the A. M. E. Church under the present pastor, Rev. Larry Thomas.

Mr. Thompson is a Christian man, a law-abiding citizen, and a true friend to his race. His neat and comfortable home is on Connally street, No. 157. May God's choicest blessings rest upon all such good and useful men.

REV. WILLIAM FINCH,

EX-CITY COUNCILMAN—PREACHER—TAILOR.

No citizen of the city of Atlanta is better known than the one whose name appears at the top of this page. All who have known him have felt themselves honored by the acquaintance.

That part of life over which he has passed has been an inspiration for good to many a youth. To say that he is a benefactor of the race is putting it mildly. No one has ever sought his sympathy and received it not. None have ever, in time of distress or trouble, applied to this man for assistance, financial or otherwise, and been denied or turned away unaided.

Small in stature, yet in his bosom rests a magnanimous heart. He bears malice toward none, and has charity for all. Even in those " cruel days," to his oppressors he was ever kind and obliging. In those trying times, when the enemy, while fighting to bind more tightly the chains of servitude, became wounded, with his own hands would William dress their wounds, administer to their wants, and soothe their sorrows. Besides exhibiting the grandeur of his soul in thismanner, he was often the instrument of saving for his master, and sometimes others, much of their gold, silver and valuables. He tells many interesting anecdotes of war times, which with his permission the writer would be glad to record.

This worthy man was born in the county of Wilkes, at Washington, Ga., during the days of servitude, and of a slave mother. At the age of twelve he went to live with Judge Andrews, in the same county. He stayed with Judge Andrews four years, at the expiration of which he went to Athens to stay with Chief Justice J. H. Lumpkin. This was the year 1848. Spending several years in the employ of Mr. Lumpkin, he afterward went to the war, where he passed through the hottest of the struggle. Returning, he again made his abode with Judge Andrews and remained with him till the strife ended, a result whereof was the liberation of six million slaves. In gratitude to the Union army for his freedom, Mr. Finch made a beautiful United States flag which he presented to the 144th New York Regiment.

He was deeply interested in the welfare and elevation of his people, and having, by his own efforts and assistance from his former owners, acquired some education, he resolved to do what he could toward instructing them. Accordingly he opened and taught the first school for the Negro in that part of the State.

In 1854 he married Miss Laura Wright, with whom he passed life happily till 1876, when death severed the union. He was apprenticed to the tailor's trade at the age of fifteen, and becoming an efficient tailor, in 1866 he

went to Augusta, Ga., to engage in the business.   He
remained in Augusta two years, when, hoping to better his financial affairs, he came to Atlanta, and, with Mr.
Danwell Brydie as partner, opened business in this city.
He came to Atlanta fifty dollars in debt and with six children whose support rested entirely upon him.   By sobriety and close attention to business he soon canceled the
debt, educated his children, and besides purchased a portion of land on what is now the beautiful Edgewood
avenue, on which he erected a cosy cottage, now worth
$6,000.

In 1881 he married Miss Minnie Vason, of Madison,
Ga., who is charming in manner and appearance.

Mr. Finch was at one time a member of the city
council, the only Negro who has ever enjoyed that honor
in this city.   While a member he used every effort to
bring about a state of affairs by which his people could be
benefited.   He was the originator of the plan to have
public schools for Negro children, and after the establishment of the same he was the first to agitate the query:
Should the whites teach the Negro children, while among
the Negroes were able, competent teachers?   Every resident of our city is aware of the result.   Every public
school in the city for Negro children is supplied with
Negro instructors.   Of course Mr. Finch met much opposition, and at times the desired result was almost despaired of; but his untiring energy failed him not, and
at last his labor was rewarded.

In July, 1848, he was converted, joined the African
Methodist Episcopal Church under Rev. Samuel Antony,
and has from that time onward been a faithful worker in
the church and cause of Christ.   March 15, 1868, he was
ordained to the ministry by Bishops Alexander and Wayman.   Lastly, he was ordained as elder of the African

Methodist Episcopal Church, by Bishop T. M. D. Ward,
May 9, 1876.

The eventful and successful career of this man is well
worth perusal. He ascribes much of his success in his
business life to the conversations which used many years
ago to occur between himself and Chief Justice Lumpkin
while he lived at Athens in the Justice's service. Many a
night until the clock would strike the midnight hour they
would be conversing, consulting and advising with each
other.

He was always fond of horses and has for several
years owned fine ones. He tells a little anecdote concerning his being able to keep them. Riding along the
streets one day he was asked by a white friend:

"How is it, Finch, that you are able to keep horses to
ride while I have to walk!"

To which Mr. Finch replied in this language:

"Do you drink beer, etc., smoke, chew tobacco; and
if so, how much does the use of them cost you?"

Receiving yes to his questions, he again remarked:

"*I do neither*. This is why I am able to keep horses to
ride. The money you spend foolishly for such things I
save. Do likewise and you too can ride."

He is a great temperance advocate, an honor to the
race, and the pride of his church.

MR. FRANK T. HOWARD,

SUCCESSFUL UNDERTAKER AND EMBALMER.

Atlanta is behind in nothing. Within her broad limits
every industry, trade, business enterprise and profession,
and everything it takes to make a city, are to be found.
In the line of business of which I now write she is sur-

passed by no city, and in this business here of the Black
Side no one is more noted than the young man whose
name is written above this article. He is the eldest son
of the well-known David T. Howard, of this city, and
was born December 10, A. D. 1871, in Atlanta, Ga.
At the age of seven young Howard was sent to the
Storrs School, which he attended till he finished the
course of study there, which he did at the age of fourteen.

Then he entered the college preparatory at Atlanta
University, and when he reached his seventeenth year
was prepared for the college course. He continued in
college till he finished the freshman year. He also attended the Knowles Industrial School, connected with
the University, and acquired the skilled use of tools.
Desiring to put into practice this valuable knowledge obtained at Knowles, he left school and associated himself
in business with his father, and to the father the son is
indispensable. He manufactures and manages the manufacturing of most of his fine caskets and coffins, some
of which equal those made at the factories of the North.
Young Howard has the reputation of being the fastest
coffin trimmer in Atlanta. He has been known to make,
paint and trim a hospital case in one hour.

He is also a skillful embalmer, and embalms for the
"State Anatomical Board of Georgia." He is successful in his business, numbering his subjects by the scores.

Aside from the more solemn works of life, he is very
fond of athletic sports. During the season of 1892 Mr.
Howard very successfully managed a baseball team,
which played in several Southern cities under his direction. He is the possessor of a very fine-blooded trotting
horse, which has made a fine record. Mrs. Ella B.
Howard, the mother of this young man, is a charitable,
Christian lady, and devotes much of her time to charita-

ble and temperance work, and is greatly loved by all
who know her.

Mr. Frank Howard is a young man of fine intellect,
jovial and courteous, and is in good circumstances, his
father having accumulated much real estate. That he
may live many years, be an honor to his race, and ascend
the ladder of fame, is the earnest wish of the writer.

REV. M. V. WHITE.

RISING BAPTIST DIVINE.

This worthy young man was born in Upson county,
Ga., March 10, 1858. Being deprived of educational
advantages he did not learn the alphabet till he was fourteen years of age.

In 1877 he went to Hampton, Ga., where he was employed as a farm laborer for the salary of $6.00 per month.
His employer agreed also to send him to school during
the three months term. Young White was very studious and soon learned to spell, read and write. He next
went to Jonesboro, Ga., at which place he also did farm
work.

Being the son of a good Christian woman the precepts
taught him in early youth, and the prayers he had been
wont to say at her knees, followed him through boyhood
to manhood, and in 1880 Mr. White was converted and
united with the Baptist Church. During the same year
he married a Miss Vinie Lawrence. It was now that
Mr. White began to realize that there was a higher
sphere for him to fill—a nobler work to do. From
Jonesboro he moved into Atlanta, and soon afterward he
felt that he was called to the ministry. To better pre-

pare himself for the great work to which he had been called, he entered the Atlanta Baptist Seminary in 1877, and while pursuing his studies was offered the pastorate of a church in this city. He accepted this, and under his wise, good guidance many souls were brought to Christ. He was next principal of the school at Tallapoosa, Ga. Here he remained till called to a church at Powder Springs, Ga. This was a poor charge, but through the perseverance and patience of this good man, the work soon revived and many came into the fold of Christ. He also at this place erected a new church which is a credit to him and the community in which it now is.

God is blessing his work and rewarding his labors by adding members to his church.

Rev. White is still attending the Seminary, which is in proximity to both of his charges, one being at West Point, the other at Powder Springs, Ga.

REV. WILLIAM H. TUGGLE,

PULPIT ORATOR—BAPTIST LEADER.

About three miles west of Madison, Morgan county, Ga., standing in the midst of an extremely poor vicinity, is an old farm-house known as the Bill West plantation. Here on the 25th of August, A. D. 1867, William H. Tuggle first saw the light of day. His early life was characteristic of honesty and frankness, for while a youth he scorned a mean act. His father being a poor farmer, William was obliged to work hard and steadily while quite small.

But amidst all disadvantages and difficulties he persevered and succeeded in obtaining a common school edu-

FRANK F. HOWARD.

REV. M. V. WHITE.

cation. Though born in obscurity and poverty he was
destined some day to become a leader among his people. When he was eleven years of age his father died,
leaving him to the care of a widowed mother. At the
time of his father's death William was unconverted, but
this death so affected him that it was not long before he
sought and found salvation of our Lord.

In the autumn of '78, shortly after his father's death,
he, during a series of meetings held at the popular New
Enon Church was converted, and received the holy rite
of baptism from Rev. Samuel Cochran. William very
soon became an ardent Sunday-school worker and his
untiring zeal knew no limit, though the cyclonic winds
of misfortune and trial blew hard against him.

In the year 1885 he was united in holy wedlock to the
accomplished Miss Ollie Coleman, of Eatonton, Ga., in
whom he finds a helpmeet indeed.

The impression during his early life that he must
preach the word of God grew stronger in him as he advanced in life, so finally making known his desire to the
church with which he was connected, he was granted
license, and began his work in the fourth district of the
Shiloh Association as Sunday-school agent. His labors
in this direction proved a success. He was next called
to the pastorate of the Baptist Church at Monticello, Ga.,
where he rendered faithful service till called to the Sand
Hill Baptist Church in Putnam county. Here he was a
successful leader for the Baptist army. His next field
of labor was at the Henderson Grove Baptist Church
where he served till a cry came down from Conyers,
Ga., calling for his service at that place. He found the
Baptists at that place far behind the times, but this only
stimulated him the more to labor, and he, with nine energetic members, went zealously to work and soon their labor

6

was rewarded by the erection of a neat little structure, which cost six hundred dollars, and that amount was soon cancelled. At this place Rev. Tuggle baptized many souls.

Finally, to the deep regret of all the charge he resigned. He was called to guide the Mt. Zion Church, at Atlanta, Ga., where with united energy, Christian zeal, patience and ambition, he still proclaims in oratorical tones the imperishable word of God. To this church, where he has been since September last, he has, by prayers and his wonderful manner of preaching, added seventy-four members. It is said of him that he has a voice like a silver trumpet, and is like unto one of the sweet singers of Israel.

REV. RUFUS H. HOUSTON,

HONORED CITIZEN, USEFUL DEACON.

Savannah, the picturesque city by the sea, is the place of nativity of the one whose name heads this narrative. He was born in the year 1845, and when very young was carried to Jackson county, Ga. His early life was spent like that of most slaves. At the age of eleven years he was sold to one John Holliday, with whom he lived until the emancipation. In 1864 he married a Miss Frances Schell, of Athens, Ga. She died in 1876. During the same year he entered the service of Major Campbell Wallace. The same year of his marriage he professed a hope in the Lord, and was baptized by the late Rev. Francis Quarles. Like the most of his fellow-brethren, at the close of the war, Brother Houston had almost nothing, his possessions amounting to six dollars in silver; and the thought which troubled him most was, what must he do with those six dollars. He could not definitely decide, so he laid them away and began working for Major Wallace, receiving as wages thirteen dollars per month. Taking out a small portion upon which to live, he saved all the rest, and by the time there was a bank established, he had quite a handsome sum to deposit. Thus he became a member of the bank, which progressed finely for a time, when finally it failed, and Mr. Houston found that he was no better off financially than when he first employed himself to Major Wallace. It was as if he had just started in life. This failure was a great drawback to him, but he did not allow it to discourage him, and he went forward with renewed energy, the result of which was that, in a few years, he had accumulated enough to purchase a cozy little home, which to-day cannot be purchased for three thousand dollars. Now he began to feel the need of education. His business arrangements would not permit him to attend school ; however, he secured a teacher, to whom he recited as often as work would allow him. Finally, a night session was opened at the Storr's School, and he had a chance to go. His object for seeking education was that he might some day be more able to preach the Word of God as he felt had been enjoined upon him. He learned to read, write and spell, and also obtained a fair knowledge of arithmetic. In 1882 he married his second wife—Mrs. Laura Boyd, a woman known for integrity, virtue and Christianity. In her he possesses a treasure.

In the year 1885 he was ordained a deacon of the Friendship Baptist Church, which position he fills creditably. In 1890 he was licensed to preach the Gospel. Brother Houston is bold and courageous in the discharge of his duty, a useful factor in his church, a faithful Christian, devoted husband, and an example to believers; an honor to his race.

REV. ISAAC R. HALL,

PAINTER, PROGRESSIVE MINISTER.

Isaac R. Hall was born near Greensboro, Ga., December 25, 1856. His parents were quiet, religious people, whose occupation was that of tilling the soil. In his early life Hall had to assist his father in field work, and this he did till the year 1875. All who know anything of farm life know it is not an easy one. Many troubles and perplexities must in it, as in all other undertakings, be borne and endured. Becoming tired of farm life, Hall learned and pursued the painter's trade for some time. During this time he became desirous of seeking and working for Jesus. These words, "Ye must be born again," rang in his ears and echoed through his heart. He obeyed them, and in the year 1882 united with the Baptist Church at Greensboro, Ga.

Having become a resident of this city, he cast his lot with the Mt. Zion Church; from which church he was, in the year 1886, ordained. While at Greensboro, Hall attended the public schools which were of short duration. After coming here, he entered the Atlanta Baptist Seminary, where he pursued, in connection with other studies, that of theology, under the efficient Rev. S. Graves, D.D. During Hall's vacation he left for the West, visiting the principal cities of Illinois, Indiana, Arkansas and California. While on this tour he was called upon at the different places to assist in religious services. After two months' travel he returned home and prepared to reënter school. In August of the same year he was called as pastor of the Shiloh Baptist Church, which had been organized four years prior to his call and was then in a state of decline. He accepted this call with the hope and intention to revive the church, whose membership

then numbered only five souls, viz : Brethren Lewis
Holmes (and wife), Linear (and wife), and Pitts. With
these Rev. Hall held worship in a small, unseated, un-
lighted, rented room. He with these labored zealously ;
the church grew in numbers and increased in strength,
and after two years a lot, 50 x 100 feet, at a cost of four
hundred and fifty dollars, was purchased, upon which a
house of worship was soon erected. In 1891 this building could not accommodate the congregation and had to
be enlarged. Rev. Hall has a wife who to him is a great
help and blessing. The Lord has bountifully blessed his
work. Since he has had charge of the church he has
raised $3,500.00, baptized three hundred and five souls,
and received one hundred and twenty by letter, making
a total of four hundred and twenty-five.

Rev. Hall is an eloquent speaker, zealous worker and
Christian gentleman. May God continue to bless him
and his work. The race needs more useful workers like
him.

REV. R. H BURSON,

STATE MISSIONARY, DEVOUT CHRISTIAN.

This godly man of whom I now write first saw the
light of day in Fair Play District, Morgan county, Ga.,
A. D. 1840.

He first became religiously impressed at the age of
five years, by his pious, Christian mother. That mother's
spirit has passed (July 1, 1888) into its eternal rest,
but the memories of her devotion to her Maker and the
Christian teaching to her son Richard are still fresh
within his bosom. Being personally acquainted with
Rev. Burson for a number of years, it is more than a

pleasure to me to be called upon to relate these few facts of his Christian life. He was born of slave parents, and was himself a slave ; but his treatment was never cruel. Somehow he was a favorite in his masters' families. In 1852 he was sold to Mr. S. Burson, of Morgan county, who was his former master's son-in-law, and with this man as his owner he spent the remainder of his days of servitude. His chief duty while a lad was to carry his master's children to and from school. This aroused the desire for an education within him ; and he set himself to wondering how he could obtain such.

He had no means with which to purchase and no ways of obtaining books. He finally decided that he would gather all the disconnected leaves of the pupils' books lying around the schoolhouse. One day, after carrying the children to school as usual and waiting till they had all gone into the schoolroom, he busied himself picking up the loose leaves which he put away snugly in his pocket, and on reaching home, obtaining a needle and thread he sewed them together, making as he said a book, and was it not a book ? Aye, to the youthful slave it was a dear book. The children were kind to him and gave him the necessary assistance, so it was not long before he could spell every word on every leaf of his home-made book.

Afterward by some means, he came into possession of a Webster's spelling book, and within a year he had mastered its contents, reading quite accurately.

Thus began his education. Let me add, his study hours were confined to the hours of the night, as he had no chance during the day for it.

In 1866 he married Miss Antoinette Virginia Veal, a woman of true worth, who has been the guiding star of his life. To them was given only one child, who having grown to useful, intelligent manhood, with a bright future before, was suddenly overtaken by a severe disease which cut him off from this life. This inestimable wife taught her husband to write, and then possessing the knowledge of reading and writing, he felt in a measure equipped to pursue his calling.

He was converted five years before his marriage, and had united with the Baptist Church of Gwinnett county.

In 1873 he was licensed and ordained to preach. He has served the following churches: At Stone Mountain, Ga., Shiloh, in DeKalb county, one at Norcross, Ga., one at East Point, Ga., and the Fraser street B. C. of this city.

He has served as missionary of the State for four years during which time he has given entire satisfaction to the chief authorities of the missionary force and is doing great work for the Master. He is still spending his days and strength in that capacity, and is not satisfied when not working for his Maker. Verily it will be said of him when he shall have finished his earthly career: " Thou hast fought a good fight. Enter into thy rest ."

REV. THOMAS M. DORSEY,

BAPTIST PREACHER.

Thomas M. Dorsey was born June 2, 1860, in Columbia county, Ga. When he was but five months old his mother died, leaving him to the care of his father. At the age of nine he began to do farm work.

Being anxious to learn and not able on account of having to work, to attend school, young Dorsey found out where a school was being taught at night and of this fact acquainted his father, who consented to send the son to

this night school.   While attending he learned rapidly.
His daily labors seemed easier to him since he felt that
he was acquiring knowledge, though at the sacrifice of
a few hours sleep at night. He was anxious to learn, for
he had already the conviction that "knowledge is
power."

The young man of whom I now write is not selfish,
he loves the race to which he belongs. Accordingly, feeling that he was able to impart knowledge to the children
of that race with God as his leader, he began the work of
school teaching.   His first work of this kind was at
Sandtown, Ga., where he endeared himself to the patrons
and pupils. Wherever he afterward taught, he was loved
and respected by those with whom he came in contact.
Mr. Dorsey at one time attended the Schofield Industrial
and Normal School at Aiken, S. C., where he was a
diligent student.

Having accepted and resolved to follow Christ and to
work for him, he united with the Baptist Church, and
was baptized by one Rev. E. V. White. He was soon
appointed church clerk, and superintendent of the Sunday-school, where he did good service for the master.
Feeling that be was one of the chosen he applied to his
church for license, and the church believing him to be
called of God granted him the necessary license.   After
coming to Atlanta, Mr. Dorsey joined by letter Shiloh
Baptist Church of which Rev. I. R. Hall is pastor, and
from which church he (Rev. Dorsey) was licensed and
ordained, the presbytery consisting of Rev. J. B. Davis,
Atlanta, Ga.; Rev. M. V. White, Atlanta, Ga.; Rev.
W. H. Tilman, Atlanta, Ga.; Rev. I. R. Hall, Atlanta,
Ga., and the writer.

Rev. Dorsey was called to take charge of the Big
Bethel Baptist Church December last.   May he be successful in this work. This church is located in Cobb

REV. W. H. TUGGLE.

REV. I. R. HALL.

R. H. HOUSTON.

SHILOH CHURCH.

county, Ga. He also was a student of the Atlanta Baptist Seminary, the inexhaustible source of knowledge.

Rev. Dorsey is a good man, worthy of his calling.
May the Lord continue to be his guide and protector
through the varying scenes of life.

REV. HENRY WHITE,

ABLE BAPTIST DIVINE.

He was born at Richmond, Va., A. D. 1854. When
he was very small he was placed upon the block to be
sold, but he used his lungs with such violent force he
was taken down. Young White knew nothing at all
about his paternal parent, his father being sold before his
birth. He was finally purchased by a man from the
State of Louisiana and carried to that State. After
spending some considerable time there, he came to Georgia and located at Lagrange. There he stayed till
1871 working on the farm. He next came to Atlanta.
Ga., and for a while worked at butchery. Thinking he
could better his financial condition by so doing, he took
up the business of draying, which proved to be successful.
His first investment in this city was in three-fourths of
an acre of land, for which he paid one hundred dollars.

Afterward sold the same for two thousand dollars. In
1885 he united with the Wheat Street Baptist Church,
and soon afterward was made superintendent of the Sunday-school. 1887 he was licensed to preach, and proving himself an efficient disciple, he was ordained.
Shortly after his ordination, he was called to the care of
a small church in South Atlanta. As pastor he has done
and is still doing excellent labor. At South Atlanta Rev.

White has erected a church-house at a cost of one thousand, nine hundred dollars, and increased the membership greatly.   He also engaged in grocery-keeping which
enabled him to push forward his education.   He is a
student of the Atlanta Baptist Seminary.   In 1892 he
accepted the pastorate of the Baptist Church at Fairburn, Ga.   Rev. White is one of the business men of
our city, and by his enery and push is able to keep the
wolf from the door.

REV. J. C. BEAVER,

DEVOUT SUNDAY-SCHOOL WORKER.

He is the youngest of eleven children, who were born
to William and Charity Beavers, and was born October
17, 1860, in Campbell county, Ga.   His early school
days were passed in the village of Campbellton, and in
this school he ranked at the head of his classes.

While he was a small boy, he would play " at preaching " to the other children about the place, and the older
persons who heard him would say among themselves :
" That boy is going to preach sure enough one day."
He has fulfilled the prophecy, as he is to-day a leader
among the Baptist army of the State.   He has taught in
several public schools and was regarded as a model teacher.
Rev. Beavers is a Christian and a trusty man ; all who
know him, place the utmost confidence in him, and believe him a true follower of Christ.   He is a great Sunday-school worker, and has done more work in that direction than any other man in West Georgia.   Has also
enjoyed the honor of being the clerk of several Associations, and has written largely for the leading Negro jour-

nal of the South, the *Georgia Baptist*. In 1889 he moved
to Lithia Springs, Ga., where he is employed as janitor
and florist of the beautiful Chautauqua grounds.

He performs his duties so well and successfully, that
those for whom he works deem him indispensable. In
1891 he married a Miss Magnolia McGraw of New Orleans, La., and during the same year was elected clerk
of the Carrollton Association. Rev. Beavers says of himself that he is a Baptist of the deepest dye. In 1892 he
was ordained to the ministry ; and soon after became the
pastor of the church of which he was a member.

He immediately began the fight against sin, and soon
had a large number to baptize. Among this number
was his wife, who had accepted Christ, that she might
the better assist her companion in upbuilding the Master's
kingdom. His highest aim is to glorify God and advance his kingdom on earth. Rev. Beavers is now engaged in erecting a church edifice, which, when finished,
will assist in adorning the already beautiful little village of Lithia Springs, Ga.

REV. J. B. DAVIS,

CARPENTER, JANITOR, SUCCESSFUL, PROGRESSIVE MIN-
ISTER OF GOD.

A few miles from Watkinsville, Ga., in a poor region
known as Farmington, near the roadside, sat an humble
cabin. In this cabin, April 15, 1857, was ushered into
this world, Jeremiah B. Davis. Being the son of slaves,
and born at the time of slavery, his educational advantages were like those of most of his people.

After freedom he lived with a white man, whose son
took pleasure in teaching Jeremiah, and each day would

give him a lesson to prepare for the next. He would get this lesson by taking with him to the field his book, and at the dinner hour would study it. In this manner Jeremiah received his first teaching. All through his earlier life he scorned wrong-doing, and never stooped to meanness. At the age of fifteen, after hearing one Rev. Shadrick preach from 1 Cor. 15: 55, he was converted. This good man, Rev. Shadrick, though not a theologian or scholar, though not able to ascend the starry heaven and bring philosophy to dwell with mankind, knew how to preach the blessed Word of God, and selecting, at that time, the above named portion of scripture was the means of bringing to Christ one more soul. After his conversion, Jeremiah lived a true Christian, and in his community is considered the leader of prayer-meetings and of the Sunday-school. Like most of his fellow-men he was obliged to do field work, but, thirsting for knowledge, he managed to attend the three months public school which had then been established.

When he was seventeen he became apprenticed to carpentry under one Mr. Mack, of Athens, Ga. He served this trade nine years. Though his early life was given to physical toil, his mind was hungry for food, and in time this food was given him.

He found a friend in the person of Rev. C. H. Lyon, D.D., who was then pastor of the Baptist church, at Watkinsville. Seeing in Jeremiah a grand spirit and believing if cultivated he would become a power for good as a pulpit orator, the church with which he was connected granted him license to proclaim the truth in Christ Jesus. Rev. Lyon now urged him to enter the Atlanta Baptist Seminary, and he, being anxious to pursue his studies, consented to this. Arranging and locking his tool-chest, he made ready for his departure. His possessions in finance amounted to only fifteen dollars, half of which

amount he gave to his wife. After paying his railroad
expenses for himself and tool chest Jeremiah had left him
the pitiful sum of two dollars and fifty cents. Arriving in this city, with comparatively no means, all
around him seemed dark and gloomy, and he knew not
where to go.

In the midst of despondencies and discouragements,
God opened a way for him, as he will do for you, my
readers, if you will trust him. He succeeded in obtaining board and lodging for eight dollars per month, from
a charitable woman who waited till he was able to pay her.
Entering school he paid his tuition of one dollar. Having
brought his tool-chest, he was prepared to follow his
trade; and this he did, obtaining work Friday afternoons
and Saturdays. By this means he kept up with his expenses for three years. At the expiration of this time,
the president, Dr. J. T. Robert, LL.D., perceiving that
Jeremiah was quick intellectually and industrious in his
habits, and knowing his financial condition, together with
the other members of the faculty made him ("Jere")
janitor of the building, allowing him as salary twelve dollars per month, including tuition. Thus, being able to
pursue his studies, he completed the normal and theological course with honor. While attending school he accepted the call of a small church at Woodstock, Ga.,
where he served as pastor for two years, during which
time he very much enjoyed his labor among the people,
who were friendly, frank and unselfish. Indeed he was
drawn by cords of love to these people, whose simplicity
attracted him.

Having a family to support, and other expenses, the income of my subject was quite limited, and because of
railroad expenses this field of labor was inconvenient for
him, and, though regretting to leave the flock he had for
two years tended, he gave up the work and assumed

charge of a church in the western portion of this city.
For this church he served in the capacity of janitor as
well as pastor, and for this little weather-beaten structure he purchased lamps, filled and lighted them, but
rang not the bell, there being none to ring.   Rev. Davis
has served this church for eight years, during which time
God has bountifully blessed his labor, he having added to
his flock two hundred and forty souls, making now the
membership two hundred and sixty strong.   Also he has
erected a handsome three thousand dollar brick structure
where the former house stood.

Rev. Davis, born amid hardships, and having traveled
at least half the distance of poverty and want, knows how
to sympathize with suffering humanity.   Having through
God's help been so successful in his work, Rev. Davis
retrospectively views the condition of the church, when
it was a dilapidated building, with defaced furniture
within, and says within himself: "Surely God is pleased
with my work, since he has crowned it with success."
He merits the respect and trust of all.   God bless such
men !

REV. DAVID S. KLUGH,

DEVOUT BAPTIST MINISTER.

I know of no one more unassuming, more unpretending and more gentlemanly than the young man of whom
I now speak.   Besides bearing these qualities, he is full
of energy, push and vim.   He first beheld the dawn of
light in the State of South Carolina, A. D. 1864.   Mr.
Klugh's father died while he was yet too young to realize
what grief was, so the son never knew the love of that
parent.

The mother was left with five children to care for, and many were the battles she fought against poverty, but she succeeded in rearing her children aright and properly administering to their needs morally, intellectually and physically. By this mother's teachings the soul of our subject became enthused with three desires: he desired first to know something, then he would work to be something, and, lastly, he would struggle to have and do something.

His first school days were spent in a rude log cabin. It was a free school, but as he lived outside the township he had to pay fifty cents per month tuition. Feeling that he must make good use of the time so as to receive the value of his fifty cents, he applied himself diligently to study and became the leader of all his classes. Mr. Klugh does not regret the money paid in those early days for his schooling, for he says it was the best investment of his life.

Leaving the village school he began farming, at which he worked five years, and during that time found it to be both profitable and pleasurable. Subsequently he entered the Normal Institute at Greenwood, S. C., and while in attendance there he was offered and accepted the position of teacher in the Pine Grove school at Hodges, S. C.; but not being satisfied with his ability as teacher he soon resigned this work and became a student of the Caflin University at Orangeburg, S. C. While here he was again solicited to take the school at Hodges, which, after some persuasion, he did.

It was now that he felt God required his labor in a higher sphere—that of minister of the gospel; so he again gave up the school at Hodges and took charge of one at Greenville, S. C., thereby having a better opportunity to exercise his ministerial talents. Feeling his deficiency for so high a calling, he resolved to attend a Baptist school of some note. Accordingly he matriculated in the Atlanta Baptist Seminary at Atlanta, Ga., where he endeared himself to the professors and students, as well as to many leading residents of the city. First in all his classes, he graduated with high honors in 1890, and his oration for that occasion was considered a masterpiece. After his graduation he became the pastor of the Morris Baptist Chapel, Greenwood, S. C., where he led many souls to Christ, and also founded the Greenwood graded school, which is still under his successful management. He has, also, charge of the Baptist Church at Promise Land, S. C., to which he gives a portion of his time, and where he is erecting a handsome church edifice.

He has recently been called to the pastorate of the Union Baptist Church at Augusta, Ga. Degrees have been offered him, but as yet he has not accepted any. One might readily see that the future of this young man is bright and prosperous. Early he obeyed the command: "Seek first the kingdom of heaven," and now he is realizing the promise: "And all things else shall be added unto you."

REV. CYRUS BROWN,

ELOQUENT MINISTER.

In the year of our Lord one thousand eight hundred and fifty-four, twelve miles from the classic city of Athens, in Georgia, was ushered into slavery life a male baby to whom was given the name we present above this narrative. Though born a slave he did not suffer to any great extent the cruelties of slavery days, for as we see, his advent into this world was not a great while before that great struggle which finally resulted in his free-

REV. DAVID S. KLUGH.

REV. J. B. DAVIS.

MACEDONIA BAPTIST CHURCH.

dom commenced. But he saw enough of the cruel treatment to others older than himself to impress him that slavery was an accursed institution; he heard enough of the cries and prayers of his elders to make him wish that they were free.

Cyrus was used as a house boy, what we now call a butler, and was more favored than many of his fellow-creatures, but possessing a tender, sympathetic heart, many were the tears he shed in secret over the wrongs perpetrated upon his people. He first learned shoe-making under his father, but after his father's death he was put to work under a Mr. Henry Horten, of Athens, Ga. In those days of superstition and ignorance the idea of children's religion was not tolerated, there were none who would believe in it ; consequently when, at the age of twelve Cyrus professed and proclaimed a hope in Christ, he created no little excitement. He was small in stature, and had to be placed upon a table in the church when telling of his conversion. He was the first child to unite with the church in the city of Athens. He became a member of the Baptist Church, and was baptized by Rev. Floyd Hill. In 1876 Mr. Brown was married to a Miss Eliza Lester. He felt that he was one of the chosen, to whom the command, "Go preach my gospel," was given; so that he might prepare himself for that arduous calling he came to Atlanta in 1882 and entered the Atlanta Baptist Seminary. Before his becoming a member of the seminary he was called as pastor of the Mt. Pleasant Church. During the same year of his entering school he was also called to St. James Baptist Church. He accepted the call and went alternately to these churches to fill the office of pastor. At neither of these places had they a decent house of worship, but under his wise management and well preached gospel both

7

communities soon erected comfortable churches at a cost
of seven hundred and eight hundred dollars respectively.
In 1888 he resigned these charges and accepted that of
the Macedonia Baptist Church at Atlanta.

In 1890 he finished his studies and was then able to
devote his whole time to his ministerial work. He is still
the honored pastor of the last named church, where he
has been instrumental in bringing many souls to the kingdom of Christ.

The names which follow are some of the worthy female
members of his church;

Mrs. Amy Simms, Mrs. Leah Hartsfield, Mrs. Susie
Eagles, Mrs. Lucy Dillard, Mrs. Mattie Sanders, Mrs.
Mahala Saracens, Mrs. Mollie Calhoun, Mrs. Cresie
Kendrick, Mrs. Chas. McHenry. Sunday-school teach-
ers: Miss Mary Jordan, Mrs. Laura Price, Miss Hattie
Rogers, Miss Culbreth; Messrs. Tate and J. C. Comer,
also trustees Rainwater and Bugg.

In 1889 Rev. Brown accepted another charge at Acworth, Ga., where he also labors vigilantly for the cause
of Christ. He owns real estate in Athens, Ga., in a most
desirable portion of the city, said property being near the
Lucy Cobb Institute. He is a zealous worker for the
kingdom of Christ, full of ambition and valor, a man of
unswerving determination.

REV. W. L. JONES.

SUCCESSFUL AND BELOVED PASTOR OF THE BEULAH BAPTIST CHURCH.

Immediately after the late rebellion, the parents of the
subject of this narrative removed from their home in
Milton county, Ga., where he was born, to the county of
Gwinnett, at Norcross.

Young Jones possessed the traits common to all youths, but was early in life religiously inclined, for at the tender age of sixteen years he professed a hope in Christ Jesus and united with the Baptist Church at Norcross, Ga. Immediately he became an enthusiastic Sunday-school worker, which he has ever afterwards been. Soon after his conversion he began to feel that he was to enter into the ministry of God. To rid himself of this feeling he left his home and went into the State of Mississippi, but while there the spirit continually impressed his mind, and after remaining there a year, he returned home and began preparing himself for his arduous calling. He was licensed and ordained, and only ten minutes after ordination was given the care of two churches.

His influence and fame as a pastor began to spread, and during the second year of his ministry, he was called to serve the third church. At one time he was the pastor of four churches. This led him to believe that God had a special work for him to do; so he began to gather together all the churches in the county in which he lived, and organized and formed them into an association, to which he gave the name of the Hopewell Association. Now it was that he felt the need of education ; so after due consideration, he resolved to attend the Atlanta Baptist Seminary. Moving from his home to Decatur, Ga., which, on account of its being only six miles from Atlanta, is nearer to the seminary, he became a member of the Atlanta Baptist Seminary. Finding it too expensive to reside at Decatur and attend school here, he finally moved to Atlanta, where he was more able to continue his studies. Soon after coming to this city he was called to serve the Mt. Zion Baptist Church, of this city. After due and prayerful consideration this call he accepted. The church building being in a dilapidated condition, Rev. Jones began to devise plans for

the erection of a new one. After much toil and labor
his efforts were rewarded by seeing a neat structure
occupying the place of the old one.

All this time he, through many disadvantages, continued in school, and also served another church at
Roswell, Ga. He remained in school till he received his
" sheep skin," when, against the protestations and tears
of his many charges, he gave them up with the intention of removing to the West. He left the soil of his
native State, but his religious influence and good works
remained behind, and during his absence he was requested to come back home and be the pastor of the
Beulah Baptist Church. Feeling it his duty to do all
the good he could at home, he returned and became the
pastor of the above named church. This church house
was also in a state of decline, but under this energetic
man a new edifice soon towered upward. This was not
accomplished all at once, for the membership was small
and the members poor; but they all persevered until the
work was completed, and now a handsome edlfice of
stone and brick adorns the community which sur-
rounds it.

Notwithstanding the many hardships through which
he has passed, Rev. Jones has had bountiful success in
all his labors. He has greatly increased the membership of this church, having baptized three hundred besides taking in others by letter. He is a man who believes that it is left with a person as to whether he will
make anything or nothing of himself, and entertaining
this view he has striven to make something of himself.

Few men there are who possess more courage and
fortitude than he. As a young man he has made his
mark in the world for good. His religion is of the liberal nature which constrains him to look after the spir-

itual and temporal welfare of his people and all who aid in any way the onward march of Christ.

Struggling against disadvantages, and knowing how hard it is for poor young men and women to acquire an education, he contributes annually to the Spelman and Baptist seminaries.

Rev. Jones has been the wise and efficient moderator of the Hopewell Associatiation for the past ten years, which fact shows his ability to rule wisely and well.

May God continue to bless him and his work, and as he advances in years, may he advance also in the love and grace of Christ Jesus.

———

MISS MABLE B. JOHNSON,

TEACHER IN ATLANTA PUBLIC SCHOOL.

The women among the Negro race who would dare to be anything to the race, have untold difficulties and trials to undergo, and if they, through perseverance do rise to any pre-eminence in the race, it is only because nature has endowed them with an indomitable will and such unswerving and natural ambition to be something. The race has not yet in general arisen high enough in the scale of culture and refinement to not show signs of prejudice to to those who would rise to honor and fame.

Long since the idea of woman's ability and position in life has crystallized itself in the minds of men and the public, that they are good for nothing more, absolutely nothing more, but to attend to babies, to cook, to entertain the husband's company, and to see after domestic affairs generally.

Such have been some of the disadvantages through which the subject of this sketch has had to pass.

Mabel Beatrice Johnson came into life surrounded by the beautiful hills of the paradise-like town of Griffin, in Georgia. She was born of parents of *ante bellum* days. Her early life was spent in the Gate City of the South. So early was she brought to this city by her parents, that she scarcely recognized the fact that she was not born in this city. This quiet, unassuming woman has gone along making her way by degrees up and up the rounds of the ladder of art, science and industry, until she stands in even ranks with those who have made in every way complete success. She has had superior advantages to many of her race in the educational line. When she was scarcely old enough to go through the streets unaccompanied, she was placed in the Haynes street school, which at the time of her attendance was taught by white teachers. After spending some years in this school, she passed to the Summer Hill public school. At this time, her mother wishing her to be taught more thoroughly sent her to the Storr's, a school of a much higher curriculum.

Here she remained till within a few months of graduating. Her parents then moved to Charlotte, N. C., where they lived some time. Returning to Atlanta in 1882, she entered the Spellman Seminary, one of the first schools for women and girls in the South.

On entering, she was able to make the Junior Normal class, and after four years, graduated with honors from the class of 1886.

After her graduation, she entered public work. She made a creditable standard before the board of education and was appointed supernumerary of the Atlanta public schools, which position she filled with credit to herself and satisfaction to the board of education, as a good disciplinarian and successful teacher. The record will show that in 1888 she was elected teacher of the third grade of the Houston street school. In the fall of 1890 she was promoted to the fourth grade at the West Mitchell street school. In 1892 she succesfully advanced and was raised in honor of her faithful and praiseworthy work, to the sixth grade.

This she has done by hard struggle and by accepting hardships and disadvantages as she met them. Miss Johnson is an expert in artistic needle work, and all her spare moments are utilized in fine lace-making and embroidering. She displays fine musical talent and on the whole is intelligent cultured and refined.

Nature has also bestowed upon her a bountiful supply of beauty, as the accompanying cut of herself will show.

REV. SILAS SMITH,

BAPTIST DIVINE.

Rev. Silas Smith was born in Pittsylvania county, Virginia, 1857. He spent the earlier part of his life in farming, and when he reached manhood he went to Danville, Va., where he was employed in a tobacco factory, where his work consisted in rolling the leaves for their further use. He worked in this establishment for some considerable time, when the desire to travel seized him, and, having saved some money, he began to make preparation for an extended tour. He purchased a magic lantern whereby he might be the better able to defray his expenses, and thus pass from place to place with ease. With his lantern he was most successful, being able to pass through twenty-two States, visiting all of the principal cities and towns in those States. With his panorama he commands crowded houses, and his splendid variety of scenes and kaleidoscopic views are enjoyed by all whose high pleasure it is to see them.

In this his chosen profession Rev. Smith stands second to none.   He has a charm about him whereby he is able to hold his audiences spellbound ; and can cause them to sing, laugh or cry at his own will.   In short, he seems suited to this profession, in which he is so successful.

During his travels he felt that he was called of God to preach the Gospel.   In March, 1892, he was ordained.

Rev. Smith now resides at Bedford City, Virginia, where he has a most beautiful and comfortable home. He is pastor of two churches, one being in the city in which he lives and the other in Roanoke county, Virginia. He pays taxes on $1,000.00 worth of real estate.   Rev. Smith is a man of broad experiences, having traveled quite extensively.   He is jovial and entertaining, a clever conversationalist.

REV. W. D. JOHNSON,

ELOQUENT PREACHER.

Among the leading Baptist divines of the Negro race can well be classed the subject of this narrative.   He first saw the light of day at Hephzibah, Richmond county, Ga., June 4, 1862.   Having a praying mother and a Christian father, his first impressions were religious. These influences were brought to bear so heavily upon him that, when only nine years old, he left his home one Monday morning and went to a great creek swamp, where he stayed five nights and days without a morsel of food or a drink of water.   Having seen the gathering of the eagles the people decided that he was dead, and

REV. CYRUS BROWN.

BULAH BAPTIST CHURCH.

REV. W. L. JONES.

a search was instituted; but when found he "had been killed dead to sin and made alive in Christ Jesus." He was then baptized into the Covenant Baptist Church by Rev. Nathan Walker. Being born of poor parents, he was never as well attired as his fellow schoolmates, but his aptness as a scholar and his Christian deportment won the respect of his teachers and demanded it of the pupils. His first effort at oratory was made at the closing exercises of the school of which he was a pupil, at the age of ten years. This attempt was a success, and then and there it was prophesied that he would one day become an orator of eminence. His parents were too poor to purchase shoes for him; thus, while making this speech, his feet were bare, and there were seen patches on the knees of his pants. At this early age (nine) he was often chosen by the older members and officers of his church to lead the prayer-meetings. At twelve he was a prominent teacher in the Sunday-school. Being impressed with the religious zeal of this boy disciple, the ministers and older Christians predicted for him a call to the ministry. Looking to this end he was persuaded by them and Rev. C. T. Walker, then his pastor, to enter the Augusta Institute, now the Atlanta Baptist Seminary. In November of 1888 he entered this school with eight dollars and a half, and in a way that he can't explain remained there six months on that sum, supplemented only by a little meal and wood brought now and then from his country home. When he left school he taught a private school in Burke county, near Green's Cut, for ten dollars per month. In the summer of the same year he resigned this school to teach at Millen, Ga., at $15.00 per month. In the fall of 1879, as the school had moved from Augusta to Atlanta, he entered Haven Normal School at Waynesboro, Ga., and remained there for several months. In the spring

of 1880 he was taken by Rev. Robert Kelsey to a very
dark section of country on the line of Screven and Burke
counties. This was a section unvisited before by any
but local instructors, and the people were almost idol-
atrous in their worship, and in every respect were
much in need of both a leader and instructor. In this
capacity he worked, gaining the confidence and respect
of both white and colored. The Bible, hymn books and
Sunday-school literature were introduced, and the people
came ten and twelve miles to be instructed. For five
years he labored in this section with almost marvelous
success. He has been styled "the father" of this country,
and to-day there are hundreds of young men and women
who regard him the greatest benefactor of their lives.
In the fall of 1880 he resumed his studies at the Seminary. Since his connection with the Seminary he has
studied modern languages, viz., Latin and Greek, both at
Paine Institute, Augusta, Ga., and by correspondence from Chautauqua school by Alfred A. Wright.
Though starting penniless he has saved up his earnings
and now owns very valuable property in Augusta,
Ga., his present home. When the grocery firm of
F. P. Johnson & Co. failed in Augusta, Ga., in 1881,
he was a heavy loser, being in school but having stock in
that firm. He is a stockholder both in the Augusta *Sen-
tinel* and the colored State Fair Company. In the spring
of 1880 he was licensed to preach (Rev. C. T. Walker,
pastor), and in December, 1881, was ordained to the
Gospel ministry. Shortly after his ordination he was
called to the pastorate of Zion Baptist Church, Burton
Ferry, Ga. Under his pastorate this flock greatly
prospered, a new house of worship being built, and many
were added to the church. At the close of two years'
labor, from 1882 to 1884, he resigned this flock, to the
regret of all. In 1883, he was called to the Murphy

Ebenezer Baptist Church, Girard, Ga., which he acceptably served two years. He was also called to the pastorate of the St. Paul Baptist Church in this year, which he served very successfully for three years. In 1884 he was called to the pastorate of the Thankful Baptist Church, Waynesboro, Georgia. This church had fallen into utter insignificance, having no land, no house, no money and very few members. It was regarded as a failure. The other churches and denominations had the town. Fifteen persons was a large congregation. By his hard work and shrewd management it has grown to be the strongest church in the town. They have purchased a lot and built a large and attractive edifice, and every service there the church is crowded to overflowing. In referring to his success there, Rev. C. T. Walker, D.D., said, "Nobody else could have done what Johnson has done." For nine years the Lord has prospered his labors there. In 1885 he was called to the pastorate of Palmer Grove Baptist Church, near Green's Cut, Ga., at which place he has built a large and substantial house of worship, paid off all of the old church debts, and baptized many precious souls. In 1889 he was called to the pastorate of Franklin Covenant Baptist Church where he was baptized, and preached three years with great success. In 1887 he was called to the pastorate of Elim Baptist Church, Summerville, Augusta, Ga., which church he now serves. This church had the sworn opposition of nearly every church in Augusta, but by earnest effort he has built a fine house of worship and largely increased its membership, and the church is now regarded as one of the strongest and most influential churches of the city. The city folks take great delight in riding three miles out to the village to hear its pastor preach. The Northern guests from the great Bon Air Hotel regard it a pleasure to resort to this church and listen to his sermons.

At the age of fifteen he was elected as a delegate to the Walker Baptist Association by his church, and served on important committees. Since that time he has been regarded as one of the leaders of that Association. For ten years he has served on the Executive Board. He is chairman of the local Board of Trustees of the Walker Baptist Institute, and has done much to bring that school up to its present degree of prosperity, and toward shaping its future usefulness. He has long served as a member of the Executive Board of the State Baptist Sunday-school Convention, and at the last session of that body was elected its vice-president. He is one of the directors of the colored State Fair located at Augusta, Ga. Prominent among the addresses and sermons delivered upon special occasions were the following: "The Needs of the Colored Ministry," delivered at the centennial celebration of the Baptists of Georgia in Savannah, 1888; "The Duty of the Colored Baptists to send the Gospel to Africa," delivered before the Foreign Mission Baptist Convention of the United States in Louisville, Ky.; and "The Enemies of the Cross," introductory sermon preached to the Missionary Baptist Convention of Georgia at Cuthbert in 1891. He has baptized more than 1,200 persons, and is still laboring in the Master's vineyard. Success to him through future life as it has been through his past.

REV. A. B. MURDEN,

STATE MISSIONARY—ELOQUENT BAPTIST DIVINE.

Few young men at the age of twenty-seven have accomplished more or exerted a broader influence for good than has Rev. A. B. Murden. He first saw the light on the plantation of Judge Howell Bunkley, near Crawfordville, Ga., August 25, 1865. He was the seventh son of Jerry and Sarah Ann Murden. Being a bright boy from babyhood, the people predicted great things for him.

The white people called him Bartow, in honor of the great Southern General, but the colored folks called him Ulysses Grant, hence the name Aaron Bartow Ulysses Grant Murden.

At the age of nine young Murden was sent to school. He soon proved to be a very bright boy; so rapidly did he learn that many offered to take him and educate him, but his mother was not willing to have him leave home. As a lad he was thoughtful and active and always wanted to earn something for himself.

A pleasing little incident is that when about twelve years old he bottomed a chair for a neighbor and received in payment an old hen. At another time he earned a goose, and from that time he began to earn money. He became quite skillful in making brooms, horse-collars and foot-mats. These articles, when sold, brought many dollars to his widowed mother.

When about sixteen years old young Aaron found himself an orphan, thrown upon the world to care for himself. He had always been a great lover of his mother, and now that she who had been his best friend was dead, he resolved to leave the old home place.

He had a great thirst for knowledge, but to gain it he

must have money, and this he had not.   He resolved to
find work on the railroad so that he might earn money
enough to defray his expenses at school one term at least.
Accordingly he left his home and came to Atlanta, but
not until the crop was gathered and he had attended to
all the business which his mother had left undone.   After
settling the debts of the farm, paying the doctor's bill and
burial expenses of his mother, he found that he had
twenty-five dollars for himself.

On reaching Atlanta he went to see his cousin, Mr. W.
A. Jackson, at whose house he left his trunk and other
articles.   Before leaving the city he deposited twenty-
two dollars in the bank, and boarded the cars for Marietta, Ga., with three dollars in his pocket.   While on the
cars, boy-like, he bought a ring for a dollar and a half.
On reaching Marietta he found he must walk forty miles
to Dallas, Ga., at which place he was to engage.   On the
way some one stole a dollar from him, so when he
reached his destination he had only fifty cents.

The E. T., V. & G. R. R. was being constructed at
that time, and he engaged at grading for a dollar and a
quarter per day.   His manliness, activity and faithfulness
to duty soon brought him to the place where he earned
a dollar and seventy-five cents a day.   At first he boarded
at nine dollars per month, but soon found this a poor way
to save money, so he built him a little shack in the woods
and did his own cooking.   He found by so doing he could
live on three dollars a month.   Some of my readers may
not know what a shack is.   It is a very small house built
of logs and daubed with mud.   It has a stick-chimney, a
dirt floor and is just high enough for a man to get in.   In
such a house our hero lived from March till August,
1882.

In this short sketch we cannot mention all the incidents,
but the reader may rest assured they were many and va-

ried.   Young Murden was the only Christian but one working on the road at that time.   Most of the men spent Sundays in gambling; but he went out and found a church into which he gathered the children and told them about Jesus, that one who died to save them.

He witnessed many crimes, and many accidents occurred.   Several times he narrowly escaped with his life.

Rev. Murden tells of one most remarkable incident.   It was the 25th of March, 1882; he had been holding the jumper from seven o'clock till near twelve, when the man who was driving the steel said, "Murden, I guess you are tired now, let me hold and you drive."   They were working in a deep cut, and a huge stone looked frowningly down upon them.   Murden had said, "Mitchell, I think that rock there is cracked."   Mitchell had proposed to examine it in a few minutes.   Scarcely had the words died from his lips when down came the massive rock upon him.   He was leaning over the jumper, and so great was the force that the steel was driven right through his breast.   His head was terribly mashed; he brought one convulsive groan and was dead.   A piece of the rock struck young Murden in the side and hurled him quite a distance.   Think, he had gotten up from the steel only about ten minutes before Mr. Mitchell was killed!   What a narrow escape and what an evidence of God's providence over those whom he chooses to do a great work in his name.

Remember, Murden was only sixteen years old at this time, and he thought this narrow escape was a warning to him, so he resolved to leave the road.   But he first went to God in prayer, and the Spirit seemed to say to him, "I'll be with you," so he decided to work until August.

It was always a glad day for him when the pay-train came.   No one knew where his bank was, but he always wended his way to a certain rock away off in the woods, under which he concealed his well-earned wages.

In August he returned to Crawfordville. Having earned enough money to defray his expenses at school, he entered the Atlanta Baptist Seminary the following October.

He had not been at the seminary long before the teachers found him to be really a promising youth. As a student he was thorough and inquisitive. He was never reproved. He realized that his opportunity was worth all the effort he could put forth, so he spent no time in idleness. As a schoolmate he was genial and loving, always good-natured, hence he was loved by all the students.

The second year of his attendance at the seminary Mr. Murden did not seek a boarding place in the city, but stopped in the dormitory, where a number of the young men did their own work. Wednesday was his cooking day. You need not think he merely cooked special things on that day; it means he did not cook anything but once a week.

During the summer vacation of 1883 Mr. Murden taught school at his home. He was quite successful as a teacher, and the people loved him as they were wont to do. He taught school five consecutive summers, and thus earned money to defray his expenses at school. Everywhere he was loved by patrons and scholars, and always made warm friends wherever he went.

In 1886 Mr. Murden was licensed to preach by the Friendship Baptist Church, Crawfordville, Ga. He at once showed marked ability as a pulpit orator, and evinced signs of becoming one of the foremost preachers in the State.

In 1888 Rev. Murden preached the introductory sermon of the State Baptist Sunday-school Convention at

MISS M B. JOHNSON.

W. G. JOHNSON.

REV. MADISON, C.B., MASON, B.D., D.D.

Savannah, Ga., which led to his being appointed State Missionary by the State Convention.

As a missionary Rev. Murden was untiring in his efforts and faithful in visiting destitute places. For four years he traveled over the State preaching the gospel and doing what he could to lift his race to a higher standard of morality, intelligence and true Christian living.

Let the reader be assured that a missionary's path is not always a smooth one. Many times has Rev. Murden had to walk twenty and thirty miles in order to meet his appointments. He was not always received by the people, and not a few times has he gone without food forty-eight hours. But Rev. Murden had a true missionary spirit, and allowed none of these things to move him. He went about doing what his hands found to do, with the firm conviction: Where there's a will there's a way. He has many pleasant memories of persons converted through his own personal influence. Many times has he known wicked men to cry out while he was yet preaching. He has that peculiar gravity which draws people; having been once heard he never fails to get a congregation.

We need not add that as a missionary Rev. Murden was abundantly successful. By his resolute will and firm trust in God he has made an excellent record and done a great work among his people. He has the honor of being called the best financier of all the missionaries of Georgia.

As an orator Rev. Murden is quite fluent, and we make no mistake when we say eloquent. His graduating oration in May, 1886, won for him quite a name as a speaker. As a preacher he is a deep and ready thinker and never fails to make an impression.

Since May 1st, 1892, Rev. Murden has been pastor of the First Baptist Church, LaGrange, Ga. He has little experience as pastor; but thus far he has been quite successful. He has won a warm place in the hearts of the people, and the prospects are that his career in the line of church work may be a brilliant one.

In October, 1891, Rev. Murden married Miss Dora A. Jackson, of Atlanta, Ga., a graduate of Spelman Seminary. Theirs was a happy union. Their home is made cheerful by a bright little boy, A. B. Murden, Jr.

Rev. Murden is a graduate of the Normal and Theological departments of the Atlanta Baptist Seminary.

May this short sketch inspire some young man of mean circumstances to rise up and make for himself a name.

REV. ROBERT SCHELL,

SUCCESSFUL MINISTER OF THE GOSPEL.

The subject of this sketch was born October 12, 1855, at Barnesville, Pike county, Ga. As a slave he was the property of the man's daughter for whom the town was named (Barnes); and was when emancipated on a farm three and one-half miles from Barnesville, and was in his tenth year. His father, Vine Schell, then moved back to town, and then it was that Robert's pilgrimage began without learning or experience. He was first hired out as house boy; after which he moved to Griffin, Ga., and entered a public school taught by Northern ladies. This was in 1866. After staying in school for a few months he was again put out in service, this time working in a barroom. Leaving that, he was then put to work on the farm, where he spent two years, and endured many hardships, being without a mother's care. In 1870 his father moved the family on a farm at Milner, Ga. In 1872 Robert was apprenticed to the blacksmith trade, at which he worked during the day, going to school at night. Eighteen hundred and seventy-four found him again in school at Barnesville. During this same year he also worked as brickmason ; after which he served as a teamster; and next as a cook in a restaurant. In February, 1877, he married a Miss Lilian Schell, and in the fall of the same year moved to Atlanta. His first employment after coming to this city was that of teamster for a Mr. F. Kicklighter. Soon after this he worked on the custom house, which was then in course of erection. When his work on aforesaid building gave out he employed himself at draying for seventy-five cents per day; finally his wages were raised to ninety cents.

In the spring of 1880 Mr. Schell was converted, united with the Friendship Baptist Church, and was baptized by Rev. Frank Quarles, who was then pastor. He was elected church clerk soon afterward, and served in this capacity for seven years. During this time he was still draying, working in the wholesale grocery of a Mr. Smith, whose place of business was on Alabama street. He had so far gained the confidence and respect of his employer that his wages were raised from ninety cents per day to ten dollars per week, and the entire business of shipping goods was put into Mr. Schell's hands.

Mr. Smith carried on an extensive shipping business, and many thousands of dollars' worth did Mr. Schell send to all parts of Georgia, North and South Carolina and Florida.

While caring for his physical wants he wished also to contribute to his mental wants; so he entered the A. B. S., but continued in the service of Mr. Smith, working for him every afternoon after school hours. Of course his wages were not so much then, but were sufficient to enable him to provide for his family and keep himself in school. Mr. Schell felt that he was called to the ministry, and he wished to prepare himself for this great and grand work. He was given license in 1886 by the Friendship Baptist Church, while attending the Seminary, and in the following year was called to the pastorate of the Shiloh Baptist Church at Dallas, Ga. In the fall of the same year he went into business with J. T. Schell (his brother) at No. 145 West Peters street. During his stay at Dallas he built a neat house of worship, and baptized between eighteen and twenty-five persons. In the spring of the next year Mr. Schell became ill, and lost all his possessions but a home for his family. In 1889 he was appointed State Missionary, which he followed two years, during which time he was instrumental in the conversion of between one hundred and fifty and one hundred and seventy-five souls, who professed to know Christ in the pardon of their sins.

He has given up the missionary work, but serves in the city whenever he can, together with serving the churches at Dallas and Douglasville, Ga. He is also in charge of the McKinley Temple in West Atlanta, and is now considering a call to the Enon Church, Campbell county.

Rev: Schell is a member of the Executive and Educational Boards of the Friendship Association.

Thus it can be seen by these few pages that Rev. Schell has already accomplished much good and proved himself worthy of the life God has given him.

REV. MADISON C. B. MASON, A.M. B.D.,

POSTMASTER — BRILLIANT PASTOR — FIELD AGENT OF
THE FREEDMEN'S AID AND SOUTHERN EDUCATIONAL
SOCIETY OF THE METHODIST EPISCOPAL CHURCH.

Rev. M. C. B. Mason was born of slave parents on a
sugar farm near Houma, La., March 27, 1859.

When ten years of age he was placed in the village
school, where he mastered the alphabet in one day.
Reaching the limit of the country schools in the fall of
1874, he entered the State Agricultural and Mechanical
College, at New Orleans, La., in January, 1875. This
being a mixed school, he received no little persecution
and ill treatment on account of color. He, however,
refused to leave, and stood at the head of his class from
March till the close of the school in July.

Rev. Mason was principal of the town school of
Houma, where he was once a student, from 1877 to 1880.
In the fall term of 1880 he entered New Orleans University, but left in the spring term of 1881 to become postmaster of his native town. In 1883 he joined the Louisiana Conference of the Methodist Episcopal Church, and
was stationed at Haven Chapel, near New Orleans, when
he re-entered New Orleans University, graduating from
the classical department in 1888. In the pastorate Rev.
Mason has been successful, as his work at Haven, Thompson and Mallalien Churches in the city of New Orleans
will show. It was, however, while pastor of Loyd Street
Church, Atlanta, Ga., that he deservedly won his popularity as a preacher and pastor. During a pastorate of
two years the church greatly prospered under his minis-
trations, more than doubling its membership during this
time.

After coming to Atlanta he became a student of Gam-

mon Theological Seminary, from which he graduated
with high honors in 1891. Almost immediately thereafter he was elected field agent of the Freedmen's Aid and
Southern Educational Society of the Methodist Episcopal
Church, being the first colored man in his church who
had been honored with such a position. He holds the
position at this writing and is doing great service for the
churches and the race.

Rev. Mason is a man of fine scholastic taste, discrim-
inating in his choice of books and the subjects which he
treats. He has been North several times on lecturing
tours, and has published several of his addresses. His
addresses are specimens of eloquence, rhetoric and pol-
ish. His life is an inspiration for those who come after
him.

MR. H. A. HAGLER,

EDITOR—STATIONER.

The subject of this sketch was born March 21, 1866, in
Fairfield county, S. C., and is therefore about twenty-seven
years of age. His parents were poor, and their residence being in the country, they were illiterate, though
possessing those sterling qualities of honor, love of duty
and strict integrity, which they have transmitted in so
large a measure to their son.

His boyhood was spent in the most arduous toil, rendered imperative by the poverty of his people and the
scarcity of money. His first visit to the schoolroom
was when, as a small boy of seven, he walked four miles
to a country school taught by an aged and irascible white
man, who assisted the young idea to shoot, with a club
and strap. Here he learned his alphabet and in two

months' time was reading. The school then closed—the closing of which was but the opening of the youthful student's study time; alone and with occasional help from passers-by and traveling workmen, he pursued his studies.

When the term opened again he had so far advanced that he could " skip" a class. The school continued only three months—another long spell of wait and study; thus passed his boyhood until he reached his fifteenth year. During this period he acquired a taste for reading every almanac, newspaper, circular, magazine, or book of any shape or size. When first he found what "*nice reading*" was in the Bible, he determined to have one of his own; having secured it, for three years he read and reread until he knew it, until his mind was full of its truth, and with texts ever ready to illustrate and prove its truths, when later in life he went to lead others in the Sunday-school and debating club, he found how valuable to him had been the carrying of that Bible in his pocket for years.

His next acquisition in the book line was a dictionary ; alone he mastered the mystery of the diacritical marks, and there in his country home, where the English spoken is a kind of *patois*, he commenced to purify his English; finding that there were different forms of speech, he commenced to study the methods and art of expression, which later gave him prominence as a writer of strong, pure English in a clear, concise style.

When about fifteen the horizon of his country home seemed to become too small, so he removed to Columbia, S. C., then the Mecca of all aspiring youths in that section. There he heard of the inducements offered by Charleston to young men and went there, but not liking the cold welcome accorded him, he hastened to Savannah where he spent eight years. By the time he reached Savannah

his money was about gone, and he looked upon a position in a barber shop—though a menial one—as a god-
send.

He was polite, he was spry, he was anxious to learn;
hence soon we see him as a knight of the scissors and
razor plying his calling.

If we are to judge the past by the present, we may
know that he shaved close and cut rapidly and to the line
in a barber shop as well as in the editorial sanctum.

Ever desirous of change, when that change promised
advancement, he seized the first opportunity to learn the
printer's trade by entering the employ of Kuckuk &
Lieman, prominent job printers, where he learned to
fumble the em quod, manipulate the shooting stick, and
explore the deep, dark mysteries of the helve box, and
knock things generally into "pi." A job office, while it
is a good place to learn to set type in, is not a good place
to learn journalism, and at last our young man has dared
to determine to become a journalist. In the office of that
great daily he saw the inner workings of a first-class paper, the association with brainy men in an air saturated
with journalistic vim, developed the fever in the young
man; once more his horizon is too contracted for him. We
are a little surprised to see him assume managerial control of the *People's Journal*, published at Rome, Ga. Here
he stayed four or five months, when an advertisement in
an exchange, the *Atlanta Times*, for a competent printer
to act as foreman and manager, determined him to come
to Atlanta, that magnetic city to which so many strong
men seem naturally to gravitate. Finding the *Times* in a
shaky financial condition, and having been disappointed in
the promised position as foreman and manager, and another installed in his stead, he worked there as a subor-
dinate until he secured a position in a white job office.
At this time, without a dollar in his pocket and not one

MISS VICTORIA MADDOX.

H. A. HAGLER.

friend in town—in fact with only a few acquaintances, with no one to aid—he determined on carrying into effect the darling project of his heart, to start a paper of his own. The *People's Advocate* was the result. Started as a monthly, soon the financial status enabled him to make it a weekly, and with the same increase in circulation through the coming time, it will not be long before the people will call it into a daily.

Most colored papers *start* (after great advertising) with a boom, then "peter out." The *Advocate*, born out of time, cradled in the editor's pocket, having for an office the editor's hat, has had a phenomenal run; each issue is larger than the last, and there are never any back copies to be had. The growth of the circulation is uniform.

The paper is Hagler, and Hagler is the paper. The paper is the best in the South, and compares in matter and finish favorably with any Negro publication in this country.

It was largely through Mr. Hagler's influence that the recently organized Negro Press Association of Georgia was called into being; he labored, wrote, spoke, and canvassed for it. As its Vice-President and member of the Executive Committee, he will have much to do with its policies and future usefulness. Thus his field is enlarging; he is a young man of promise; look out for him in the future.

Believing that the home is the chief corner-stone of the State, Mr. Hagler married early. His was a love marriage. His wife, M. Francessa, is a dutiful, sympathetic, intelligent and helpful helpmate, and it is said is one of the most competent compositors ever employed in the office. Two beautiful children, a girl and boy, have blessed this union. In his home Mr. Hagler is a model husband, kind, gentle and loving.

After the establishment of the *Advocate*, he had associated with him in his job office Mr. Moses Amos, a thorough business man and pleasant gentleman, the leading Negro pharmacist in the State in point of ability and experience. After continuing the pleasant business relations for sometime Mr. Amos retired, Mr. Hagler purchasing his interest. Thus Mr. Hagler runs the best Negro paper in Georgia, the only Negro job office in Atlanta, and the largest Negro bookstore in the South. He has made Negro literature a specialty since his opening business.

If we judge a man by what he has overcome, keeping in view the obstacles which he has surmounted, the depths from which he has ascended and the heights attained, then no fair, impartial man could withhold from this man the claim of heroism which is justly his due.

His mind is still growing; in his editorials there appears more profoundness of thought; his investigations are still going on. What may we not hope from the future of this man who has triumphed so grandly in the past ?

PROFESSOR W. H. CROGMAN, A.M.

William Henry Crogman, who occupies the chair of Latin and Greek in Clark University, in this city, in Christian character, scholarship in his department, literary ability, general culture, and distinguished services, stands, it is not too much to say, the equal of any of the great educators of the country. He is thoroughly capable to honor a professorship in any college in the land.

Professor Crogman was born in the year 1841, on the beautiful little island of St. Martin, in the West Indies. In his fourteenth year he left that island with a gentleman by the name of B. L. Boomer, at that time first mate on a vessel. Mr. Boomer from the first became very much interested in young Crogman, and after returning home in Massachusetts, sent him to the district school, where he made a good record. He afterwards followed the sea along with Mr. Boomer's brother, who was also a sea-faring man and captain of a vessel. In this way the boy Willie, as he was then called, had the privilege of visiting many lands, England, Sweden, Germany, Australia, Calcutta, Bombay, Brazil, Argentine Republic, Peru, Chili, and many other places. Being observant and thoughtful, while even a lad, Professor Crogman obtained a wide knowledge of men and things.

Just here I insert a few words from a letter from Mr. Boomer, read at Professor Crogman's fiftieth anniversary:

"It has been my good fortune to know our good friend all the way from his fifteenth to his present fiftieth year, and it would afford me the greatest satisfaction if I could feel that his great success in all these years had, in any manner, been furthered by me. On the contrary, his untiring perseverance, diligent, wise and studious use of his time and money made him from the first independent of all save our love, respect and never ceasing interest."

In 1866, at the suggestion of Mr. Boomer that an academic education would make him more useful, the young man Crogman began to earn money and lay it away for this purpose. In 1868 he entered Peirce Academy, Middleboro, Mass., where he took a course of study comprising the higher English branches and French. He also took a commercial or business course in a commercial college at that time connected with the academy. While attending this school he had to encounter (though not in the school) that fiendish race prejudice which everywhere among white people in this country ostracizes the Negro. Nevertheless, he completed his course with honor to himself and credit to his race.

Professor J. W. P. Jenks, of Brown University, Providence, R. I., who was at that time principal of the academy, writes these good words in reference to his splendid scholarship and rapid progress made under him. He says:

"Beginning with me in the elementary English branches, I may safely say, in them all, he accomplished in one quarter as much as the average student did in two, mastering almost intuitively, and with equal facility, both mathematical and linguistic principles. So rapid was his progress in his classes that I formed him into a class of one, lest he should be hindered by the dullness of other students. In the third quarter, he commenced French, and, as I have often said, surpassed every one of the hundreds of students in both rapidity of advancement and accuracy of scholarship. I need say no more, except that his record since leaving the academy, taking all the extenuating circumstances into account, has reflected greater honor upon me as its principal, and his almost sole instructor while connected with it, than any other alumnus."

Having completed his studies at the academy, he turned his footsteps southward in order that he might devote the energies of his life to the elevation of his people. In the fall of 1870 he was employed in Claflin University, Orangeburg, S. C., and taught there three years. Desiring to render himself more proficient in his chosen work, he came to Atlanta in the fall of 1873 and entered the Atlanta University, from which institution he graduated in 1876 in the first class of young men that came out of that school.

Professor Frances, of the Atlanta University, on Professor Crogman's fiftieth birthday, in a speech, paid the

Professor a most glowing tribute both with reference to his scholarship and his conduct while a student. He said that the Professor had carried away as his bride one of their noblest, most gifted, and cultured young ladies, Miss Lavinia C. Mott, of Charlotte, N. C.

In September of that same year, 1876, he was called to a position on the faculty of Clark University, where he still remains teaching with great acceptability to students and employers, the classic tongues of Greece and Rome. It is safe to say that the name of Professor W. H. Crogman has done more to win respect for Clark University and draw students to it than the name of any or all who have been connected with the institution.

In token of respect for this great man and his services, on his fiftieth birthday, at a reception given him by Dr. Thirkield, he received many valuable gifts from different parts of the country, North and South. Among these were an elegant gold watch, a set of beautiful Carlsbad china, nine handsomely bound volumes of ancient classics, along with a large ornamental inkstand, from which rolled one hundred dollars in gold. The china was especially appropriate, as it recognized the merit of Mrs. Crogman, who is the queenly helpmeet of the noble subject of this sketch, and presides over one of the most cultured homes of this land. She is a worthy mother of seven children.

In 1884 Professor Crogman was elected one of the secretaries of the General Conference of the Methodist Episcopal Church. To this office, which he filled with great efficiency, he was again elected in 1888. Rev. D. S. Monroe, D.D., the chief secretary, who nominated him, says, "I was certainly fortunate in securing the services of one so efficient, educated, modest and gentlemanly as Professor Crogman.

Rev. Charles H. Payne, D.D., Secretary of the Board of Education of the M. E. Church, says of him, " I have

watched his course with a brother's interest, and have
rejoiced to see his loyalty to principle and his fidelity to
duty. Few men in our church have rendered more useful service in our educational work than he. Few men
have maintained a more straightforward and manly
course, or acted more wisely under all circumstances, than
has he."

Another distinguished man said of him, "He is an
honor to the human race. I wish the world were full of
such men."

These tributes show that by fidelity to right principles
one may make his life useful, admirable, grand.

Some years ago, a university of good standing, wishing
to do honor to Professor Crogman, conferred upon him
the degree of LL.D., which degree he, nevertheless, re-
spectfully declined. Professor Crogman has also won
great distinction for himself and great respect for his
people by his wonderful power and gift of speech. On
manifold occasions he has had the honor of addressing
the most cultured audiences with greatest acceptability.
At Ocean Grove, at Henry Ward Beecher's church, at the
National Teachers' Association, and many other places
of note, Professor Crogman has spoken, and has never
failed to come up to expectations.

In conclusion, and for the benefit of the rising generation, we may say that the life of this remarkable man is
only an illustration of the truth of Scripture, which saith,
"Blessed is the man that is diligent in all things; he shall
stand before kings."

MISS ———— MADDOX.

No person can ever tell how much the world owes to
its mothers and good guardians. We can never be too
grateful for the unwearying love and care of them. And

on the other hand, they can never think too highly of that grand work of training children, for they never know for what glorious work they are training them. The mother, grandmother and Spelman Seminary have given to Georgia, in the person of Victoria W. Maddox, a woman in which the race might be justly proud. Her progress is an eminent example of that perseverance that in its onward and unwearied march conquers all difficulties, and makes what would be stumbling-blocks to ordinary women stepping-stones to prominence. The record of her life is full of interest, and it is impossible to give her justice in this small sketch. We must simply satisfy ourselves to speak of some of her common characteristics which have caused so many to admire her.

Miss Maddox was born at Stone Mountain, DeKalb county, Ga. She was the daughter of Ned and Betsie Maddox, who lived on a farm near Stone Mountain. Her father died when she was but four years old, leaving her widowed mother to provide for her small children. The difficulties she encountered in trying to care for them are too numerous to mention here. Her parents were both members of the Baptist church, her father being a deacon. Before the mother had been left long to face the stern realities which every widow experiences in caring for their children, God saw fit to remove her from a life of toils and disappointments, and this left the children (three in number) to care for themselves.

Through the kind providence of God they managed to provide for themselves and to surmount the hills of adversity until they reached the age of maturity. Miss Victoria was always a quiet, modest and sweetly disposed girl, easy to be instructed, and it was by this that she was influenced in the right direction. A short time after the death of her parents she joined Bethsaida Baptist Church at Stone Mountain, Ga., under the pastorate of Rev.

E. R. Carter. Her Christian life was exemplary. Many were her disadvantages, but, like a woman, she surmounted them all, and to-day stands shoulder to shoulder with the leading young women of her race.

Miss Maddox became a member of Spelman Seminary in 1881, when the school was in the basement of Friendship Baptist Church, Atlanta, Ga. Her eagerness for an education, her devotion to her studies, her deportment and Christian character soon won the love and respect of her teachers, classmates and schoolmates. Her teachers soon recognized in her one who gave promise of being a large factor in the uplifting of her race. She graduated with honor in 1888. She was retained as teacher in her Alma Mater in 1881 and 1889. She taught successfully in Howe Institute, Memphis, Tenn., and in many other places. That genial and compatible disposition, that earnest desire to lift her race intellectually and morally, has caused her to be admired in every place where she has labored. In 1891 she entered the Missionary Training Department of Spelman Seminary, then opened for the first time, and completed the course in 1893. She has ever been found to be firm in her religious principles, never swerving from the right to please others. Being just in her decisions she was often called upon by her classmates and schoolmates to decide questions of difference among them. A noble Christian worker, she lives to-day an ornament to her race.

A. O. LOCKHART, M.D.

Among the men of the race who are able to annex the title M.D. to their names is found this one, of whom Atlantians should be justly proud. No one of whom we have spoken is more worthy of space in this, the "Black

A. O. LOCKHEART, M.D.

MOSES AMOS, PH. M.

Side," than he.   No one deserves more praise for having
surmounted obstacles than does A. O. Lockhart, the subject of this narrative.   He is a self-made man, having
from early boyhood up to the present depended entirely
upon his own resources for a livelihood.   Few there are
who are willing to suffer and endure what he did to gain
an education.   Not many would have braved the fury of
the tempest and not succumb.   But our hero looked beyond the means to the end.   He fought to obtain the
prize, and nothing short of that would satisfy him.   Consequently he ranks to-day with the leaders of the race,
and that race should be appreciative of such leaders.

In the village in which he was reared young Lockhart
was considered no ordinary youth, and a bright, useful
future was predicted for him.

To prepare himself for real life-work he, in 1879, entered
the Atlanta Baptist Seminary, where he took a complete
course of all the studies there taught.   He had little or
no ready means of support, but by hard, honest toil succeeded in accomplishing his desires in the line of education.   Having completed his course at the A. B. S., and
desiring to be a man of profession, he went to Meharry
Medical College in pursuit of the needed information.
Gaining that, he has returned to us ready and equipped
to fight against the diseases which sometimes hold sway
over these earthly tabernacles of ours.

Dr. Lockhart is proficient in his profession, thus receiving a pretty good amount of practice.

He possesses a strong will and nerve, and believes that
victory attends the daring, success awaits the persevering.   All honor to such men!

Albert Owen Lockhart was born near Hampton, Henry
county, Ga., November 24, 1860.   Soon after the war
the family moved near Jonesboro and sett'ed on a farm.
9

Here this young man resided till twenty-one years of age, working on farm and doing other work to assist himself to acquire the much-needed education.

He is now one of Atlanta's noted physicians and druggists, and bids fair to be successful in his profession. Success to him.

IRWIN W. HAYES, M.D.,

BRILLIANT STUDENT, SUCCESSFUL TEACHER, GRAND DEPUTY FOR THE STATE OF GEORGIA, ABLE PHYSICIAN AND SURGEON.

Among the many young men of the State of Georgia who have risen above the clouds of ignorance and superstition that overshadowed their birth and early life, and are destined to write their names high upon the pages of history, and equally indelibly upon the hearts of men, perhaps none looms up with more promise than the subject of this sketch. Irwin W. Hayes was born at Tennille, Washington county, Ga., May 5, 1865. He was the second son of Charlotte Hayes, and at quite an early age gave signs of promise and future usefulness. Being of Negro, Caucasian and Irish extraction he possesses to some extent the peculiarities of each. His early life was passed at Tennille and Sandersville, Ga., and it was at these places that he first began to study books. At the age of eight he was hired upon a farm four miles in the country, and was assigned the work of a "shepherd boy," watching cattle upon the pastures. While thus employed he was seized with the desire to know something. He finally obtained a spelling-book and was not long learning to spell, then to read, and next to write. At the expiration of two years he secured a position at Sandersville which enabled him to attend school at night, though he had to work during the day. Being an apt, swift pupil, at the age of twelve he entered the common school under the principalship of Professor J. A. Butler, and completed the course in two years. Next he obtained employment in the National Hotel at Macon, Ga., as bell boy at night, and during the day attended the Lewis High School. He did not remain here very long, being summoned home on the account of sickness. Subsequently, being without sufficient means to return to Macon, he taught a small school during the summer, but realizing so little cash from this he left for Savannah, where he hoped to secure work whereby he might be able to help his mother, and at the same time continue his studies. Failing to secure such work in Savannah he embarked upon the steamer "Halyson" as cabin-boy. During his two years' stay with this vessel he recited daily to the captain (who was quite a learned man), and in this way completed all the principal English studies, besides enriching his life by traveling.

During his voyages he touched the shores of the great continents of the earth. In 1881 he returned to this country, entered Cookman Institute at Jacksonville, Fla., where he completed the course of study in two years, graduating at the head of his class. In this institute he was considered as being the only student who could break and make classes at will. October, 1883, he matriculated in the Clark University at Atlanta, Ga., but being in poor health and with limited means, his career here was uneventful. He, however, completed the higher mathematics, all the sciences and most of the languages. In 1885 he had some altercation with the faculty of the university, which grew out of a misunderstanding between himself and a teacher. Having been indefinitely suspended he demanded a proper dismissal, entered Benedict College at Columbia, S. C., and gradu-

ated from the scientific course with the degree of B.S.
the following spring. He returned to Georgia and began the work of teaching in Greene county. Soon after
was elected President of the Teachers' Institute of
Greene county, which position he very creditably filled
for two years. It was now that he turned his attention
to the study of medicine. Accordingly he became a
student of the Leonard Medical College of the city of
Raleigh, N. C. He took two courses of lectures and
one summer's course of study, after which he graduated
with the degree of M.D. Was twice elected from this
school to represent the medical fraternity before the Missionary Association of North Carolina. This he did in
such an able manner that he elicited the praise of the
whole body.

Leaving Leonard Medical College he came to Georgia, and during the summers of 1889 and 1890 taught
school and practiced medicine in Hapeville, Ga. Hearing of the opening of city hospitals of Nashville, Tenn.,
to colored students, he determined to avail himself of all
the clinical advantages possible. Thus, on the first of
November, 1890, he entered the Clinical Sanitarium of
Nashville, paying strict attention to surgery, gynecology
and pharmacy, and again was awarded the degree of
M.D. February, 1892. During his stay at Nashville he
won not only the prize for excellence in practice, but carried off the gold medal which was offered by the Inter-
Collegiate Association at their annual oratorical contest
of 1892. Since his last graduation he has located in
Atlanta, Ga. Dr. Hayes has proven himself a thorough-
going and able physician, and has already won a reputation of which any young practitioner would be proud.
He takes well with his people, commands a large practice and is highly respected by all. During the past few
months he has, for reasons best known to himself, refused

the proprietorship and management of two drug stores. At the Biennial Conference of the Colored Men's Protective Association of Georgia, held at Atlanta, July, 1892, he figured conspicuously in advancing plans for the bettering of the association, and was unanimously elected Grand Deputy for the State of Georgia. This position he still holds to the satisfaction of all. May this young man live long that he may do much good for the race of which he is a member.

MOSES AMOS,

PHARMACEUTIST.

In the city of Atlanta there lives a young man who has established himself in the drug business, and whose standing in the community makes him a fitting representative of the State of Georgia and the city of Atlanta.

He is considered as one of the solid young men of the city, and the success which he has made during his short life should not be kept from the public. The number of business men among our people is small at best, and when we have one whose deeds are worth recording let us record them.

We have orators, divines and professors in abundance, but our business men are few, and especially in the line of business represented by the named person.

Not many launch out in this enterprise, but here is one who is well equipped in the business. Mr. Moses Amos first saw the light of day at Haynesville, Ga., in the year 18—, where his early days were passed.

In 1876 he came to Atlanta, and shortly afterwards entered Storr's School. He remained a student of this school till he completed the course of study in 1885.   In the fall of the same year he entered the Atlanta University, making the junior "prep." class.   After passing awhile as student of that institution, because of business engagements, he was not able to finish the course.

The life of this enterprising young man is a history in itself.   Quite early in life he was employed by Dr. J. C. Huss, by whom he was given a thorough knowledge of pharmacology.   Seeing that Moses was of quick perception and would doubtless be of great service to him in his business, the doctor took great care in teaching him pharmaceutics, little guessing that at some future day he would put this knowledge into practical use for himself and his people.

This was even then manifested by the fact that most of the customers of the store were the patrons of Mr. Amos and not of Dr. Huss.   He remained with Dr. Huss until that gentleman sold out the business to its present owners, Drs. Butler and Slater.   When they assumed charge of the business, they retained Mr. Amos, finding in him just what they desired.   At first his salary was small, but at the expiration of a few months, it was raised to quite a handsome sum.   Mr. Amos is still with this company to whom he has rendered great satisfaction.

He is one of the shrewdest young business men in the city, and for his true worth well merits the honor and respect shown him.   He is interested in several paying enterprises, and an owner of much of Atlanta real estate.

THOMAS HEATHE SLATER, M.D.

In the town of Salisbury, N. C., December 25, A. D. 1865, Thomas H. Slater came into this life.

His early life was passed at his North Carolina home,

where he received a complete knowledge of the rudiments of an English education. Having gone over and over again the same studies, young Thomas began to think of going to Shaw University where he could secure a higher course of study. Just as the necessary preparations for his leaving were completed, death came unannounced and robbed him of his father.

This was in 1882, and of course all thoughts of school were temporarily dismissed. In 1882 Rev. F. C. Potter, a graduate of Lincoln University, suggested the idea of going to that school, and volunteered his assistance in securing a scholarship for the doctor. In this Rev. Potter was successful, and in September of the same year the young man bade farewell to his mother, his friends and the home of his childhood and took leave for Lincoln. He entered the university as a "prep." in the "A" class.

That indomitable spirit of conquest and victory began to manifest itself, and he began to strive for honors. Early he comprehended the words, " Knowledge is Power." As he succeeded in accumulating knowledge, he found himself more and more in the possession of power, and to stand first or second in a class followed as a necessary sequence of this power. At last, after five years hard study, he was graduated in June, 1887, with first honor and the captor of the Bradley medal, a prize offered for the best average in a five years' course of the natural sciences.

While at Lincoln he was very fond of the classics, and delivered the Greek salutatory on Class day and the Latin salutatory on Commencement.

From Lincoln his thoughts turned to Philadelphia, the Mecca of the followers of the medical faith. Here he received his first blow from the shillalah of prejudice. The Medico-Chirurgical College of that city is a dissatisfied offspring of Jefferson Medical College, the

Gibraltar of Southern opposition and the hotbed of
Southern prejudice. The faculty of the former school,
after admitting him, summarily informed him that they
could not admit him on the ground that it was not ex-
pedient for that year. The truth was that the white
students did not want to contend with a Negro for class
leadership. The fear of "Negro domination" is a bugbear up there too.

Nothing daunted, he resolved to go elsewhere, and
through the kindness of Dr. G. W. Hubbard, the Dean
of the Meharry Medical College, he was allowed to enter
that school in the autumn of the same year, 1877. In
this school he evinced the same spirit as of yore, and
with his present partner and former classmate, Dr. H. R.
Butler, succeeded in capturing "the gold," Dr. Butler
winning the medal for excellence in dissecting and surgery, and Dr. Slater the one for excellence in obstetrics.

Immediately after graduating from Meharry, he came
to Atlanta, Ga., where he began the practice of medicine,
and with Dr. Butler, opened the first drugstore in the
State of Georgia, owned and operated by colored men.
'Tis safe to say that they are doing a larger retail drug
business than any Negro drug business in the United
States. His practice, scattered among Atlanta's best
class of Negro citizens, has steadily improved in value.
The doctor's ability, scholarship and talent is a strong
denial of the lie that a Negro has little or no talent. His
intellect towers above that of ordinary men as the church
steeple above the brick chimney of the ordinary house.
His success is sure and a bright future awaits him.

I. W. HAYES, B.S., M.D.

T. H. SLATER, M. D.

DR. H. R. BUTLER, M.D.

H. R. BUTLER, A.B., M.D.

The subject of this sketch was born in Cumberland county, N. C., April, 1862.

His early life was spent on the farm. About 1876 his parents moved to the city of Wilmington, N. C. Shortly after reaching the city, he secured employment with the lumber firm, then known as Colville, Taylor & Co.

Here he worked himself up from the most humble position to be one of their most reliable men. Business becoming dull with the firm, Mr. Butler pushed himself out, not being a man to wait for something to turn up, and applied to the Wilmington Compress Company for employment. He was received, and worked with this company for six or seven years, during which time he worked himself up from a hoop-straightener to a cotton tier, and was said to be the soberest man in the employ of the company. It was in this latter position he made the money to start him in school.

Having spent only three months in free schools, his education was of course limited. Professor E. E. Green, now Dr. Green, of Macon, and his wife, gave him a few months of private instruction at night, preparatory to his entering the University.

In January, 1883, Dr. Butler bade his many friends good-bye, saying he intended to make a man of himself, God willing. He reached Lincoln University January 3, 1883, and after spending five and a half years in hard study, and often in need of the necessaries of life, he was graduated with the class of '87 with the degree of A.B. In the fall of the same year, without money enough to put him through the term, he entered Meharry Medical College, Nashville, Tenn. While there he won the H. T. Noel gold medal for being the most proficient in operative surgery and dissecting. Five days after receiving his degree of M.D. and diploma, he left Nashville for Atlanta, Ga. Here he put out his shingle and is now enjoying a large and lucrative practice. In January last he was appointed by the democratic governor of Georgia surgeon to the Second Battalion of Georgia Volunteers, colored, with the rank of first lieutenant. He is also one of the leading business men now of our race. He and Dr. T. H. Slater, also of North Carolina, are doing the largest retail drug business of any colored drug establishment in the United States.

Dr. Butler and his partner were the pioneer druggists of the Negro race in the State of Georgia, and hence hold the first pharmacy license ever issued to Negroes in the history of the State of Georgia.

EDWARD J. TURNER,

PHARMACIST.

The hope of the nation is the young men, whose aspirations are such as will develop them into good and loyal citizens.

Their habits, conduct and common pursuits will decide what home, society and government will be.

And when we, who are more experienced, more acquainted with the ways of life, see younger brothers striving to press their way to the front ranks of the race, we should open file and let them in line. One calculated to benefit his race, full of ambition and loyalty, is the subject of this sketch. Until Edward was six months of age his parents were in easy circumstances, his father being the leading barber of the town in which he lived;

but the father died, misfortune came, and their possessions were swept away, and the mother found herself in straitened circumstances. She toiled arduously for the maintenance of herself and child, and was successful in providing for him intellectually, as well as morally and physically, until he was old enough to assist her. The home, which to the mother had been so pleasant during the father's life, was now broken up, and Edward, having arrived at the age when he could steer alone, launched his boat out upon the broad sea of life. Coming to Atlanta, Ga., he entered the Clark University that he might prepare himself for life's work. His financial condition would not allow him to remain an inmate long at that institution.

Having a knowledge of pharmacy, he was offered a situation as druggist in the firm of Drs. Asbury, Taylor and Company. He accepted this offer, and is rendering satisfactory service to all concerned.

Mr. Turner is a steady, upright young man, and by his gentility and agreeableness of disposition, he is destined one day to be an honored citizen.

He is quite a young man, not yet eighteen years old. Thus, before him lies a whole lifetime of usefulness, and the writer hopes that he will exercise his ability and talent to do good wherever and whenever needed. Mr. Turner speaks most tenderly of his mother, and the precepts taught him by her he cherishes fondly, and says whatever goodness or greatness he may attain will be due to the teachings of his Christian mother and adviser. He is a native of Enterprise, Miss.

MR. WALTER H. LANDRUM,

ONE OF ATLANTA'S HONORED CITIZENS—A MODEL MAN.

One who has made rapid strides up the ladder of success is the subject of this paper.

He started at the lowest round, but by perseverance, industry and toil he has already reached a height of which the most ambitious might well be proud.

His mother is Mrs. Eliza Landrum, a woman of firm purpose, who used great care in the training of her children, of which Walter is the second.

From his mother he inherited a spirit of thriftiness, for while he was yet quite young he would peddle about with cakes and pies, or do any sort of work which would bring him the honest dollar.

When he was but nine years of age he was apprenticed to the brickmason's trade, but in this pursuit money came in too slowly for Walter, so he obtained a more lucrative occupation with Mr. Wesley Darden, who paid him a salary of three dollars per week. He desired to do even better than this, and began to search for work which would pay him better. Finally, in 1876, he secured work with the Central Railroad of Georgia, and has been in the service of said railroad for sixteen years. Every one who is acquainted with Mr. Landrum knows he is the embodiment of prudence, economy and discretion combined.

Before engaging in any action he first considers and investigates most thoroughly, and whatever he may realize from any movement he does not readily throw away. In short, he exercises wisdom and judgment in all his undertakings. His dealings with his fellow-men are characteristic of fairness and equity. In truth, it may be said of him that he is one who practices the "golden rule."

As a worker in benevolent organizations he has few equals. Has for years been identified with the I.O.O.F., in which body he has held the highest offices in its gift. Passing through all degrees, he has filled every office and is now Patriarch. He is also allied with the Good Samaritan Lodge, in which he has also occupied conspicuous places. Mr. Landrum is charitable and benevolent, refusing help to no one who is needy; an advocate of every movement having for its object the elevation or advancement of the Negro. He is associated with several enterprises of this city, and possesses no little amount of her soil, owning many desirable lots on some of the principal streets. His home residence, on West Mitchell street, as seen in the cut, is attractive, and on entering it one's eyes are made to feast on beauty and art. An amiable, affectionate wife presides over his household in which two lovely children scatter sunshine.

Aside from his possessions in the city, Mr. Landrum owns a productive farm consisting of fifty-five acres. This land lies along the Central Railroad and is within three miles of Jonesboro, Ga.

He is a member of the Friendship Baptist Church, and an honored and trusty deacon, a teacher in the Sunday-school, and, on the whole, a devout worker for the kingdom of Christ. He pays taxes on fifty-five hundred dollars' worth of property. Mr. Landrum was born at Wintersville, Ga., February 19, 1859.

MR. JOHN T. SCHELL,

ENTERPRISING, PROGRESSIVE, RISING CITIZEN.

In that lovely month of the year when Nature puts off her sable costume for one of emerald, when the buds

begin to unfold themselves to our view and the grass
peeps up from the soil, in the year 1857, John T. Schell,
the subject of this narrative, came into this life.

Without doubt he is one of the most assiduous in business that it is my pleasure to know. He is also benevolent, having built a house of worship, which, unfortu-
nately, was destroyed by fire some months ago. Mr.
Schell is a native of Barnesville, but until the emancipation lived three and one-half miles from that town. His
mother is   , his father Colonel Wm.
Fletcher, a lawyer by profession, and from him our subject inherited the business talents which characterize him·

His mother having married a man by the name of Schell,
he took his stepfather's name, which he still bears. In
1865 his stepfather removed the family to Barnesville,
and he was sent to live with an aunt in Griffin, Ga. His
aunt hired him out as an errand boy, but he had opportunity to attend school part of each day, and, being apt,
he learned quite readily. He remained with his aunt till
1867, when he returned to his mother, who apprenticed
him to the shoemaker's trade. Working at that till he
served out his apprenticeship, he came up to Milner, Ga.,
and opened a shop for himself. While at this place he
met and married a Miss Sarah Fambro, a charming girl
in the bloom of youth. After his marriage he stayed on
for a while, when, thinking he might· better his financial
condition, he came to Atlanta. After reaching this city, he
found it exceedingly hard to find employment at his trade.
He searched and searched for work, but all in vain.

The few cents he had brought with him had nearly all
been spent, and he had not the means to open a business
of his own. He had a wife now who was dependent
upon him; what must he do? Finding he could not
secure work at his trade, he began to look about for
other employment. Finance was at a low ebb, and he

must get work of whatever nature. Accordingly he
engaged as a paint-washer at the Markham Hotel. One
day, while at his work, he discovered that the hotel boys
were ridiculing him because he did not wear the stylish
" tooth-pick " shoes. Being humiliated at this, he spent
the last dollar and cents he had for a pair. Then the
idea of drudgery and " tooth-pick " shoes became dis-
gusting to him, and he resolved to seek another field of
labor.

This time he was more fortunate than at first, as he
succeeded in getting work at his trade with a Mr. Tines.
His wages were poor, but he remained with Mr. Tines
till he was offered more money by Mr. Latham, with
whom he went to work. He was soon able to move his
family to Atlanta, which he did, but the expense of caring for it decently was more than he could do with his
small wages; thus he left his trade, purchased a receipt
for making a patent soap, and by this enterprise he realized enough cash to start some line of business. So he
opened up a small grocery, with a shoe shop attached, on
Peters street. This was his starting point. His business flourished, and ere long he became the owner of the
building in which his business was carried on.

Signal success has attended him ever afterward, and
he is now classed with the wealthiest citizens of the Gate
City of the South. He is a member of every prominent
enterprise in the city, an extensive dealer in real estate,
and an owner of much of that real estate. He has a
snug bank account, and, on the whole, is a progressive
and rising young man. A cultured and amiable wife presides over his pleasant, beautifully arranged home, in
which four bright, merry children mingle their happy
voices.

Mr. Schell is a leading spirit in political, social and
financial matters in this city, and his industry and atten-

tion to business, his urbanity and sobriety, characterize him a model man. In addition to his vast amount of real estate he owns a well supplied dry goods establishment. He is master of his trade, having followed it for twenty-six years. In connection with his dry goods store is a shoe store, and he has another in a different portion of the city. Wonderful has been his success in so few years. Mr. Schell is also owner of a neat, three-storied brick building which adorns that portion of the city in which it is located.

MR. THOMAS L. LYMAN,

A RISING, INDUSTRIOUS YOUNG MAN.

Newnan, Ga., in Coweta county, was the scene of this young man's birth, and the year was 18——. He only spent four years of his early life at this place, after which time, his father having died, his widowed mother sent him to Marietta, Ga., where he was to live with his grandparents. While in Marietta he attended school, which was under the supervision of a Mrs. Johnson. After spending five years in Marietta, he returned to Atlanta. Leaving Atlanta, he went to Opelika, Ala., and while there attended school, and after school hours clerked in his brother's store. Staying with his brother till misfortune caused him (his brother) to close his place of business, he then returned to Atlanta to care for and assist his mother. In 1888 he married Miss Cora Boswell, a gentle, refined, intellectual lady, who, together with a bright little boy of two years, makes his home a comfort and joy.

Mr. Lyman owns a most beautiful home in a very desirable portion of the city, the hospitality of which many friends enjoy.

RESIDENCE OF W. H. LANDRUM.

THOMAS LYMAN.

He is a model young man, thrifty and saving; and his industrious, economical wife shares equally his sorrows and his joys.

Mr. Lyman, of course, did not have the many disadvantages and difficulties to encounter which so many others have had, but nevertheless he was a poor boy, and accumulated what he has through industry, toil and perseverance, and that is saying a great deal for him.

MR. JAMES C. ODOM,

A THRIVING MERCHANT.

Among the thorough-going young men of this city who are full of energy and pluck can be classed Mr. James C. Odom. He is genial and courteous, and possesses in no little degree that quality which is termed grit. His parents, perceiving in him an aptness to learn, placed him in school so soon as he was old enough to attend. They were soon rewarded by James having, at an early age, completed with credit his studies in the grammar school, and being prepared to enter a school of a higher course of studies. Consequently, he entered the Atlanta University, where he applied himself diligently for a number of years. Then, deciding that he had received so much from his parents it was now his duty to assist them; accordingly he left college and began teaching school. He taught for a successive number of years in the State of Florida. While in that State his father died; he gave up his work there and returned home that he might care for and comfort his mother. He is a lover of home, and has the peace and protection of it at heart. Mr. Odom struggled under the disad-

10

vantages common to all colored young men, and by which so many of our young men are carried down the abyss of ruin; but possessing an indomitable will he managed to keep his head above the sweeping tide ; and to-day is a model young man. In 1890 he commenced the grocery business. This was known under the names, Goodlett & Odom; but Mr. Odom, in a few months, bought out Mr. Goodlett's share and is now sole owner of the house. This has not proved a failure, but the stock of two hundred dollars with which he began has increased eight times its value. He makes a splendid living for himself and family, and has no mean supply laid by for days which may be rainy. For one of his years Mr. Odom has done remarkably well; and how well he may yet do is for the coming years to decide. The future is big with promises for him. He believes that he can do what others have done. He has no place in his vocabulary for "I can't."

Recently Mr. Odom was married to the accomplished and amiable Miss Pickens of this city, in whom he possesses a jewel of much value. He is not a native of Atlanta, having first beheld the light of day in Carrollton, Ga., A. D. 1864.

MR. PETER F. HOGAN,

ANOTHER RISING YOUNG MAN.

Were two-thirds of the Negro population of Atlanta made up of such thrifty men as is the subject of this sketch, it would be *well* with the entire city; for he is one who possesses in a considerable degree the requisites for the advancement of a people like ours. He did not live

during the days of bondage; but while justice was de-
manding the liberation of the slaves and injustice was
struggling to fasten more tightly the shackles which
already bound them, Peter first opened his eyes to the
light of this world. He experienced some sadness during his early life. When only seven years old his father
was burnt to death. After the death of his father, he,
with his mother and brother, went to live with his grandfather. Soon after they had settled themselves comfortably at their new home the summons came for the
grandparent to join the innumerable caravan gone on before. Then the family was once again dispersed. The
boys, though young, undertook farming, but with no help
except that of a mother found it a difficult task. There
was a school being taught in their little village, and they
were both anxious to attend; but the mother could not
spare them both; so she sent one son one week and the
other son the next week; thus trying to do her duty by
both. Finally, she was advised to give Peter as much
advantage in school as possible, as he displayed a quick
and clear perception ; so Peter was sent daily to school.

In 1886 he came to Atlanta, thinking that in this city he
might have better opportunities to become a more useful
man. His ambition was to assist in the elevation and the
advancement of his people; and with this cherished hope
in his bosom he entered the Atlanta Baptist Seminary to
prepare himself more thoroughly for the work. He first
felt that he could do the most good for the race by
preaching the gospel; then he decided that perhaps this
was not his talent, and that he could the better preach to
his people by teaching their children. Accordingly, for
quite a number of years, he taught school in different lo-
calities, when he finally decided that he would invest the
proceeds of his labor in some line of business. Consequently, he began grocery keeping with a small stock,

which stock has increased to the amount of three or four thousand per year.

In 1890 Mr. Hogan purchased a lot on Greenferry avenue, on which he soon had erected a two-story building, the lower floor of which is used as his storehouse, being 20x90 feet. He has a considerable amount of cash and some valuable real estate, all of which was accumulated in five years. He is a member of the Salem Baptist Church, and an untiring Sunday-school worker; a useful and law-abiding citizen. He hails from Lincoln county, Leathersville, Ga., and was born in the year of our Lord 1864.

LEWIS H. COX,

SHIPPING CLERK, STENOGRAPHER, MERCHANT.

Without doubt no occupation of the mind is so pleasant as that indulged in when one looks over the lives of industrious, devout and Christian young men, who are unpretending, unassuming and gentle in manner. Mr. Lewis Cox is a young man of this make–up. He was born at Meansville, Ga., nine miles below LaGrange, December 10, A. D. 1864.

His parents remained at the home of his birth till the year 1869, when they came to Atlanta, bringing with them their two children, Lewis and Laura. Being industrious and economical they soon saved enough of their earnings to purchase a comfortable home. In 1884 the father died, leaving Lewis and Laura to the care and protection of the mother. The son then felt that the care of his widowed mother and his sister rested upon himself, and being of a sufficient age to seek work, he sought and obtained employment with Mr. W. Darden, working on the farm, and in this line became a professional farmer. During portions of the year he attended the Storr's

School, where he applied himself diligently to study and wasted not a moment. All of his hours of rest from his labors were spent in study. In this way he acquired a pretty fair education.

In 1879 he entered the A. B. S. with a view to completing the Normal Course, but scarcely had he begun his studies, when because of ill health his mother could spare his assistance no longer. This noble son gave up his cherished hopes of continuing his studies, left school and again sought work, which he found with the firm of Duncan & Camp as a shipping clerk. He served the firm in that capacity for several years, giving, by his strict attention to business, entire satisfaction.

In 1890 he accepted the position as bookkeeper and clerk in the grocery business of Mr. Nick Holmes, who finds him indispensable, so successfully and thoroughly does he execute his tasks.

Some years ago Mr. Cox professed the hope of Christ, was baptized by the distinguished Rev. E. R. Carter, and united with the Friendship Baptist church.

His promptness to the services, his punctuality and activity, combined with the devotion displayed in the meetings, soon won for him a warm place in each heart, and the whole body of the church desired his services as clerk of the church. He was made clerk, and to his honor it is said that one more faithful in the discharge of his duties is yet to be found.

Mr. Cox studied shorthand under the Rev. Samuel P. Smith, of Halifax, England, and in it became quite an expert.

The writer cannot do justice, in the small space set apart for this narrative, to this young man. All he might say will be praiseworthy, but this little sketch will show that Mr. Cox has made the beginning which marks for him a bright future and a glorious end.

J. W. COX,

DEVOUT CHRISTIAN, USEFUL CITIZEN.

This gentleman was born, A. D. 1819, in Murray county, Ga. Though born and reared during slavery days, his treatment was better than that of the average slave, as his master was his father.

Very early in life he married Miss Martha Ray, a free woman, and to them were born five children. Soon after the birth of the fifth child, the mother died, leaving the father and children to lament her loss. Some years after her death, Mr. Cox met and married Miss Emily Griffin of the State of Alabama. To this union were given ten children.

Soon after the surrender Mr. Cox was chosen chairman of a committee. This was the Reconstruction Committee. He fain would have accepted this honor, but being illiterate, said he was unprepared for the duty involved therein. Feeling the need of education, he resolved to pursue the road to the acquisition of knowledge. Thus he began to study, but the duties and cares of life came so heavily upon him that he could not long continue his studies.

In 1872 he removed to Atlanta, at which place he lived till his death, which occurred a few months ago. He began work in this city by running hacks, and getting a start in life by this means of employment, he went into the shoemaker's work. Serving out his apprenticeship of several years, he opened a business of his own, hiring his own help, paying them from seventy-five cents to one dollar a day. This line of business proved a success, and soon in connection with it he opened up a beef market and a grocery store. His success was rapid and steady. Selling his property at West Point, which he owned, he invested the proceeds in real estate in Atlanta, and soon became the possessor of valuable land in this city. During all his life he proved a model husband, devoted father, a worthy and useful citizen.

This good man passed from this life not long since, after bearing uncomplainingly for several months the severest illness, to the "Home beyond the skies." He leaves a wife and several children to grieve his absence. He was connected with the M. E. Church (Loyd street) of this city, in which he was a most devout and useful worker. He left his family in easy circumstances, having accumulated, by hard, honest toil and industry, several thousand dollars' worth of property.

He fought the good fight, finished his course, then entered his Master's rest. He was connected with a lodge of Odd Fellows, being P. N. F. of his organization.

MR. GREEN W. WILSON,

ARCHITECT AND BUILDER.

He is a young man of acute business talent. Though comparatively young he has had to encounter many disadvantages, and has come in contact with many obstacles, but his indomitable will and unswerving energy have made him successful in life thus far. He has never given over to disappointments, has never yielded to failures; the result of which is that he ranks with those who are fast approaching the front in the accumulation of this world's goods. He is a mechanic of the first order, applying his skill to the architectural part of the profession. With his clever knowledge of drawing he is able to make all his plans for his work. He is also a skillful bridge builder, and for several years followed this pursuit in the

West.   He married a Miss Bomar in 1891, and in her
possesses a charming, industrious and intelligent helpmeet.   Mr. Wilson is a man full of pluck and nerve; he
believes that the way to success is through perseverance,
and says that he alone falls who gives up the struggle
and holds not out to the end.   He was born March 31,
1856, at ———

He owns twenty-five acres of fertile land, which he
has purchased and paid for himself.

In 1891 he opened up a butcher's business on Tattnall
street, which he finds to be very lucrative.   This business his helping wife attends during the day while he is
at his profession.   May he continue in the road to success and prosperity.

MORGAN McNAIR,

REPAIRER OF ALL KINDS OF SEWING-MACHINES.

The subject of this narrative was ushered into this life
in DeKalb county, Ga., August 31, 1862.   When only
three months old his mother died, leaving her infant son
to the charity of the world.   His mother's mistress, being interested in the baby, had him reared in her own
family, and cared for him till he became of a sufficient
age to "paddle his own canoe."   His first real work was
that of farming, which he followed for some years, when
he left and went to a place called "Snap Finger" to seek
work.   Here there were a saw and a gin mill owned by
a Mr. Van Winkle (the same now does business in this
city), who employed him, and with whom he remained a
year, working around the house of Mr. Van Winkle
and assisting at the mills.

P. F. HOGANS.

JOHN W. COX.

JOHN TREMBLE.

At this time, young Morgan's brother, who was older than he, began farming, the farm being near Atlanta, and desired the services of his brother; so Morgan left Mr. Van Winkle and went to live and work with his brother. They worked together two years, when, having saved some money, they turned their faces Atlanta-ward, thinking that they could save and make more money. That they might not be out of employment while seeking work, they bought each an axe and went from house to house chopping wood. While thus engaged Morgan one day met Judge A. Speer, who then lived on the corner of Rawson and Cooper streets. The Judge employed Morgan to cut wood, and told him to come over the next morning and clean his yard and wash and curry his horse. Morgan did his work so well that both the Judge and wife were pleased, and being without a coachman the Judge hired Morgan in that capacity, giving him a salary of six dollars per month. Morgan remained with Judge Speer till his (the Judge's) death. Judge Speer and wife were exceedingly kind to Morgan, sending him to school two terms, after which they gave him lessons themselves every night. The result was that he learned to read and write very rapidly. Judge Speer was of no little prominence, and being with him Morgan came in contact with the better class of whites and blacks.

After the death of the Judge, Morgan apprenticed himself to the brickmason's trade, at which he worked for a considerable time; then he obtained a situation with the Singer Sewing-Machine Company of this city and worked with this house seven years. While with it he learned all about the work and became machine adjuster. He served as foreman until July 6, 1891, when he opened the same kind of business for himself.

In 1887 he married Miss Jennie V. Payne, with whom he has from that year to this spent a happy life. Mr. Mc-

Nair is well versed in the sewing-machine manufacturing business; is fully able to renovate all machines out of repair. He also sells and buys machines, and will give as good satisfaction as any white machine dealer. Let all of us who have work in his line to be done give our patronage and thus help him instead of our white brother, who needs our help less. His place of business is No. 43 West Mitchell street. He has a neat, comfortable home which he has purchased and paid for since his coming to Atlanta.

Besides being industrious, Mr. McNair is courteous in manner and a pleasant conversationalist.

MR. JOHN A. TREMBLE,

CARPENTER.

This Christian young man was born at Covington, Newton county, Ga., A. D. 1864. In Christian character, sterling worth, he cannot be surpassed by any young man who was reared without the tender, watchful care of parents.

The mother of this young man died when he was an infant. When he was but ten months of age his father went to the war, never returning, and he was never heard of by the son. Young Tremble was then left to the care of his grandmother, who also died when he was only nine years old, leaving him to be cared for by her daughter. After living with this relative for two years, she also died, and he was again left alone in the world.

Being now eleven years old, he resolved to find employment whereby he might support himself. After many days of careful search he succeeded in obtaining work at a very small salary. In 1881 he secured employment with the drug firm of Sharp & Brother, for which he received better wages than he previously had. With these men he worked till 1884, when he was employed by the C. R. R. of Ga., where he remained several years.

Mr. Tremble is a model young man, sober, industrious, energetic and persevering. He was converted in 1886, and united with the Friendship Baptist Church of this city.

In 1890 he became apprenticed to the carpenter's trade, and after completing his apprenticeship, went to work with contractor Geo. Thomas.

By good, careful management he is able to surround himself with the comforts and necessities of life. His education is limited, but sufficient to enable him to be classed with the leaders of the race.

A bright and prosperous future lies before him, which, if he continues in the path in which he now treads, he will doubtless realize.

JOHN OLIVER ROSS.

MERCHANT.

John Oliver Ross is a native of Austin, Texas, born A. D. 1863.

Soon after his birth his mother moved to North Carolina, where his early life was passed.

When he was but thirteen years old his mother died, after which he went to Raleigh and engaged in farming. This was the beginning of his career. He first attended night-school till he realized enough cash to enable him to attend daily. His first (day) instructor was a Miss Hayes, who, becoming interested in him and wishing to aid him, made him janitor of the school building.

By this means he was able to pay his board and tuition. While studying here he became equipped for a teacher. He taught for one year and earned enough to enable him to become a student of Shaw University.

After a time he had to return to work, and was employed in the office of the Secretary of State of North Carolina. He stayed there till he earned enough to come to Atlanta, Ga.

In 1882 he became a member of the Atlanta University, where he acquired a pretty good education and a thorough knowledge of shoe-making. Following this line of work he made enough cash to keep himself in school, paying his board and tuition.

In 1885 he went to Valdosta, Ga., to engage in the mercantile business, which he carried on for two years, when he was made principal of the Academy of that town.

Returning to Atlanta in 1889 he engaged in the grocery business, which he now follows. He married the refined, highly cultured and intelligent Miss Mahoda Hill, a graduate of the A. U. and a former teacher in the Atlanta public schools.

Mr. Ross has traveled extensively through most of the States of the Union.

His business is in a flourishing condition.

He is a young man of good repute, highly respected by all good people who know him.

It may be interesting to some readers to know that this young man, coming to Atlanta with only forty dollars, and depending upon the money earned by his trade for his support, by industry and attention to business, has been able to purchase the beautiful home residence of the late beloved president of the A. U., for which he paid three thousand dollars. In this home, where are cherished memories so dear to all A. U. students, reside this happy pair, to whose keeping God has given two lovely little children.

CORNELIUS KING,

INDIAN AGENT.

Cornelius King, the eldest son of George and Phyllis King, was born March 17, 1861, in Mississippi. His mother was a Cherokee Indian, and was stolen from her parents at the age of six or seven and sold a slave in Mississippi. Here she grew to womanhood, met and married George King, who, being a carpenter and mill-wright, saved money and bought his wife and two children, Cornelius and Alice, and sent them to Jackson, Tenn., in 1863. Here the children attended school, and 1870 Cornelius was put to work at a machine shop, and developed a great talent for the use of tools. Captain Jacobs, the head master mechanic, noticed this and found that he had learned the use as well as the names of many of the tools. He at once offered to teach him the trade if Mr. King would agree that the boy could stay with him long enough. The offer was accepted and Cornelius was given the trade. He worked here until the death of his mother in 1876. This was a terrible blow to him, the effect of which still remains fresh in his memory. He always refers to his mother in the most endearing manner, and hopes to see her again in the beautiful home, where parting is no more.

His father now prepared to move to Ft. Smith, Ark., and sent Cornelius on ahead. A young white boy accompanied him. They traveled in a wagon. At this time the Mississippi and Arkansas bottoms were alive with wild animals. This was very dangerous, and he and his companion often despaired of ever reaching their destination. Three days and nights they traveled through these bottoms without seeing a living soul. The waters had subsided, and the high water mark was twenty feet

above their heads. Though homesick and often discouraged, they traveled on, and in twenty days after
they started they reached Arbuckle Island, where the
white boy, John P. Perkins, now a leading young lawyer
in Ft. Smith, found work. King, however, finding none
there, went on to Ft. Smith. The only machine shop
there was owned by Philip Millberger. He applied to
this man for work, and obtained a situation which he held
until 1880, when a company, known as the Arkansas
Oil Mill Company, built one of the largest mills and
cotton compresses combined in the South. This company employed Captain Jacobs (who had taught King
the trade) to put in all the machinery and boilers and
put the mill to running. He employed Cornelius and Jim
Childs to help him. They made all the water and steam
connections, and when these were tested not a defect was
found. This gave Cornelius great prominence, and he
was sent from mill to mill to do general repairing until
1887. This year he married, and as Arkansas City was
a very unhealthy place, and fearing his wife's health, as
well as his own, would be endangered, he resigned and
took work with the Iron Mountain Railroad Company,
with headquarters in Little Rock. Here he remained
until the death of his mother-in-law, Mrs. Bishop Turner,
in 1889. The bishop being thus left alone, requested
him and his daughter to move to Atlanta and keep house
for him. This they did. He hoped to secure work in
some of the machine shops here. Having *excellent* letters
of recommendation from the best business men and com-
panies in the State of Arkansas, he presented them to
several different shops, and, to his great surprise and dis-
appointment, was told that Negroes were not allowed to
work at a bench, as the white workmen would all quit.
He was compelled to accept a position from the Western
and Atlantic Railroad Company. Here he stayed until

he was injured in a wreck at Dalton, Ga. He brought suit against the road and the jury gave him five hundred ($500) dollars, though many thought him entitled to as many thousand. He has recently been employed as private detective in the law office of Messrs. Hoke and Burton Smith. The former, now Secretary of the Interior and thus a member of the President's cabinet, moved to Washington and still kept King in his employ in that city in the pension office.

He has deeds to some one hundred and sixty acres of fine farming lands in Arkansas and some to his wife's property in Georgia. His father holds his claim of one hundred and sixty acres in the Indian Territory, which comes through his mother. Each of the other children has the same share. His father, stepmother, his only brother and youngest sister now live in a beautiful home on the edge of a large prairie thirty-two miles from Ft. Smith in the Indian Territory. Victoria Turner King, to whom he was married in 1887, visited the home of Mr. King, in company with her father, then Bishop of Indian Territory, in 1882. Here they were betrothed, and were ever, before and after marriage, devoted and happy in their choice.

Three bright boys blessed their union, Henry McNeal, George Turner and Cornelius Victor. The two oldest died before their mother, the youngest one month after. Her death was a shock to the entire community. She was well known throughout Georgia and in many of the other States. She attended school at Wilberforce, O., and Berea College, Ky. She spent much time in Washington City and traveling with her father. She had the happy faculty of making friends wherever she went and was very popular. Many hearts were saddened as the news of her death was read in the papers. They were married December 14, 1887. She died May 28, 1892, and is buried in West View Cemetery, Atlanta, near her mother and beside her three children.

The following is clipped from the Atlanta *Journal* of May 30, 1892:

DEATH OF A BISHOP'S DAUGHTER.

"Lincolnia V. King, the wife of Cornelius King and daughter of Bishop H. M. Turner, will be buried this afternoon from Bethel African M. E. Church, on Wheat street. She was born August 25, 1864, and died at 2 o'clock P. M., Saturday, the 28th inst.

"Her father said to-day that she was bright and possessed an unusual tendency to politeness from childhood. She was educated at Wilberforce University, in Ohio, and Berea College, Kentucky. She was happily converted about seven years ago during a revival conducted in Bethel Church by Rev. Richard Graham, now presiding elder of the Milledgeville district. She married some five years ago Cornelius King, of the Indian Territory, and for a time lived at Little Rock, Ark., but after the death of her mother, Bishop Turner's wife, she and her husband came to Atlanta to keep house for her father. She lived a consistent Christian and died most happily.

"A short time before she expired, she called for her infant baby and kissed it good-bye, commending it to the keeping of the Christ in whom she put her trust, and then in turn kissed her father, husband, sister and niece, and requested them to meet her in heaven, being conscious of all she was doing and saying until the breath left her body. She was generous to the poor, sympathized with the suffering and a worker for her church. A stream of persons were coming and going all day yesterday, many of whom wept profusely as they looked upon her remains. Bishop Gaines and other ministers of prominence will conduct the funeral services at Bethel

JOHN ROSS.

C. KING.

MRS. VICTORIA KING.

church.   She leaves an infant only two months old and
a devoted husband to lament his loss."

After holding an important position in the Pension
Office for more than a year and a half, Mr. King was
appointed a Special Indian Agent, with headquarters at
Muscogee. This is an important and honorable place,
only to be held by men of undoubted ability and well-
tried fidelity.   This appointment was extensively noted
and commented upon by the press throughout the country, and many letters and telegrams of congratulation
were received from distinguished colored men all over
the country.

Before going to his new field of activity Mr. King was
united in matrimony with Miss Tina Culver, one of the
most cultured and affable leaders of the best society of
Washington, who accompanied him to his home at Muscogee, I. T., after visiting through the East and South,
stopping at most points of interest.

The elements which show themselves in Cornelius
King are patience, industry, sterling honesty, acute ana-
lytical powers, powerful memory, large generosity and
kindness of heart, invincible courage and indomitable
will power.   These qualities of head and heart, coupled
with a strong body and economical habits in his business
and personal life, will in time carry him to the top whence
he can look back from his already exalted post with a con-
sciousness of duty well discharged and that success
is the price of worth and activity.   His life is an incentive to younger men to educate and apply themselves,
thereby to rise, as King has risen.

11

MR. WILLIAM M. ALLEN,

SHOEMAKER, MUSICIAN.

He was born at Athens, Clarke county, Ga., in the month of December, Christmas day, 1860. At the emancipation he was sent to live with his grandmother, and while with her he went to school and learned the alphabet. His next school days were spent in the city of his birth, and these schools were taught by the first missionaries. At the early age of eleven years he was apprenticed to the shoemaker's trade under a Mr. Adam Malone. He was so apt and swift in this that by the time he reached his fourteenth year he had served his apprenticeship. Then he went back to school, and later, took the examination for county schools, received license, and taught in different counties. He did not fancy school-teaching, but had a desire to be a business man ; so in 1880 he entered the Atlanta Baptist Seminary to better prepare himself for a business life. Subsequently he received an appointment as mailing clerk in the post-office of Athens under Postmaster Madison Davis. This position he filled with credit and honor to himself. In the spring of 1884 he resigned his position as clerk, returned to Atlanta and resumed his trade, which he followed till 1891, when, having taken the Civil Service examination, June 6 of same year, was appointed U. S. letter carrier by General J. R. Lewis, postmaster. His other duties were so urgent upon him that he found it very necessary to return to them. Accordingly, he, on the twenty-second of same month, tendered his resignation. He received a very flattering letter from the postmaster, who regretted his (Allen's) hasty action. Mr. Allen is full of enterprise, being a member of all the leading organizations of the city. For two years he was

the honored Secretary of the South View Cemetery
Company, which position he filled with credit to himself
and benefit to the Association.   He is also a member of
the Georgia Real Estate Loan and Trust Company,
which is one of the strongest organizations in the South,
having a capital of $50,000.

Mr. Allen is a lover of music, and performs with great
skill on the violin, zither, mandolin, cornet and other instruments of music.   He is the organizer of the first
orchestra of this city, and on the whole is what might
be called a talented young man.   He has, by his habits
of industry and sobriety, accumulated considerable property.   Being a first-class shoemaker, he is in the employ
of the premium boot and shoemaker of the State, viz.,
A. J. Delbridge, and is the leading workman in the shop.
Mr. Allen is a great advocate of all young men learning
trades of some kind, and, having learned them, to stick
to them.   Too much cannot be said in reference to his
spirit of energy and daring, for few possess these in a
greater degree than he does.   It is hoped that he may
ever be useful in life and achieve greatness in the end.

G. H. FARMER,

A PROGRESSIVE BUSINESS MAN.

G. H. Farmer, the subject of this biographical sketch,
was born in Madison, Morgan county, Ga., December
25, 1859, and is thirty-four years of age.   At an early
age he attended a high school taught by Bost Howell,
but his circumstances rendered it necessary for this
bright genius to forsake the school of learning before his
collegiate course was completed.   He took favor to the
music of the anvil and delighted in the wheelwright's
trade, and by assiduous work he became master of both

trades. Under H. R. Goldwire, of Madison, he started his trades in their different branches, and proved a competent and accurate workman. In 1888 the firm of Geo. D. Harris & Co., of Augusta, gave him work, at which place he stayed until 1891, when the fame his business characterized by remarkable success, went widespread, and Atlantians, who are ever on the alert to secure that which is best, did not miss the opportunity of having him join their number. Here he opened with a business of his own, and is very extensively patronized by all who need work in his line. Success has attended his every effort, and both Morgan and Fulton counties receive a considerable amount of taxes on real estate. He is generous to a fault, the friend of all workmen, the enemy of none, lending help when and wherever he can. Such is the character of this business man of whom we write. In 1885 he married a Miss Janie Jones, a woman faithful and true. God bless all such good men, for they in their turn are a blessing to any community. Young men, follow in his footsteps.

MR. JULIUS ALEXANDER,

NEGRO-ARTISAN.

He was born in the State of North Carolina, in the year 1843, of slave parents. At the tender age of five years he was sold from his parents, and thus grew up without their tender care and protection.

Julius passed through all the trying scenes of Southern slave life. It was his lot to be the property of both kind and cruel masters. At the age of twenty-one he emigrated to Georgia, and locating at Griffin employed himself to a man under whom he learned blacksmithing. After leaving Griffin he came to Atlanta and secured employment from the G. R. R. Company, for which he worked three years. He next obtained work at the Winship Brothers' Foundry, in whose employ he stayed several years, after which he opened a business of his own. He now has an establishment, where he runs two forges, on corner of Ivy and Lyon streets.

In 1871 Mr. Alexander united with the First Congregational Church, in which church he was treasurer for both church and Sunday-school. At this time Rev. Cyrus W. Francis was pastor.

His first wife was a Miss Lula Nunnally, to whom was born eight children, two of whom he educated in the Atlanta University, these being Stephen and Annie. In the year 1881 Stephen died. His daughter Annie, a graduate of the A. U., is now a successful and accomplished teacher in Florida. His first wife dying, he was married in 1889 to a Miss Edwards, who by habits of economy and industry renders him great service.

At the surrender Mr. Alexander was entirely illiterate, but by diligent and hard study, chiefly at night, he has acquired a good business education.

His mother was a devout Christian woman, a member of the Methodist church, and though Mr. Alexander was deprived of her gentle training, he seemed to have partaken of her Christian nature.

He is a good man, a useful, law-abiding citizen, and is esteemed and respected by all who know him. When freedom was declared he would not take his former master's name, and instead of using his full name, Julius Alexander Pledger, he cut off the surname, which was his master's, and used his first and middle names. Thus we know him as Julius Alexander.

He has some real estate ; pays taxes on one thousand four hundred dollars' worth. Mr. Alexander is still a useful factor in the church, law-abiding, and respected by all who know him.

MR. THOMAS GOOSBY,

ARTISAN AND MERCHANT.

The subject of this sketch, Thomas Goosby, was born November 10, 1840, in Oglethorpe county, Ga. He was born of slave parents, and lived during the "dark days" of slavery, but as it was his lot to fall into the hands of a good, Christian owner, a man who possessed a heart and realized that all other human beings possessed the same organ, he fared well, and did not experience the cruel treatment or feel the lash of the Negro driver's whip as so many of his slave brothers did.

In his early life he worked on the farm and at the carpenter's trade. During the war he worked at shoemaking.

December 1, 1865, Mr. Goosby received his first wages, which consisted of one pound of meat and twenty-five cents per day. He was married in the year 1863 to a Miss Martha Eberhart, who has been a constant helper, adviser and sharer of joys and sorrows to him. This union was prolific of five children, two of whom are graduates of the Atlanta University, Miss Mary, who is now employed as public school teacher at Athens, Ga., and Mr. Wm. H., who is now in the government service, being U. S. letter-carrier. Mr. Goosby moved to Atlanta in 1866, and at once obtained work at his trade (carpentry), receiving one dollar and twenty-five cents per day. He was, as is now, a master workman, and during the rebuilding of the city had as much as he could do. He assisted in erecting many of the first structures in the city. Was employed in the erection of the present Kimball house for two years, also on the State capitol, and aided in the erection of the steeple on the Trinity M. E. Church (white).

In 1876, having professed a hope in Christ, he united
with Wheat Street Baptist church, and was baptized by
Rev. W. H. Tilman. Mr. Goosby is an important factor
in this church, serving as trustee, treasurer, finance col-
lector and deacon. He is a man of sober habits, integrity and industry, and numbers his friends by the scores.

In 1889, with his son as partner, Mr. Goosby commenced grocery keeping, in which, for so short a time,
he has built upon an excellent trade, carrying on an extensive business in this line.

He owns a most cozy cottage home on the principal
thoroughfare, Wheat street, near which is his place of
business. Mr. Goosby pays taxes on more than $6,000
worth of real estate. He is a man of fine parts, gentle,
faithful in duty, earnest in business, respected by all
who know him.

MR. FLOYD GRANT SNELSON,

PRINCIPAL OF THE MITCHELL STREET GRAMMAR SCHOOL.

The subject of this sketch, Floyd Grant Snelson, was
born at Ellaville, Schley county, Ga., December 19,
1865. His father is Rev. Floyd Snelson; his mother is
Mrs. Nancy Snelson. Grant is the eldest of three children, all of whom are living. He is brother to the thriving, successful practitioner, S. C. Snelson, of Savannah,
Ga., who graduated from Howard Medical College at
Washington, D. C.; also brother to Mrs. Mary Snelson
Cooper, a graduate of the Atlanta University.

Grant first entered the A. M. A. school at famous An-
dersonville. He next attended the Beach Institute at
Savannah, while his father was pastor of the Congregational Church in that city in 1874. During the winter of

1874 his father moved to McIntosh, Liberty county, where he constituted the Dorchester Congregational Church and established the Dorchester Academy. Grant then entered this school, where he remained a student till the fall of '83, when he entered the Atlanta University. While at his home he was secretary of his church for four years, an assistant deacon and a religious worker, frequently aiding his father as exhorter. He was organist for five years, and the leader of the boys and girls in assisting to raise funds for the erection of the large Congregational Church which his father afterwards erected at Snelsonville, a village of two hundred inhabitants, named for the family of Snelson.

Grant began his career as teacher at the age of twelve years by assisting in the academy he attended, hearing three classes regularly each day under the supervision of Miss R. M. Kinney, who was then in charge of the Dorchester school. The principal frequently commended before the entire school the excellency of Grant's work, and he was considered the "boy royal" of the times.

After two years' experience in his own schoolroom as a tutor, at the age of fourteen, in company with others, including his brother, Grant went before the County School Commissioner to take the examination, which was both oral and written. Hon. S. D. Bradwell, the present S. S. C., who was at that time President of the Institutes for whites, was called upon to assist in examining the applicants. In the presence of a large audience he gave Grant a rigid problem in taxes to solve upon the blackboard. This Grant did so quickly and accurately that the C. S. C., Hon. Benj. Dorsey, observed: "This boy is an exceptional Negro, for he has the brain of a white man." Grant answered readily all questions put to him by the white students of the institute, and it is needless to say received first grade license. This was

WM. ALLEN.

G. H. FARMER.

RESIDENCE OF THOMAS GOOSBY.

remarkable for a boy of fourteen. He was so small in
stature that his mother prepared for him two home-made
dusters in which to teach, that his small figure might not
be so noticeable to his pupils. Signal success has followed
and attended him ever after in the schoolroom. In the
summer of 1888 he was compelled to leave his school
after teaching three weeks, on account of the "crackers,"
who had most of his patrons employed, and who told
them that if they sent their children to school to Snelson
they would not hire them (the patrons) to work for them.
It was election year, and the "crackers" claimed that
Grant would teach the children Republican doctrine. So
he was persecuted in this way, an account of which appeared in the State papers of color.

In 1877 the father of Grant was called to the missionary work in West Africa under the auspices of the A.
M. A. Grant accompanied the family in visiting Africa,
the fatherland. He remained there fourteen months, attended school with the natives, one of whom, Mr. A. B.
Jarrett, has since graduated from Fisk University.

Grant in Africa, as in America, was first in his class,
and was well spoken of by the principal, Rev. A. P.
Miller, now pastor of Congregational Church at New
Haven, Conn.

He frequently accompanied his father about among the
African villages, talked with the natives, gave Bible
lessons, and was generally found doing good.

In rhetoricals he was pointed out as "the model" for
all the boys, and was fondly considered by the notables
in Sierra Leone, among whom was the royal governor
who predicted that Grant would some day be a "good
and grand man." The English commandant called him
his "little American beloved," and when Grant was preparing to return to America he presented him with a fine
jack monkey and a copy of Robinson Crusoe. On their

return homeward, while in New York City, Grant's father took him to Henry Ward Beecher's church.

This eloquent divine placed his hands upon Grant's head, blessed him, and prayed that God would give him a life of usefulness, long and full of good deeds.

Entering the Atlanta University in 1883 he spent seven years in this institution, graduating in 1890, just nineteen years after his father's graduation at the same university. While an inmate of this institution he led an exemplary life, always stood well in his classes, was religious and had the respect and confidence of the entire faculty.

In the college literary societies he was always ready, with his wit and genius, to contribute to the occasion, and whenever his name appeared on the program for emancipation or other public exercises, there was sure to be assembled a large audience to greet his appearance on the rostrum.

His ability as an author is wothy of mention: his productions being "Starlights of the Ages"—a historical essay on slavery; "Universal Conflict"—a philosophic oration touching upon the great movements of mankind; "Eulogy on General U. S. Grant," his distinguished namesake, and the "Development of Modern Liberty," which was his graduation oration in which he surpassed himself, and which was pronounced to be the treat of the occasion.

Immediately after his graduation he was called to the principalship of the Columbus High School, at Columbus, Ga.

Very untoward circumstances greeted him at the opening of this work. They were subjective as well as objective. Subjectively he was discouraged, because his plans for entering a Northern seminary had collapsed.

He left home with only means to secure a week's lodging; without money and with little to cheer, he took upon himself the labor of building an institution of learning.

Objectively the work there was in a shattered condition. The fears within this educational enterprise were greater than the foes without; but notwithstanding this he labored to unite all elements in the city, visited all churches, preached and lectured to all congregations and Sunday-schools, and in ten months had increased the school from a membership of nineteen pupils to one hundred and fifty.

His addresses and lectures were inspiring and elevating in no little degree, and were always largely attended. On one occasion he received an invitation from the white people of an adjoining town to lecture to them, which invitation he accepted. He held an immense crowd spellbound, and received unlimited applause, his address being encouraging to both races, practical, eloquent, and serving to teach the colored heroism in all that develops the race, and to teach the whites generosity, fair play and equity, to an aspiring people.

January, 1891, Mr. Snelson delivered the Emancipation Oration at Columbus. The occasion was a brilliant one. The address was published abroad and was favorably commented upon by the public press.

At the dedication of the high school building at Waycross, Ga., in 1889, he delivered the dedicatory address, which was complimented most freely by the town paper, as well as all who heard him.

Limited space will not allow us to recount every achievement in his public career; let it suffice to know that he figures conspicuously in all public gatherings which have for their object the elevation, morally and mentally, of the Negro race.

His address delivered before the State Teachers' Association, held at Macon last June, was considered one of the best of the session.

He is now the successful principal of the West Mitchell Street Grammar School, of this city, and is identified with all that tends to better the race.

Mr. Snelson is connected with the A. M. E. Church as a member of Class 1894 of Gammon School of Theology. He is blessed with the companionship of an educated, refined and faithful wife; ambitious like himself, she encourages and lends inspiration to him in all his efforts, and is building for him a house of true love which shall bless his coming years with progress and peace; a fine baby-boy has sealed their union and united their spirits for life.

MR. JAMES LEE HONEYWELL,

CIGAR MANUFACTURER—U. S. LETTER CARRIER.

The amount of enterprise shown in the life of this young man of whom I now write is worthy of commendation. It is not an every-day occurence to find one of so few years as he who has passed through the many varying scenes of this complicated life of ours. He was the only child of Mrs. Mariah Gay, and first opened his infant eyes to the light of day at Quincy, Fla., January 28, A. D. 1868.

His mother was not strong physically, and young Honeywell had to be put in service at an early age to aid in her support. Thus, when he was eight years old, he was employed as errand-boy and clerk in a grocery store. His next work was that of stationary engineer, and from this he went to the hotel work. Possessing a spirit of enterprise and daring, this life soon grew monotonous, and he began to look about for other employment.

Accordingly he met Mr. A., of Maine, a retired millionaire, who engaged Honeywell as companion for himself.   Honeywell was eager for the hour to arrive when his employer and himself would begin what was to be to Honeywell a round of sight-seeing.

With the millionaire he traveled for more than a year, visiting every State in the Union, Canada and Mexico.

After leaving Mr. A.'s service he did not care to locate at any particular point; so he secured work over a prominent railroad as sleeping-car porter.

One day while in New York City a stranger approached Honeywell, and in language which was not all English told him that he was in distress and wanted to go home, and asked assistance of him.   This stranger was a native of Cuba.   Mr. Honeywell complied with the stranger's request; and, while conversing with him concerning his home, expressed a desire to go to Cuba himself; but added that he had no friends or relatives there, and did not know how he would fare among the natives.   Whereupon the Cuban persuaded him to go, telling him he would see that he (Honeywell) was cared for.   Accepting the invitation, Mr. Honeywell, in due time, with his friend, reached the Isle of Cuba.

All was strange and new to him, but he trusted his Cuban friend.   True to his promise the Cuban secured Mr. Honeywell employment in a cigar manufacturing establishment, in which were employed one thousand persons, whose language he could not comprehend or speak a word.

Among these strangely speaking people he had peculiar experiences.   When he desired anything he either had to go out and search for his Cuban friend, or pay an interpreter to make known his wishes.   This, however, did not last a great while, for soon Mr. Honeywell mastered the Spanish language, which he now speaks most fluently.

After spending two years in Cuba, working in the cigar business, he returned to Atlanta, Ga., where his mother was then living. Soon after his return to this city, she became ill, and lingered for a year. During her illness he proved to be the most devoted son. Indeed he performed the parts of husband and son. No wish of hers was denied. The best medical attention was furnished her; and finally, when death claimed her, the devoted son's grief was most poignant.

During the latter part of 1892 he was married to Miss Mattie Duke, a very amiable young lady, who, during his hours of sadness, shared equally his sorrow.

He is a son of whom the fondest mother might be proud; a husband to whom the loving wife can look with reverence.

He has established a cigar business here, which is carried on with great profit to himself. He also occupies a government position, being a United States letter-carrier.

My personal opinion of Mr. Honeywell is that he is a model young man. He has a pretty fair education, and his experiences gained through traveling are interesting and various.

His only teacher was the Rev. E. K. Love, now of Savannah, to whom he went seven months.

The remainder of his education he acquired himself, with sometimes the aid of perhaps his different employers. He is what might truly be called a self-made young man. During his young life, so far, he has performed many noble acts, which if he continues to do until he shall have reached a ripe age, when he is summoned to join his mother, there will be written opposite his name many noble deeds.

MR. ELIJAH RICHARD GRAVES,

THE CANDY MANUFACTURER.

To many, perhaps, the biography of this man will be particularly interesting, as he is the only one of the race with which he associates in this city who is engaged in, and owner of the above business. His father was a Jew who bore the cognomen of Allison Deikle. His mother, in whose veins flowed Anglo-Saxon and Indian and a few drops of African blood, married a man by the name of Belvin Graves, and it is from him that our subject takes his surname.

Early in life he was bereft of his mother and left to the care of his step-father. At the time of Hood s raid through Georgia, young Graves refugeed from Atlanta to Macon, Ga., and then joined the United States hospital train, which was then going through the country taking up the dead and wounded soldiers. It was then that he lost sight of his step-father. Leaving the hospital train at Nashville, Tenn., he returned to Atlanta and soon after became quite ill. He was then adopted into the family of Festus Flipper, where he was nursed back to health. By his many good traits young Graves soon won the hearts of the entire family, and was liberally provided for by Mr. Flipper, who sent him to the Storr's School, where he received instruction from the best teachers. In his early life he worked at photography under one Mr. R. N. Lane. Mr. Graves has had a checkered career, in which has been mixed both sorrow and joy. He at one time joined a minstrel troup at Athens, Ga., which soon dissolved, and not having the necessary means, he had to walk the entire distance from that city to Atlanta. On another occasion he was compelled to walk ninety-three miles. He was employed as butler in the National Hotel, at Atlanta, but desiring to acquire a knowledge of some occupation or profession, he began to work at the baker's trade; but his lungs being weak, he feared the constant dealing in flour might more seriously affect them. So he gave up this vocation, and took up that of candy-making.

He found employment with the F. E. Block & Company manufacturing establishment, where he worked quite a number of years, mastering entirely the candy-making art.

So proficient in this art is he that he has established a business of his own, which he conducts and carries on most successfully and with profit to himself.

In 1876 he led to the hymeneal altar a Miss Georgia Anne Sims, whose father was Dr. Thos. Sims, of Clayton county, Ga. The marriage vows were solemnized by the eminent Rev. Wm. Finch, ex-councilman of Atlanta. The morning succeeding their marriage Mr. Graves gave his wife fifteen cents, which was half of his entire possessions, and said to her, "As I give you this I will give you more." With the aid of his brave, industrious wife, who has proven a constant source of comfort and joy to him, he has accumulated a bountiful supply of this world's goods.

His neat little cottage home on Magnolia street, near which is located his place of business, is attractive and inviting.

Space need not be taken to comment further upon this man's life. The facts here given show the amount of industry, enterprise and grit in his make-up; and if his future be as progressive as has been his past, he will have ascended to the topmost rung of the ladder of finance. He has some valuable real estate, and also some cash.

He is a native of Richmond, Va., where he was born A. D 1855. Mr. Graves pays taxes on three thousand dollars' worth of property.

F. G. SNELSON.

JACKSON M'HENRY.

MR. DANIEL L. ANDERSON,

A RISING MERCHANT.

Mr. D. L. Anderson was born in the year 1865 in DeKalb county, Ga. His parents were industrious, thrifty and religious people, who, though they were, or had been, debarred of educational advantages, resolved to do their duty by their children in this line. By their industry and economy, they had accumulated something of this world's possessions, thereby enabling them to educate their children.

Accordingly Daniel was sent to the village school till it was found to be necessary to send him elsewhere to one of higher studies.

Finally it was decided to send " Dan " (as he was called at home) to Atlanta, and after doing so he entered the Atlanta University, where he spent five years, during which time he made rapid progress, so that when he left this grand institution of learning he was equipped to fight life's battles.

While a student of the Atlanta University he would spend his vacations in teaching that he might help himself in school and not depend entirely upon his parents, who had several other children to educate.

From both parents " Dan " inherited that spirit of thriftiness which so plainly characterizes him. Since living in Atlanta, he has borne an untarnished name, and is ever found on the side of right.

He was converted and joined the A. M. E. Church in 1875. Faithfulness in the discharge of his religious duties brought him to the office of steward and then secretary in his church. These positions he held for a number of years with credit to himself and satisfaction to all.

12

In 1891 Mr. Anderson married Miss Macie Gill, a sweet-tempered young lady, who is a helpful adviser and counselor to him.

In 1888 Mr. Anderson opened a grocery business with a stock of thirty-six dollars. This business has grown steadily till he now does a business of six thousand dollars per annum.

For one so young, he is fast coming to the front ranks of the race. It furnishes me no little pleasure to be able to record the good deeds of our coming young men, those who will take their places beside the worthies of our race, as the subject of this paper will no doubt do.

JACKSON McHENRY,

ENTERPRISING AND PROGRESSIVE CITIZEN.

There is no man in the city of Atlanta who bears a greater flame of anxiety in his bosom for the progress of his people than does the subject of this paper, Jackson McHenry.

His very existence goes rushing out, as an uncontrollable flood, for the elevation and welfare of the young of his race. He is not a man of letters. The "King's English" is not at all safe when it falls into his mouth; but in common sense, wit and humor there is not a man born who can surpass "Jack."

He is a born orator. When he is speaking, words of wisdom fall from his lips like an April shower. It is almost marvelous to see a man with no more education than he has with such power of speech. He can electrify and entertain any assembly of people, political or religious, ignorant or educated, as well as any man of superior attainments.

His business career in the city of Atlanta has not been in any certain line. He, like his fellow brethren, is hedged in by race prejudice. The assistance which Negro men of the South need is shut out from them wholly because of color. A great number of colored men in this city, of unflagging industry and energy, would soon be lifted to wealth and distinction, were it not for Southern sentiment. On account of this state of affairs, he has had to keep feeling until he found it safe to hold on to one certain line of business.

He came to Atlanta in 1868 with seventy-five cents in his pocket, and feeling himself rich in the possession of that amount. Possessing an indomitable will, and being of a high spirit, no class or kind of work "downed" him. He soon began blacksmithing with his brothers, serving the trade till he became an acceptable workman; but desiring to do better, he took his earnings and purchased an ox and cart and began hauling and selling wood. After a time he was able to dispose of his ox and secured a mule; finally he sold the mule and obtained a horse. Then accepting a position as office porter under H. I. Kimball at $40 per month, he gave up the team to his two brothers.

This he held till he was engaged as janitor for the financial committee of the Legislature of the State of Georgia at a salary of $30. He pursued this till the Democratic administration, after which he obtained the agency for the Wheeler & Wilson Sewing Machine Co., receiving $75 per month and 10 per cent. on every machine he sold. He was thus engaged ten years, and was able to repair machines and do work connected therewith.

In 1891 he was made head janitor at the custom house of this city, for which his salary is $300 per year. He is a military man, being Captain of the Governor's Volunteers. Under him this company has progressed, winning the first and second prizes. Mr. McHenry is the oldest captain (in position) in the State. He was married at the early age of seventeen to a Miss Louisa Moore, who died in 1871, after which he married in 1873 Miss Ellen Brown. In 1872 he united with the A. M. E. Church, of which he has ever since been an active member. He pays taxes on between two and three thousand dollars' worth of property. Mr. McHenry was at one time an owner of several hacks and cabs. This pursuit proved very lucrative. Was also at one time engaged in the express business.

In 1870 he was nominated for councilman, but was defeated by sixty votes. Eighteen hundred and seventy-six found him a nominee for the Legislature, and received the largest number of votes ever given a colored man. He has filled the position of bailiff, and has been a delegate to every District Convention; also a member of the State Central Committee. In 1888 he was elected as delegate from the Fifth Congressional District. It is seen by this that he has occupied many positions of honor, which he filled honorably.

REV. FREDERICK LAWRENCE CARLETON,

A GREAT EVANGELIST.

One of the bright stars that beamed forth with brightness and shed its rays in a portion of Clarke county known as Bashire, in Alabama, is Rev. Frederick Lawrence Carleton.

He was ushered into this life December 11, A. D. 1837. At the age of six weeks he was sold for the sum of $100. He became religiously impressed when he was just three

years old, by one night hearing his mother shouting
and praying. This impression was so deep that from
that time he became a Joseph boy. He talked constantly
of things pertaining to the other life, but was not then
conscious of the extent of his knowledge concerning that
life.

His mother was permitted to stay with him until he
reached the age of seven years, after which time she
was sold from him, and he was left to the care of a
drunkard. He remained with this drunken master one
year longer, when he was again sold, this time bringing
the amount of $850, and with this owner remained until
he was emancipated through Lincoln. Being a bright,
active lad at the age of twelve years, he was placed in a
blacksmith shop to learn the trade, which he accomplished by the time he was sixteen years old. He was
then taken from blacksmithing and put to engineering,
at which he worked till his stoppage was necessitated by
his having lost his sight. For a number of years he
could not see at all, then a period of partial blindness set
in, during which time he worked at the mill.

In 1862 he became converted and was immediately
called to the ministry, while between the plow handles in
the field. He began preaching then and there; threw
aside his plow, went to the house and told his master of
his call; whereupon his master got upon his horse and
rode all around to the different plantations, telling the
people not to molest Frederick, but to allow him to
preach wherever he went. There were many souls converted under him even before he was baptized. He was
afterward baptized by the Rev. Cerrine, at Elam Baptist
church, remaining a member of that church till freedom
was proclaimed. During this time he went about from
plantation to plantation, preaching the word of God, and
causing many to turn from the paths of sin.

At this period it was discovered that he was endowed with the evangelistic gift. In 1856 he was married to Patsey King, and with her lived till '59, when they became separated by her having been sold to a different plantation and another put in the house with her. He next married in 1870, Miss Elizabeth Griffin, his present wife, after which he moved to Mobile, Ala., where he received license to preach from the Central Baptist church. After receiving license, in six months he raised a church, caused the conversion of many souls, who were baptized by Rev. C. C. Levi.

A council was called, by which he was ordained from the Shiloh Baptist church. He served as pastor there three years, then going to Scranton, Miss., organized a large church, which he pastorated till the yellow fever epidemic. He then returned to Alabama and established another flourishing church.

Leaving here he went to Chunchula, Ala., and there built from the bush arbor a large church, remaining pastor two years, and also caring for the Starlight church, of same place, for twelve years. This church deciding that he had the evangelistic call, sent him out as an evangelist. It was then that his evangelistic tour commenced, which afterward became so extensive. He went to the States of Florida, Louisiana and Texas, where he organized and erected churches and baptized many souls. He met many Associations, all of which co-operated with him in his work. He did and said much toward preserving the purity of the Sabbath, and much gospel work generally.

The education of this godly man is limited, on account of his partial blindness for so long a period. He attended college at————————for a time, when his sight failed. He next pursued a course of Theology under Professor Warner, when his sight again failed. Applying himself

at different times to diligent study, and information gathered from his extensive travels in nearly every State in
the Union, have made him a well informed man.

Rev. Carleton came to Atlanta, Ga., October 26, 1892,
purchased a desirable lot, beautiful for situation, erected
thereon and occupied a neat cottage, in less time than
one month. He owns forty acres of fertile land in Mobile
county, Alabama. He has been solicited by the Sunday-
School Convention to visit the entire State of Georgia.
The blessing of God ever attend his work.

Rev. Carleton ranks with the world's great evangelists;
is a most profound Biblicist of this day, knowing it from
Genesis to Revelations, and is prepared at any time, without any previous warning, to quote exactly any passage
required.

Below are given clippings from some of the leading
journals of the day concerning him, and showing forth
his vast knowledge and good works:

"By request we visited and listened to a lecture Monday evening, on the Scriptural Sabbath and its Proper
Observance, by Rev. F. L. Carleton, of Chunchula, Ala.
To say that we were surprised, is putting it mild. His
familiarity with the Bible is indeed wonderful, and his
lecture would do credit to more pretentious divines, and
he is instructive and entertaining to any audience. We
are informed that he has appeared before white congregations in many places and astonished them with his reasoning and ready reference to scriptural passages from
Genesis to Revelations, sustaining his arguments. He
requests his hearers to bring their Bibles with them,
refers them to different chapters and verses and calls
upon them to read aloud during the progress of his lecture. He seems to know the whole Bible by heart."—
The American, Lake Charles, La.

"On Sunday evening, the 18th inst., the Rev. F. L. Carleton lectured to a congregation of whites and blacks, at the Skating Rink, on the Observance of the Holy Sabbath and Training of Children. This lecture was indeed a gem, and so pronounced by all present. The Rev. Joel T. Daves, pastor of the M. E. Church (white), commended it in the highest terms, saying in the course of his remarks that it was a duty for the colored people to send this colored divine forth over all the country, and if they failed to do so, God would be angry with them. I testify to these things for the simple reason that I know they are true, and that I believe that the Rev. F. L. Carleton should receive encouragement and support wherever he goes, from the white people as well as his own race, whom he is so capable of elevating and enlightening."— W. C. McClanahan, Editor *American*, Lake Charles, La.

"Rev. F. L. Carleton, the Evangelist, of Chunchula, Ala., has been traveling in Alabama, Florida, Mississippi, Louisiana and Texas, and has met with great success."

MR. JOHN W. WILLIAMS,

SUCCESSFUL DYER.

Among the earliest records of the human race we find that there was a great appreciation of the brilliant hues displayed by natural objects; and in those days of wisdom, men were not long in finding out ways of appropriating these hues for the adornment of wearing apparel. The art of dyeing extends back to the days of Jacob and Joseph; for we are told that Joseph had a coat of many colors. Moses, when making the Tabernacle, was commanded to use "blue and purple and scarlet and the ram's skin dyed red."

REV. F. L. CARLETON.

JOHN W. WILLIAMS.

POLITE ATTENTION
FIRST CLASS WORK ALWAYS
"AT"

Bob Steele's

BARBER SHOP

No.18 MARIETTA ST.

ATLANTA·GA·

J. O. CONNALLY.

When Solomon's Temple was being built, the Tyrians
sent one of their number skilful to work "in purple and
blue and in fine linen and in crimson," to assist in this
line.

During the time of the Roman emperors a kind of
coloring was so highly estimated, that cloth which had
been twice dipped in it, was sold for a sum equal to
about one hundred and fifty dollars per pound weight.
We are told that in the fourteenth century, in the city of
Florence, there were two hundred dyeing establishments.
These facts give an idea of the importance of the art of
dyeing in those early days. The man who dyes will live,
because he is indispensable. Realizing this fact, he
whose cognomen appears at the top of this paper chose,
for his part in life, this art. Of course he did not accomplish it all at once ; he did not step from the lowest to
the top round of the ladder; he ascended it step by step,
and this too through many disadvantages, and over
many obstacles. In making the ascent to this accom-
plishment, Mr. Williams first employed himself to the re-
nowned Mr. James Lockrey (white), with whom he
staid five years. He next worked under the most professional dyer in this State—Mr. James Watson, remaining with him a considerable time, after which, feeling
that he was able to stand alone, he began a business for
himself. This business he carries on with the greatest
accuracy, and satisfaction to all customers ; his patronage
is large.

Mr. Williams' early years were spent as house-boy in
his master's family. In 1865 he became apprenticed to
the hatters business, and says he made many woolen hats
during Federal days. His first wife was a Miss Mattie
Hardie, with whom he passed four happy years, when
death claimed her as his victim. His present wife was a
Mrs. Ophelia Marsh, in whom he finds one well able to

fill her station in life. Being a man of sound intellect
and good judgment, his advice is often sought. He is
treasurer of one of the largest orders in the city, admin-
istrator and guardian of the estate of Mr. Edmond
Thomas, and an esteemed deacon of the Zion Hill Baptist church. He was born at Griffin, Ga., A. D. 1850.
The real estate of Mr. Williams and wife amounts to
four thousand dollars.

DAVID W. RYAN,

PICTURE FRAME MAKER AND DEALER IN BRONZE, OX-
ODIZED OAKS, COMPOSITIONS AND MOULDINGS.

David is the first child of John and Jane Ryan, and
was born in Edgefield county, S. C., November 30,
1861.

Young Ryan was placed in school at an early age, and
being ready in his studies made rapid progress, so that
when but eighteen years old, he was employed as teacher
in one of the public schools of his county. He taught
three years, after which time his mind thirsted for more
extensive knowledge; so he left his nativity and came to
Atlanta, Ga., and entered the Atlanta University. Here
he pursued his studies two terms, then left this institution and became a member of the Clarke University.
While a student of Clarke he began the business of
framing pictures, which he did so accurately, that it in-
sured for him immediate success, so much so that he
had to leave school to give his whole time to his work.

Mr. Ryan deserves commendation for the manner by
which he learned the first steps in his now lucrative business. He gained his knowledge of the art of framing
by watching a man do the same work, and he said to

himself that he saw no reason why he would not do the same. His invincible will assisted him. He applied himself to the task, and the result is that he now carries on the business with great profit to himself, and satisfaction to the patronizers. Mr. Ryan's patronage is not confined to his people and to this city. He does work for both people, and for different cities. When David was fifteen years old, his father gave him one hundred and ten acres of farming land and three horses. He undertook farm work, but it not being congenial to his nature, he sold out his possessions and invested the proceeds in the above mentioned business, which he now follows.

He was converted at the age of twelve years, and has since lived a Christian life. He was only seventeen when he married Miss Amanda Hardy. He met her when she was but nine years and he only twelve years old. They loved at first sight, and their affection for each other increased until they were wedded. She survived only one year after marriage.

Mr. Ryan has acted as secretary for the Building and Loan Association of Syracuse, New York, and has held other positions of honor and trust.

His business increases rapidly and is carried on quite extensively.

Wishing to unite with some order, Mr. Ryan joined the Free Masons' organization, and is now a Master Mason. Success to him continually.

ROBERT STEELE,

THE PRINCE OF BARBERS.

One who has made success in the tonsorial line in this city is he whose name heads this page. He is one of Atlanta's most enterprising citizens, and justly deserves the title given him above, for the manner in which he governs his business. Among the corps of workmen in this line of work Mr. Steele is surpassed by none. He has splendid equipments for shampooing and baths, and after going through this treatment under his skilful hands, one feels new energy, new life again.

His place of business, located on the thoroughfare, Marietta street, is inviting within, and, at a glance, one sees that it is operated by master hands in this vocation.

Mr. Steele is a man who exercises great common sense in all things, and of extreme politeness. Exercising these traits, he has been able to draw around him a host of the best citizens of both races of the city. His patronage is white, and consists of the best of that race in this city. His work is done in the latest and most modern style, and satisfaction is always given.

It must not be inferred from the above assertions that Mr. Steele is not a race man. To his people he is kind, benevolent and generous, exercising a great deal of charity towards them.

He is also a Christian gentleman, a member of Bethel A. M. E. Church, in which he is a class-leader and useful worker.

Mr. Steele is a trustee of the Carrie Steele Logan Orphanage. Mrs. (Steele) Logan, his mother, did much to help him along in life, but to himself was left the greater part of the struggle to fight.

Being of a good disposition when a lad, he met with favorable circumstances. Was apprenticed to the barber's trade, and, marked for his wonderful aptness, he soon rose to the position of barber, having a chair of his own.

Laying aside his blacking-box, he began the work in earnest, and with a desire to better his condition and accomplish his calling. After working sometime at his

trade his health began to fail, so much so that he was
obliged to leave off work of that kind.   Accordingly he
accepted a position as porter in the National Hotel.
This work he followed for sometime.   When his health
was restored he went back to his trade, which he has successfully pursued ever since.

In 1872 he was married to Miss Emma Brown, in
in whom he finds a thorough-going, economical wife,
and to her noble traits and characteristics he says he
owes much of his success.

Mr. Steele is an honored member of the Masonic
Lodge, and also of the Afro-American Historical Society.

He was born December 4, 1846, at the historic little
town of Milledgeville.   He is a man of fine and commanding appearance, to whom Dame Nature, in bestow-
ing elegance of person and manner, has been kind.

JAMES W. PALMER,

A STAUNCH FRIEND OF HIS PEOPLE.

Mr. James W. Palmer, the subject of this sketch, is
one of the staunchest Republicans belonging to the
party.   Doubtless, no young man of the Republican in-
clination has sustained more disadvantages for the sake
of the party than he has, and none has proved more true
to the cause.   He was born in Hancock county, A. D.
1854, and was the property of one Henry Farley.   His
earliest days were spent in the capacity of errand boy for
his master's family.   After the surrender he was sub-
jected to many and various changes, going from one
place to another, till, finally, he located at Milledgeville,
where he was employed to one Dr. White as porter and

messenger boy.   He remained at this place till 1866, at
which time he went to Augusta, Ga., and found a position as waiter in the Planter's Hotel.   Subsequently, he
was employed as cabin-boy on the steamer ———.

In 1873, Mr. Palmer came to Atlanta, in the same
predicament in which so many before him had come,
viz., without money, and with only one suit of clothing.
He soon found work under Inman & Co., cotton dealers,
as sampler of cotton.   For this firm he worked success-
ively till 1890.   In 1892 he was employed by the United
States government as an assistant engineer at the Custom
House.   Two years previous to this he served on a
County Executive Republican Committee, also as assistant chairman of the first ward of this city.   He has also
been in the race for councilman of Atlanta, and was
among the first to apply for a policeman's position, stood
a fine examination, but only on account of the color of
his skin was not appointed.   Mr. Palmer is a man of fine
physique, congenial, pleasant in manner, entertaining in
conversation.   If allowed the chance he would fill high,
honorable positions in the city in which he resides.
Will race prejudice never cease?

MR. J. O. CONNALLY,

SAUSAGE GRINDER, SUCCESSFUL BUTCHER.

In days of bondage, we were what our white brothers
made of us.   In this day of freedom and opportunities
we are what we make ourselves.   From the earliest period it has happened that those born amid hardships and
in poverty often amass the most in this world's goods.
So it is with the man who bears the name of this paper.

Near where the famous historic battle of Chickamauga was fought, in Walker county, was born on July 20, 1855, J. O. Connally. At the early age of ten Connally was left an orphan, his parents having died of that devastating disease, smallpox, which then infected the city of Chattanooga, Tenn., to which place they, after leaving Walker county, had gone. With no kindred, save a cousin, young Connally was thrown upon his own resources. He lived with his cousin, assisting him in farm work. This relative, being in poor circumstances, had not the necessary farming implements, and with only the hoe did not make this vocation a success. With an intention and a desire to make something of and for himself, young Connally left his relative having staid with him about seven years, and with not a penny in his pocket he walked to Atlanta. He worked at whatever he could find to do, receiving little remuneration. Finally he succeeded in obtaining employment under a white butcher —a Mr. Shields. On account of his small stature, Connally was first refused by Mr. Shields, but afterward was taken on trial. The work proved to be very hard for him. Early and late had he to grind away at the sausage mill. No day was his, not even Sunday, as that day—as all others—was spent at the slaughter-house or the market. How well Connally performed his tasks is shown by the fact that he remained with Mr. Shields for ten years. On the occasion of Mr. Shields's refusing to increase Connally's salary he left Mr. Shields, and having saved his earnings he was able to start a business of his own. Knowing more about it than any other, he decided on butchery. He has made it a success. Thus, while grinding at the sausage mill from early morn till late at night, though weary and faint at times, this man was shaping his destiny, and grinding, as it were, dollars and cents, which have enabled him to take a place among the

property holders of the Gate City of the South. His
property values about three thousand dollars. His business is in a most flourishing condition.

LANDY EMBREE.

FROM A CANAL DIGGER TO A TRUSTY, WORTHY PORTER IN THE SUPREME COURT ROOM.

The subject of this sketch was born at ——————,
May 15th, A. D. 1854.

He remembers a few incidents of slavery-life. On one
occasion his mistress, having become angry with him,
declared that she would sell him to the meanest man she
could find. Accordingly he was sold to a Mr. Horton.
Landy was then but ten years old. He staid with this
man 'till freedom was declared. Contrary to his mistress' expectation, Mr.Horton treated Landy with great
kindness, and seemed to like him very much.

After the emancipation he went to live with his uncle,
with whom he staid two years, and receiving no pay for
his services, his mother took him home. He lived with
her five years, when she hired him for fifty dollars per
year. This employer was a negro-hater, and one day
while Landy was at his work, his employer became enraged at him for some trivial offense, and threatened to
flog him. Landy resisted, whereupon his employer put
a pistol to Landy's temples, and made him yield.

He felt that he could not stay with this man and take
such cruel treatment, so he decided to return to his
mother.

When he reached home and told his mother of the
mistreatment he had just received, she told him that he

J. W. PALMAR.

LANDY EMBRY.

could go about and pick cotton for a livelihood. This he did, and during the year made twenty-five dollars by it. He had to divide this money between his mother, himself and nine brothers and sisters.

He kept for himself five dollars, which was the largest amount of money he had ever received or possessed. After that he left home and went to Augusta, Ga., where he was employed to assist in digging the canal. His next employment was dish-washing in a hotel; then a butler. Up to the time he was twenty-three years old he had saved nothing. Leaving Augusta he went to Madison, where he obtained work at the Female College; his wages being eight dollars per month.

In 1881 he came to Atlanta and was employed in Capt. Langston's family as cook. After that he went to work for the E. T., V. and Ga. railroad.

In 1882 he returned to Madison to receive his bride, Miss Maggie ————.

Mr. Embree is a useful member of the Friendship Baptist church, a Mason and an Odd Fellow; and in each institution gives valuable service. Having married an industrious woman, with her assistance he has accumulated quite a snug little fortune. When he first came to Atlanta he had only twelve dollars in cash; now he pays taxes on five thousand dollars property. By these few points in this man's life one can easily see that life is what we make it. He never attended school but five weeks during his life. Born amid the disadvantages, he persevered; pressed forward to make himself something and to make something for himself. He waited not for opportunities, but searched for them, and having searched he found them awaiting him. Go ye, do likewise.

He also has six shares in the Mutual Aid Loan and Investment Company.

13

MR. WILLIS SMITH,

PROGRESSIVE MECHANIC.

The subject of this sketch, Willis Smith, was born in Walton county, Ga., in the year 1835, under the yoke of slavery. His lot was the same as that of his fellow bondsmen. Deprived of liberty, he had not the opportunity to gain an education. When a mere lad he was anxious to learn something in books; and so soon as he found opportunity, he by some means obtained a Webster's spelling book, and with the aid of an old man whom he called "Uncle George Peters," Willis was soon able to spell anywhere in the book, but could not read a sentence. One day, uncle George asked him why he did not read. Willis replied, I do not know how; whereupon the old man took the book and began reading about the old fat hen feeding her chickens. This so amused Willis that he took the book and after trying for a while, began then and there to read. Ah! it was no easy task in those days of darkness to learn to spell or read. In this day we look with amazement upon those who cannot read; in those days those who could read were considered as being wonderful (of course I refer to slaves), and when they, with all the difficulties and threats through which they had to pass, were so persevering as to accomplish such, methinks that if we, who have everything prepared for us, neglect such chances, shall be justly punished for opportunities wasted. Willis went to the war in 1860, as attendant for Mr. Calvin Naul, and remained during the years '61, '62, '63 and '64, when he returned to the place of his nativity (for the slave has no home). In 1866 he came to Atlanta. He had just enough money to pay his railroad fare, so when he arrived here he was penniless. He borrowed five dollars from his sister and with it set himself up in the business of selling pies and cakes, but this proved a complete failure, leaving him as bad off financially as at first. Having a knowledge of carpentry he resorted to the use of tools, and was successful in realizing ten dollars. This stroke of good luck encouraged him greatly, so he engaged a job at twenty-five dollars. In 1869 he began bridge-building, and with following that and house-building together he was soon able to purchase a piece of land, on which he built a small house, into which he moved his mother and sister. In 1871 his mother died, and the next year Mr. Smith was married to a Miss Adaline Sims. His work was profitable and thereby he was able to buy a more desirable lot than the first. Accordingly his present lot on Tatnall street was bought, and the house on the former lot was moved to this one.

Soon after this Mr. Smith became ill, but Providence saw fit to prolong his life, and soon he was again at hard work. In 1874 he began car-building, and worked at that till 1881, when he became the junior partner of Mr. Harrison Coles in the undertaker's business. In this was invested twelve hundred dollars. They did well for a time; finally Mr. Coles died, and when his affairs had been settled, Mr. Smith found that he was involved about thirteen hundred dollars. Of course this was enough to deprive him of courage, but possessing that quality in no little degree, he struck out anew, continued the same business until he could arrange matters satisfactorily. Then he resumed the work of carpentry, in which he engages now.

Mr. Smith is a great advocate of education. He has educated his wife, who took a thorough course in the Normal department at the Spelman Seminary, under that matchless woman, the late Miss Sophia B. Packard. He and wife have no children, but aid greatly in the education

of others; having educated his sister's children. Mr.
Smith and wife united with the Friendship Baptist
church of this city, having been baptized by the Rev.
F. Quarles.

He claims that much of his success in later years is due
to the help of his industrious wife. He has renewed and
enlarged his home; making it a six-room residence.

In the family of Smiths with which he was connected
the name of Willis was much valued; the grandfather,
the father and the present Smith, all having the name
Willis.

Mr. Smith pays taxes on two thousand dollars' worth of
property.

WALTER A. WRIGHT, JR.

Walter A. Wright was born in Athens, Ga., October
15, 1872. His father is Rev. W. A. Wright; his
mother was Mrs. Hattie Wright. His father being a
minister of the A. M. E. Church and a member of the
Conference, young Walter had the advantage of travel.
So soon as he was old enough he was sent to school,
where he spent his early days.

Conference finally gave Rev. Wright a charge at his
old home, Athens, from which he had been sent for a
number of years. So the family moved back to Athens.
At this time the religious wave was sweeping over
Athens, and during this period young Wright was converted and united with the church of which Rev. D. G.
McGhee was pastor. While at Athens he attended the
normal school under the regime of Rev. C. H. Lyon.
This school he attended two terms, during which time
his mother died. After her death he became dissatisfied
at Athens, and went to Albany, Ga., to live with his

uncle. While with his uncle he learned the woodturner's trade. He began by earning fifty cents per day, and was soon able to earn two dollars per day. By this occupation he was soon able to purchase a lot of three acres in Watkinsville, Ga. At the time of the purchase the property was worth only three hundred aud fifty dollars. Now it is valued at just twice that amount.

Leaving Albany, he went to stay with his father, who was then at Acworth, Ga. He did not long remain here till the desire to return to Athens seized him, and gaining his father's consent to this, he went to that city to live with his aunt. Then it was that he became a zealous Sunday-school worker. He was sent as a delegate to conventions at various times.

He next worked at the barber's trade, but seeing that he would not make a success in this line, he gave it up and coming to Atlanta, entered the Clark University.

Soon after his entrance to this school he became quite ill and remained so for several months.

After his recovery he was anxious to make money, so he employed himself to the Dobbs Lumber Company as woodturner. Here he stayed thirteen months. His next place of labor was at the Western Union Telegraph Company, at a salary of thirty-five dollars per month. Next he worked for the Advance Publishing Company, giving entire satisfaction.

Mr. Wright is a Christian young man and is destined some day to be an honor to his people if he continues to pursue the path he has chosen.

Since coming to Atlanta he has united with the Friendship Baptist church under Rev. E. R. Carter as pastor, and is an important factor for one so young May he hold out faithfully to the end, thereby winning the prize.

MR. GEORGE W. HATSFIELD,

GROCER.

Somewhere in Richmond county, Ga., A. D. 1850, George W. Hatsfield came into this life. His early days were spent in the capacity of house boy. He afterwards went to the war as servant to his master, who was most kind to him, and by whose family he was used most kindly. In fact, his master and family were so good to him that after the surrender he remained in their service, receiving as wages ten dollars per month.

In 1871 he conceived the desire to come to Atlanta. He had not the means with which to do so, and so borrowed his railroad fare. Arriving in this city he was not long in finding and obtaining employment under one Mr. Pelligrini, who ran the terra cotta business. Under this man he made all sorts of statues, images, etc. By his industry and aptness in this work, he has from time to time, received as much as two dollars per day. He well understands this work and pursues it at no mean profit to himself. In 1875 Mr. Hatsfield was united in holy wedlock to one Miss Deys, and their union has been blest with ten children, six of whom are living.

His chances for education were those of the average man who was born a slave, but his perseverance in this line aided him in acquiring a pretty fair knowledge in the common branches of study. Many nights, after hard day's work, he would walk some distance to attend night school, that he might the better fit himself for life's great work, which none but those who are blest with some education can successfully accomplish.

Mr. Hatsfield has at heart the welfare and elevation of his race, is a strong advocate of all which pertains to the good—morally, mentally and financially—of his people.

He is in possession of some fine property on Chapel street, which consists in a comfortable residence and a well-paying grocery, which business his industrious wife superintends during the day, while he is at work at his trade. His grocery business grows rapidly and yields a profitable income. Mr. Hatsfield pays taxes on twelve thousand dollars worth of property. Thus from a poor boy has risen a man of respectability and means.

CHARLES WILLIAM THOMAS,

CLERK IN U. S. COURT ROOM, PRIVATE SECRETARY OF U. S. MARSHAL.

Many things of value, because of their apparent insignificance, have been considered of no value. Hence, what was a fortune to some, became a misfortune to others by neglecting it for its outward appearance.

Three persons in company with each other were passing through the streets of a city, when they all espied an ordinary package lying at their feet. One passed it by with only a slight glance at it. Another concluded it was only a bundle of rubbish. The third stopped, looked down upon it, and deciding its contents may be of value, picked it up, and on opening it found therein things of value.

Like the hero of the preceeding narrative, many sons and daughters of the race, because of no striking outward show, are passed by unseen, unknown until, perhaps, a good Samaritan chances to pass by who discovers in them noble traits, which only need the proper development

Taken in, sheltered, nourished, they proved to be

worthy, industrious and ingenious. Thus it will be seen in this brief sketch of the life of Charles Wm. Thomas. The first person to take any notice or manifest any interest in this young man was Miss Amy Williams, the inestimable instructor of the Storrs' school of the good days of yore. She discovered in Charles an intellect which needed only training to perfect its magnitude—a business talent which required the least cultivation, and many grand traits. She put forth every effort to aid him in preparing to meet the tasks of this life successfully.

His mother was a poor woman who maintained a livelihood by cooking. As much of her earnings as she could spare went toward the support and education of her son. She desired to see him fill a *man's* sphere, in the true sense.

With the ennobling influence of Miss Williams and the teaching and prayers of a good mother, our hero launched out toward the shores of success. And to those who know the Charles W. Thomas of to-day, it need not be told that success has attended his young life thus far.

When he left the Storrs, Miss Williams secured a position for him with Colonel A. E. Buck. After having two months' instruction in stenography (from Miss C. B. Ball) the quick genius of this bright youth immediately exerted and displayed itself, and it was not long before he became an expert in stenography. He could take speeches of any one with ease and rapidity.

During the campaign of President Harrison he was appointed Chairman of the State Central Committee.

In 1890 he was made a Master Mason ; in 1891 made Grand Worthy Chief of Crystal Fount Lodge of the Good Samaritans.

C. W. THOMAS.

RESIDENCE OF A. PERRY.

A. HAMILTON.

Since the death of his step-father, in 1884, he has been the sole support of his mother and sister.

During his short life he has filled many places of note and honor, and served as clerk in the United States Marshal's office. He is an important member of the Real Estate Loan and Trust Company, and member of the board of South View Cemetery. He has acquired the knowledge of calligraphy and writes very skillfully from dictation. Has been clerk at the Sixth ward polls for three terms. Also notary public. He is the first negro who has ever acted in the capacity of record clerk in the clerk's office; also United States Court. His position now is that of private secretary for the United States Marshal.

This serviceable, intelligent young man, in whose short life so much genius has been displayed, is a Georgian by birth, LaGrange being the place of his nativity, the date of his birth, February 11th, 1867.

A glorious future awaits him, to which he is prosperously approaching.

MR. AARON PERRY,

INDUSTRIOUS FARMER BOY, SUCCESSFUL BAKER THRIVING RESTAURATEUR.

"We may live without poetry, music and arts,
We may live without conscience and live without hearts,
We may live without knowledge and live without books,
But civilized men cannot live without cooks."

Neither can civilized women; and when woman does not engage in the art of cooking, man must.

Different minds choose different spheres. Some engage in various occupations; some in enterprises, others ascend to the starry heavens and busy themselves in the science of Astronomy; while others descend and busy themselves in the science of Gastronomy.

To the last class belongs the subject of this narrative, Aaron Perry. He was born one and a half miles southeast of Columbus, Muscogee county, Georgia, August 17, 1858, where he remained until he reached his ninth year. His parents then moved farther out and began the work of farming. Being unsuccessful in this line of labor, they left Georgia in the year '70 and moved to Alabama. Here they remained four years, after which time they returned to Georgia, locating sixty miles north of Atlanta. In the meantime, Aaron went back to Alabama, where he labored as a farm hand, receiving as salary $75 per year and board. Till now he had never had an opportunity to attend school, but began to realize that to do so would be a great blessing. Accordingly he purchased a blue-back spelling book, and with the assistance of one Mrs. Mulkay, a white lady, soon learned to spell quite accurately. So anxious was he to acquire learning, that he carried with him daily his book to the field, studying it at odd times while plowing.

In 1876 Aaron returned to Atlanta, at which place he was employed in a colored restaurant. He next obtained employment with the Jack & Holland Candy and Cracker Manufacturing Co. Aaron was desirous of learning the baker's trade, and soon mastered it so thoroughly that the firm made him foreman baker. In this capacity he served until he was given a position which had never before been given a person of color in the establishment.

His wife was a Miss Bettie E. Holsey, youngest daughter of Robert and Sallie Holsey, of Athens, Ga. She is an accomplished and refined woman. The fruits of their union are three children: Glovina Virginia, Robert Aaron and George Edwin.

Mr. Perry continued the baker's business for two years after his marriage. In the spring of '87 he was seized with a severe illness, which kept him confined for nearly a year. Convalescing, he went to Chicago, where he spent five months. Returning to Atlanta, he began business by peddling pies on the street. He followed this for a year.

In 1889 he became proprietor of the neat, inviting restaurant at No. —, West Mitchell street. Here Mr. Perry constantly keeps on hand a bountiful, fresh, palatable supply of food, which satisfies the taste of the most epicurean; also niceties and dainties of every kind.

By sobriety and strict attention to business, Mr. Perry has realized great success, and is prepared against a rainy day. He pays taxes on $1,500 worth of property.

MR. JAMES SIMONTON,

EMINENT MERCHANT.

In the little village of Watkinsville, Oconee county, Ga., on July 25, 1851, the subject of this sketch was born in slavery. When he was but four years old his parents were sold from him, but being the property of Judge Thos. Simonton, young James was cared for by the judge until slavery was abolished. Having not the guidance and tender care of parents he drifted to and fro till the year 1867, at which time he came to Atlanta and secured employment in a hotel as butler. He was next apprenticed to the carpenter's trade, and at the same time engaged in butchery, to which he attended at night. Toiling away at carpentry during the day, working at butchery through the night, he was soon able to deposit some of his earnings in the bank. His first deposit was three dollars, but little by little he added to this till he had what was then to him the snug little sum of one hundred dollars. At this juncture the bank failed, but prior tothe failure, Mr. Simonton had drawn out all of his deposit but a few cents. So he lost only eighty-eight cents by this failure. Soon afterward, the " Citizens' Bank of Georgia " was established, in which he also made deposits, and when this bank failed he lost sixty-seven dollars. Possessing a nerve of iron, he did not allow this straw to stem the tide of his progress, but regarded it as an incentive.

In 1889 Mr. Simonton was employed as clerk in the grocery of one Foster Mitchell, with whom he staid till death of his employer. Having gained four years experience in this line of business, he resolved to pursue it for himself. At the opening up of his business, his total stock amounted to eighty dollars. According to the late census it is now more than two thousand dollars.

Mr. Simonton's wife was a Miss Lizzie Chatman, who is industrious and economical, and renders him great service in his business-like life. They were the first for whom the marriage ceremony was performed in the present Friendship Baptist church, of this city. Their union resulted in four children, Benjamin Hays, Andrew Jackson, James Escott and Russell Hugh.

A more useful, active, progressive business man than Mr. Simonton is hard to find. He has occupied more places in life than one, was at one time captain of the Atlanta Light Foot Infantry, also on the United States jury, also in the Superior Court. It can be said of him what cannot be said of everyone: He grew up without parents, with no father's strong hands to point out the dangers of life, no loving mother's tender care to guide him.

Does not he merit the respect given him for having made a man of himself ? Mr. Simonton's education is limited, he having attended school at the Storrs for a short time, and the school conducted by the Rev. D. L. Delamotta; but he is a man of broad experience. His business tact is unsurpassed. Industry, thrift, energy and push are stamped upon him, as may be shown in the fact that he came to this city, among strangers, a penniless youth, and now possesses more than four thousand dollars' worth of real estate.

Young men of advantages, you should waste not your time and talent. Be sure you put them to the proper use; and to you, who have no other source of help but yourself, I would say do not be discouraged. Before you give up the struggle, consider the hardships of the subject of this sketch, consider through what disadvantages he passed. Fight, and you too will win.

MR. FELIX BROWN,

PROFESSOR OF THE CULINARY ART.

Of the men who are respected for their moral and religious qualities, certainly no one can object to such a worthy character as Mr. Felix Brown for companion.

He lacks greatly in letters, but in being charitable, generous and benevolent, he lacks nothing. Of industry and thrift, of enterprise and progress, and all which tends toward the development of his race, he is the very embodiment. He possesses a broad heart, and in that heart there is room for the poor and needy. There is no time when Mr. Brown is not willing to make some effort to render some one's condition better. He is a great institutor of all kinds of charitable orders, and sustains rela-

tions to many of these institutions in this city.   He is a
Christian gentleman, a lover of home and of the church,
easily entreated, gentle in manner.   He was born A. D.
1844.

While quite a small boy his father died and his mother
was sold from him, so like many others of his fellowmen
he was thrown among strangers.   Early in life he
learned the profession of cooking, and is now a cook of
the first order.   He has filled that capacity in all of the
leading hotels in Georgia and many in other states.

From the old reliable National Hotel in the city of
Atlanta to the magnificent Markham House, Mr. Brown
filled well the sphere of a first-class cook.   In fact he has
been employed in most of the leading hotels of the
South.   It may be interesting to the reader, and also
serve to show this gentleman's reputation in this line, for
me to give the names of some of the cities in which he
has ruled over the culinary department: Atlanta, Augusta, Savannah, Macon, Gainesville, Rome in Georgia;
Chattanooga, Tate Springs, in Tennessee ; Birmingham
in Alabama; Asheville in North Carolina; Jacksonville,
in Florida; Watch Hill in Rhode Island.   Surely he
is master of his profession.

Mr. Brown has been twice married, his first wife having died leaving two children.   The fruits of his second
union are two children, also.   The first two children he
has given a fair education, and is educating the other
two younger ones.   He is a man of some means.   Owns
property on the beautiful and popular Eegewood avenue,
valued at eight thousand dollars; also other real estate
and some cash.   It pays to be industrious; it pays to be
economical.   He has been engaged in hotel business
since the year 1866.

ALEXANDER HAMILTON,

CONTRACTOR AND BUILDER.

In the dark days of reconstruction, when men of worth for the race were comparatively few, among those who stood boldly in the cause of the defense and interests of the race, was Mr. Alexander Hamilton. Though his opportunities for an education were very limited he, nevertheless, used to a great advantage those talents with which he was endowed. In political life he then wielded a great power, and that to the betterment of his people.

In 1862 he was in the army, remaining one year in the South, then transposing to the North; he participated in several engagements. In peace as in war, he exemplified great courage.

In —— Alabama, his former home, he married a Miss Mattie Crocker, now deceased. They had born to them five sons, three of whom are now living.

He was a member of the Legislature of Alabama, serving a two years' term ; ran as a member of the city council of Eufaula, Ala., and was regularly elected ; was foreman of a jury of Barber county, which position is seldom given to a man of color.

In 1877 he came to Atlanta, his present home. Not long since he married Miss Grant, a genial, cultured lady, of Charleston, S. C.

Mr. Hamilton ranks as one of the best contractors in the city. He was superintendent of the work of W. L. Trainer & Co. for several years. He also was the contractor of Morris-Brown College, and many of the most beautiful houses in the city, on Peachtree and Washington streets. The brick structure of the Good Samaritan building, on Ivy street, was erected under his supervision.　In fact, Mr. Hamilton stands fair as a prominent factor in these lines, and the numerous structures all over the city which have been built under him are enough to recommend to all that skilled labor is amply repaid.

Mr. Hamilton is a gentleman of considerable wealth, and stands in high estimation among the representatives of the races.　If there be one who, by his own labors, through hardships and difficulties, has won his way from servility to honor and confidence in the estimation of both races, it is the subject of the above sketch.

In commenting on his life we can but speak generally, for the benevolent enterprises and acts relative to the race, in which he engaged, are too numerous to here mention in detail.

He is in possession of some very valuable real estate. The handsome residence recently erected by him is an object of " beauty " and attraction.

Mr. Hamilton is a Christian gentleman, and is held in high respect and esteem by all whose good luck it is to know him.

REV. JAMES BUCHANAN BORDERS,

SUCCESSFUL TEACHER, DEVOUT BAPTIST PREACHER.

It is a pleasure to me to be able to relate the following facts, as I know them, of this godly man's life:

He was a student of the A. B. S. at the same time the author was, and we were classmates.　During those days he manifested a true Christian character and was never known to deviate from the path of rectitude and duty. He took no part in frivolity, but was always diligent and attentive to his studies.　The consequence was that he made rapid progress and graduated with honor.

FELIX BROWN.

REV. J. B. BORDERS.

JAMES SIMONTON.

The elder Borders was a pious man, who gave in the
days of slavery a large portion of his time preaching to
his fellow men, who, unlike himself, were held as slaves.
From both the father and mother young Borders inherited the spirit of Christianity, which has characterized
him so prominently. At quite an early age he sought
and found Christ as his Savior, and was baptized by his
father.

In 1884, during the month of October, he was ordained
to the Gospel ministry by the Rev. E. K. Love, D. D.,
G. H. Washington and Jeremiah Spence. In 1886 he
was chosen principal of the Jackson Academy at Forsyth,
Ga., which position he held honorably for a year, when
he resigned to accept the pastorate of the Liberty Baptist church at Cuthbert, Ga. During his term of principalship of the above named school, it was said by the C.
S. C. and patrons of said school, that he gave better satisfaction than any of his predecessors; and many were
the protestations when he tendered his resignation.

After serving this church acceptably for a year, bap-
tizing many souls into the membership thereof, he accepted the charge of the Saint James Baptist church, at
Forsyth, Monroe county, Ga., thinking that he could do
more good in a larger field of labor. Thus against the
wishes and prayers of the members of Liberty church,
he became pastor of the one at Forsyth. During his
pastorate of four years at Forsyth, he gave good satisfaction as leader and pastor, and was the instrumental in
bringing many souls to Christ. At one time he baptized
more than one hundred souls. He also renovated the
church house at a great cost, making it a neat and attractive house of worship.

In 1891 he was chosen Secretary of the Middle Georgia Baptist Association, which is one of the largest in the

14

210 THE BLACK SIDE.

State, with about eighty-five churches and a membership of eight thousand. He served in this capacity two sessions, when his work becoming too burdensome, he resigned, against the will of the entire body. A committee was appointed at the time of his resignation to draft resolutions thanking him for such efficient service while being clerk.

In 1892, October 24th, he was called to the pastorate of the Mt. Olive Baptist church at Macon, Bibb county, Ga. This is a very strong church, owning property worth more than fifteen thousand dollars. Rev. Borders did not accept the call to this church at once, but waited as is his custom for the guidance of the Holy Spirit. Finally, after several weeks premeditation, he resigned his congregation at Forsyth, and accepted the church of which he is now pastor.

No man has undergone more hardships than Rev. Borders; but being a man of God, and one who trusts fully in God's guidance, he has overcome so far all obstacles, and is now carrying on a successful work for Christ. It can be said of him, and with truth, that no servant and follower of the Master labors more zealously in His vineyard than does he who represents this narrative.

Rev. Borders is a man of unblemished character, and is a Christian gentleman. May he live long to do much work for the Master, is the wish of the writer.

MR. JOSHUA SHARP.

A RISING YOUNG MAN.

He was born in Green county, Penfield, Ga., A. D. 1859, and was the son of Daniel and Emeline S. His mother was a Christian lady of the Baptist faith.

When he reached the age of fourteen he was sent to the village school, but being the only help of his mother, he could remain in school but two weeks.

He employed himself for twenty-five cents per day, his work consisting in cutting and cording wood and burning coal; by this he was able to contribute to the support of his mother and three sisters. He also purchased an acre of land upon which he built a cottage.

Though he had to toil incessantly for a livelihood he did not neglect to contribute something to his mind, but availed himself of every opportunity to increase his small store of knowleege, which resulted in his obtaining a pretty fair common education. In 1881 he married Miss Lena Laster and came to Atlanta, Ga., to reside. The union was blessed by one child.

When Mr. Sharp came to Atlanta he had in cash only three dollars, which he paid out the day after his arrival or house rent. He was then without a penny, and had to borrow one dollar and seventy-five cents with which to pay for his baggage. Owing to his persevering nature he was not long a dweller of this city before he succeeded in getting employment on the E. T., V. & G. R. R. He next engaged himself as coachman to a private family, for which he was paid twenty-six dollars per month and board. He served in this capacity for nine months, after which he went to learn the brick mason's trade. He first worked at this for eighty-five cents per day, but because of his promptness and energy his employer increased his wages to one dollar and twenty-five cents per day. Completing his apprenticeship he began to take contracts; the first of which was the Girls' High School, on East Mitchell street. He realized quite a snug little sum from this work, which he deposited in the bank.

The bank failed and he lost. Nothing daunted he was soon ready to make deposits in another bank; but preferred to invest it in real estate. In 1886 he was baptized by the writer and united with the Friendship Baptist church, in which he is a useful member.

He pays taxes on twelve hundred dollars' worth of property.

W. A. HARRIS,

DEALER IN LUMBER.

W. A. Harris, son of Elijah and Mary Harris, began life near Senoia, Ga., A. D. 1861. At close of the war the father died, leaving the mother and eight children to the cold charity of the world. Soon after the death of the father, the mother became quite ill and lingered a year or more, when death freed her. Thus the children were left to fight life's battle alone.

The subject becoming of an age when he could work for his support, sought immediately for employment. Having to make his own support, he had not the opportunity of attending school but a very short time.

But he seized all the information which he had a chance to do, thereby being able to make his way through life thus far a success. Coming to Atlanta, he employed himself to W. J. Willingham, the lumber dealer. His sobriety and integrity won the respect and trust of his employer, and he was made foreman and salesman for the firm, which position he still holds. He is also a man of some means, being in possession of some neat cottages on Chapel street. As it is seen by this, now and then our brother in white, seeing the real worth of his brother in black, opens his heart and the avenue to places of honor and lets him in. Thus it has been with the hero of this narrative.

Hasten onward, oh time, in your flight, when a man will be a man "for a' that and a' that."

PROF. WILLIAM E. HOLMES, A. M.

The character of this sketch is one that there cannot be too much said about. If we speak of his interest in the race advancement—progress, thereis none to equal him. If of his scholarship, he is the equal of any. If of character, as far as human beings can be pure, he is that in character. If of manners, he is as polite as an angel. He would take the prize any where. An able, genial, noble man is the subject of this sketch. He was born in the city of Augusta, Georgia, January 22. 1856. His parents were slaves, his father belonging to one family and his mother to another. Separated as they were, the care and responsibility of rearing him devolved upon his mother. Fortunately for her, in the immediate ser- vice of her master, who was a planter, she never spent a day. From early youth to the close of the war she was hired out, and the family in whose employ she passed the last fourteen years of her slave life, consisting of a father, mother and son, were very kind. The head of the family was a contracting carpenter, and did business on a large scale, and, as is characteristic with most Southern men, lived an easy, free-going life, never thinking of expenses in providing for his family. There being but one child on his premises, he took a liking to William at an early age, and made a pet of him. He ate at his table, slept in his bed, and accompanied him in his walks. In this kind treatment his wife and son vied with him. His home was indeed a pleasant one. Books and papers were not kept from him, or, indeed, anything which was elevating and ennobling in its tendencies. His mother being able to read, early inspired with love for books, had taught him to read. During the last years of the war she sent him to school, carefully concealing his books under his clothes to avoid arrest, for even the elementary instruction of Negro youth in slavery was forbidden, and the authorities were ever on the alert. All over the South they were preparing, in this secret way, a host to go forth and raise up their people, for had this not been the case, our race would never have made such progress in so short a time. From 1865 to 1871 he continued his studies under some of the best teachers from New England. On account of ill health he suspended his studies that year, and was hired to a cabinet maker and undertaker, in whose employ he continued two years, but still kept up his studies. On December 10, 1874, he was converted and joined the Thankful Baptist church at Augusta, and on the 7th of February following was baptized in the Savannah river. That year he began school at the Augusta Institute, prosecuting his studies for seven years without interruption—four years in the city of Augusta, and three years in the city of Atlanta, after the removal of the school to that city and its incorporation under the name of "The Atlanta Baptist Seminary," Dr. Joseph T. Roberts, President. He was a trustworthy disciple to that good man, to whom he owes much for his instruction. Shortly after he entered the institution he was gradually promoted until graduation, when he was made a full professor. Besides doing the work of the prescribed course of literary and theological studies, he has had thorough instruction, careful preliminary instruction in the Hebrew language. He went to Chicago and was favored with the personal training of Dr. William R. Harper, the learned professor of Oriental languages at Yale University, and for two years he pursued the study of German under a gentleman who completed his education in one of the German universities, and French under a graduate of Colby University. He was licensed to preach on the 21st of June, 1878, and on the 2d of

September, 1881, was ordained to the ministry in
May, 1883, he was elected to the corresponding sec-
retaryship of the Baptist Convention of Georgia, which
position he held one year. Recently he delivered a lecture before the Spellman and Baptist Seminaries, his
subject being "The Negro Problem." It was well received. He has at various times been called to fill positions of prominence and trust. He is secretary of the
faculty of the Atlanta Baptist Seminary, corresponding
secretary for the State of Georgia of the American National Baptist Convention, member for 1888 of the committee to report to the American Baptist Home Mission Society on the colored people, member of the Local Board of
Trustees of Spellman Baptist Seminary. The degree of
Master of Arts was conferred upon him by the University of Chicago June 11, 1884. He is worth about five
thousand dollars. He married Miss Elizabeth Easley,
a graduate of the Atlanta University, July 15, 1886, who
taught in the public schools of Atlanta. He is a man
universally beloved and admired by all who know him.

THE Mt. OLIVE BAPTIST CHURCH.

This church is situated on the east side of the city, in
the Fourth ward, on the corner of Harris and Butler
streets. It is one of the most elegant, unique and attractive church edifices in the city. It is beautifully
adorned on the inside with most adapted colors in wall
papers of the modest kind for church purposes. The
walls are richly reflected by the exquisite variegated
colors from the cathedral glass. Its vestibule and belfry
are arranged in taste and symmetrical beauty. The
pulpit is also arranged in equally as great a taste and
harmony with all the other portions. This church was

founded in 1886, with fifty-six members, by Rev. W. R. Clemons. Since the date of its organization it has steadily increased in its membership and power for good. Since the day of Rev. Clemons it has had two very able pastors, whose labors cannot be too highly spoken of, viz.: Rev. C. H. Lyons and the present pastor, Rev. E. J. Fisher. Under Rev. Fisher the membership has increased to six hundred from its organization. Among those that make up this membership are some of the best and most refined people of our city; all of which is due to the eloquence of its able pastor and his power to draw. This affable Christian gentlemen and gospel minister was called to the pastorate of this church October, 1889. Since that day there have been brought into this church some of the strongest and most devout Christian men and women of any church in the city. Among them are N. L. Black, the efficient and genial superintendent of the Sunday-school.

The following are those who compose the deaconry: C. B. Banks, L. Wellon, R. Coles, I. A. Thomas. The Dorcases and those in whom the spirit of mission work is found, Miss L. L. Turner, Mrs. Eliza Johnson, Miss Lula Harris; all of which is due to the indefatigable leadership of their learned pastor. He has baptized over twelve hundred persons, and has traveled and labored in evangelical work in this State and others.

Rev. Fisher is a man of more than ordinary culture and the best element of success. Notwithstanding all the pastoral and ministerial work he has accomplished, burdened at the same time with a large family, he has accumulated considerable property, so that now, from a financial standpoint, is in good condition.

MT. OLIVE BAPTIST CHURCH.

READ STREET BAPTIST CHURCH.

ELLA P. WILSON.

The subject of this sketch was born in Atlanta, where she has lived the greater part of her life.

She was educated at Atlanta University, where she graduated in 18—.

The greatest part of her labor has been among the youth of this and surrounding counties, until her election to a place in Gray Street school, five years ago.

Ella (Baker) Wilson is a woman of large sympathy, fearless courage, strong will, strict religious convictions and transparent truthfuluess. She is no idealist, but having had acquaintance with the stern actualities of life, is a true realist. Her devotion to her church, her creed and her God is something beautiful to contemplate, while her devotion to her family and friends is full of self-sacrifice and self-forgetting. Her energy shows itself in every lineament of her countenance, upon which character is written in legible characters, and in her every movement, which seem full of suppressed force, needing but an occasion to flash forth and scintilate in energetic action.

She has been since a child a true and consistent member of Friendship Baptist church, where she is ever seen, taking a lively and sensible part in the lay work of the church.

Her ambition always seems to be to be exact; this shows itself in her scholarship. Without any vain attempt at display or egotistic pretensions to splendid natural parts or superior acquirements, she has, by merit and merit alone, gained the reputation of being one of the best informed and most accurate scholars among the ladies of our city, and having a masculine mind, many men fear her trenchant logic and evade the collision of wits with her.

By pursuing researches in biblical work, and examining theological questions, her mind was turned to biblical criticism. Her " Thesis on Luke " was the outcome, for which she received a certificate of merit from Dr. Harper, of Morgan Park, Chicago. This is but one of the numerous monographs from her able and fertile brain.

As a teacher, from the time that she first wielded the birch in a country school to the present time, she has been a decided success.

Her re-election to Gray Street school, the finest school in Atlanta, for five successive years, attests the value attach ed to her services by the principal and the Board of Education of Atlanta Public Schools, who engineer the finest sys tem of schools in the South, and one of the best graded and regulated, as well as most effective, in the United States.

Her pupils get the benefit of the best methods, and are brought directly under the finest discipline. They do well, and reflect credit on their teacher

Taken all in all, her character, worth and work reflects credit upon her town, her school and upon her race.

REED STREET BAPTIST CHURCH.

The Reed Street Ba ptist church, the subject of this sketch, is a hou se of worship that shows taste in its plan and arrangement, bea uty in its architecture. This church was fir st known as Pleasant Grove Baptist church. At the tim e it bore this name, Rev. Robert Epps, one of the most t horoughgoing, energetic and eloquent preachers, was i ts pastor. For many years Rev. Epps took the forem ost lead, and ranked among the best brethren, and, in fact, was one of the st rongholds in Zion, and in the work of the State. He was a preacher among those who preached the best, noble among those who were noble, honored among those who were honorable. He was often chosen to preach the leading sermons of the Baptist Convention of Georgia. His fame as a preacher went far and wide. Whenever it was known that Rev. Epps was to preach, the people came from every direction to hear the great preacher. This church was organized by Rev. Epps in 18—, which he served for some considerable number of years with signal success.

In 1876, Rev. Charles O. Jones was called pastor of this church. Rev. Jones, the present pastor, has greatly improved upon the house of worship of the day of Rev. Epps. The house in which these good people worshipped was an old wooden structure. This has been torn away and a more commodious house, built of brick and on modern order, with cathedral glass windows, with a seating capacity between five and six hundred. The plan of the floor is that of an incline, and the seats are so arranged that all who sit in the rear can see as well as those in front. The walls are overlaid with beautiful paper, which gives an air of pleasantness and cheerfulness to those who come to worship. Too much cannot be said about the noble pastor of this church. He is a man of great patience, long suffering and of great endurance. He is a graduate of the theological deparment of the Atlanta Baptist Seminary. He is an exceptional preacher, of indomitable will and very courageous in all of his work. With these characteristics he has accomplished much for himself, people and Master. He has succeeded wonderfully in imparting this spirit to his people, old and young.

Just here we mention some of the prominent and affable members of this church. As mothers of this church we mention Mrs. Beasley, Mrs. Nettie Lary, Mrs. Nancy Mitchell, Mrs. Jenkins, Mrs. Piler Anderson. As

leading and thoroughgoing, energetic men of this church,
is the able and efficient superintendent, Milton Washburn, and the inestimable assistant, J. H. Brooks. Deacon
W. A. Jones is a young man of high aspiration, and one
who takes very great pride in the work of his church.
Doubtless there is no man that has done more for the upbuilding of that church.   However, I would be guilty of
gross injustice were I, by the slightest attempt, discoun-
tenance, or in any way speak disparagingly of the work
of the other grand and noble men of the deaconry, viz.:
David Render, Willis Jones and Knowlley. Equally as
much may be said about the following brothers and sisters : R. L. Jones, who is the able clerk of the church;
Daniel Jones, R. B. Jones, Rev. Willis Craver, Owen
Jones and Miss Emma Jones.   And then there is a grand
choir of some of the most worthy and enterprising young
ladies that would be an honor and credit to any church
to have in its membership.   Miss Laura Maddox is one
of the brightest scholars in the city, and is one of the
teachers in the public schools of Atlanta, and was for the
first term assistant principal. The other young ladies
deserve praise for their labor and work in this church:
Miss Mary Williams, Miss Lena Davis, Miss Mamie
Washburn, Miss Lula Washburn, Miss Bessie Washburn,
Miss Janie Carr, Miss I. Lee Williams.

These and a host of others are the able and efficient
workers of the Reed Street Baptist church.

SKETCH OF THE PASTORS OF BETHEL A. M. E. CHURCH, ATLANTA.

The Allen family is one of the largest in the world—
many different climes on this broad earth can boast of
its children. We shall speak of those members of this

family who, from time to time, have taken up their abode
at one of the family residences in our city. The first to
take charge of this sacred house, then on Jenkins street
(see fifth chapter), was Rev. J. A. Wood, who labored
with might and power to build up the family. Times
were different then to what they are now, so he labored
under many difficulties, but success was his. Next came
Rev. W. J. Gaines, who saw at once that this part of the
family needed a new residence, so set to work to build
one on Wheat street (he yet seems to have that power to
see quickly what is needed). This house is useful yet,
though crumbling with age. He had great success, and
won many souls. After his time was out he went to
take charge of another house. We had in his stead Rev.
F. J. Peck, who aroused the family by his learned talks,
and many flocked to hear him. He saw that this residence needed an addition to hold the children, so he added an up-stairs room (the gallery), which helped the cause
very much. The next head of the family was Rev. C.
L. Bradwell, who came with all earnestness and worked
with all his might. The children, too, seemed to be in
earnest about their work, seeing their father so willing
to help them. When his time was out he left to take
charge of another house. Rev. W. D. Johnson then took
charge. He spent a short while with the children, but
made them feel very happy, and many shouts of amen!
and hallelujah! were heard while he was here. Rev. S.
H. Robertson was at the head of this family next. He
worked hard to point the children to the Better Land,
and felt their interest in every way. He left in a short
while to talk to another part of the family. Rev. F. J.
Peck then returned to the house, and as before, carried
on the good work to the delight of all. The next man
of the house who called the children in to listen to his
words was Rev. R. A. Hall. He wanted to instill in

them the qualities which he possessed—dignity and pride.
So, said he, "We are too proud to live in this residence
without a steeple or bell." Then the children began to
feel so too; so up went the steeple, and in it was placed
the bell. It soon sounded forth to the delight of all.
Again he said: "Some people think that if I have you
change this way of sitting, the male members of the
family on one side of the house and the female on the
other, you will sit and talk while I am instructing you in
your christian duties, but you will be too dignified for
that I know." So the change was made, and now we
like to see ladies and gentlemen sitting together much
better than the old way. He also told the children to
honor the celebration of the death and sufferings of
their elder brother by removing their right hand glove
before catching hold of the cup. Many children were
added to the family during his stay at the house; they
came in so fast and in such large numbers the doors
of this house were not closed for three weeks, but stood
open night and day. Those who came in then will always have pleasant recollections of his tender care and
of the sweet songs he sang to them while they were coming in. Dr. W. J. Gaines then had charge of the house for
some time, and his work was felt, not only in the family,
but throughout the city. Said he, one Sunday, "I always feel more like preaching in the mornings than at
any service during the day ; let us make true the words,
' Lord, in the mornings Thou shalt hear my voice ascending on high.'" He urged that all would try to make
morning service the best of the day. He succeeded
in this. If you do not believe it, go to every other house
in the city, on Sunday mornings then come to this one,
and see if the attendance is not greater than at any
of them. After doing a noble work, he was called
to another house. Then Rev. R. Graham walked in

to take charge of the children. He was with them a short while, but labored as best he could. He possessed a true Christian character, and the children needed more of this than they seemed to possess at that time. Next came Rev. J. S. Flipper, who set about to please the children; he then worked to help them pay their honest debts; he was of the opinion of St. Paul, owe no man anything; he also taught the members punctuality. Who of you can remember the time when the last bell was ringing for the children to gather to listen to his counsel, that you did not see him, as regular as a clock, walk up these aisles, take the book and begin as soon as the last sound of the bell died away? He spent some time with us, then was called to take charge of another part of this family. I have said that Rev. W. J. Gaines seemed to be possessed with the power of seeing ahead that which is for the best. He had become Bishop at this time, and when Rev. J. S. Flipper left, this great head of the family sent the heroic builder to us, Rev. L. Thomas. His work is so great, and he has pleased the children so well in building a fine two-story residence on the corner of an avenue, for them to live in, that they searcely know how to behave themselves. Of course there is much more to be done to this house before it is completed, but that is easily done compared with what has been done. This good man of the house tried with all of his might to impress upon the children the importance of holding up virtue and morality. He will long be remembered. He has gone to take charge of other children. The head of this family now is Dr. R. M. Cheeks. He comes willing to help the children in paying their debts and encourage them all he can. He has aroused the "nursery" since his coming, and such joy and merriment we've not heard from this part of the house in some time. The little folks are up early and dressed, ready to hear his kind words. We wish him much success.

Thus ends the line up to 1894.

The following are the Bishops who have cared for us since our organization:

Bishops D. A. Payne, A. W. Wayman, J. M. Browne, T. M. D. Ward, J. P. Campbell, I. W. F. Dickerson, J. A. Shorter, W. J. Gaines, A. L. Grant.

Nine in all. Six are with the Church Triumphant. Three are left, who still carry on the work.

The Presiding Elders who have helped to counsel the members of this part of the family are :

Revs. H. M. Turner, Andrew Brown, S. B. Jones, A. W. Lowe, D. T. Green, W. J. Gaines, S. H. Robertson, R. A. Hall, D. T. Green (second time).

Eight of these. Two of this number, Rev. H. M. Turner and Rev. W. J. Gaines, have since become Bishops in the church. The former has dared to cross the ocean and find his brother in foreign lands. His name will ever live as the great missionary of this family. Three others have finished their work on earth; they live with that part of the family that have crossed the river.

To bishops, elders and pastors:

> "Ne'er think the victory won,
> Nor once at ease sit down,
> Thy arduous work will not be done
> Till thou hast got the crown."

GRAY STREET SCHOOL.

THE FIFTH WARD GRAMMAR SCHOOL.

Gray Street School building was erected in the spring and summer of 1890. The building is a substantial brick edifice, with stone basement of rubble, random range. It is trimmed with rock-faced granite and terra cotta

REV. E. J. FISHER.

BIG BETHEL CHURCH.

Bruce & Morgan
—:Architects:—
ATLANTA, GA.

FIFTH WARD GRAMMAR SCHOOL—E. L. CHEW, PRINCIPAL.

Romanesque designs. It is finished throughout with Georgia pine, hard oil finish; has large, commodious rooms, airy halls, Venetian blinds, and is fitted out with Smead's system of heating, and furnished with first-class desks for pupils and teachers, with all the latest educational aids in the way of maps, globes, numeral frames, charts, etc.

The cost of the lot was $2,500 ; the cost of the house, $15,750.

It is said to be the best arranged building for grammar school purposes in the city, as well as being the best workmanship. It was planned by the well known firm of Bruce & Morgan, architects.

When the school opened there were four hundred and fifty pupils present. A. L. Gaines was principal, with Misses Helen Coles, F. M. Beale, M. A. Hill, C. T. Johnson, Mrs. E. P. Wilson, Misses E. D. Coles, C. E. Pullen and H. Jenkins as teachers. This was a strong corps of teachers, and soon made their school felt in the city.

By resignation, later, of some of the teachers, Misses E. L. Holmes, A. E. McNeil, M. M. Sloan, S. H. Porter, L. J. Maddox, R. M. Bass, E. M. Adkison received places in the school.

Mr. Gaines, after a successful stay as principal, resigned in 1892, to assume the pastoral charge of Bute Street A. M. E. Church, Norfolk, Virginia, one of the largest and best appointed churches in the State of Virginia.

E. L. Chew was elected as principal to succeed Mr. Gaines. Mr. Chew has kept the school up to the high standard reached and held by Mr. Gaines.

The present corps of teachers are E. L. Chew, R. C. Deveaux, C. E. Pullen, E. L. Holmes, E. P. Wilson, L. J. Maddox, E. M. Adkison, L. C. Davis, M. A. Ross.

15

Most of the former teachers of Gray have, by some peculiar coincidence, left the school as brides. In fact, there are several happy homes in which are one or the other of its heads learned and practiced the power of control in Gray.

The percentage of attendance has been on the increase since the first year.

The scholarship and discipline have had an even, uniform and encouraging development since the founding of the school.

A close scrutiny of this school and its corps of trained teachers, its building, with its elegant modern appointments, will convince even the most unbelieving that the white Board of Education cares and works for the education of the Negro child.

To the thinker this institution is pregnant of much good feeling, and promises much good for the future of our ward and city.

Then, too, it is a tangible evidence of that spirit of equity and broad philanthropy which, in its last analysis, concedes to the Negro the discharge of those duties and responsibilities for which he is fitted, and guarantees to him the environment most calculated to develop in him the highest powers of a man.

The school is young, but already her sons and daughters are taking leading rank in the school sand colleges of our city.

This fact, coupled with the intense love of her principals and teachers for her good under the fostering care of the Board of Education, will in time develop Gray Street School into one of the most important feeders to the various colleges of Atlanta.

G. M. HOWELL,

A FIRST-CLASS MERCHANT TAILOR.

The gentleman of whom we speak in this narrative is one of the brightest young men in business of the race. He comes into prominence as a root out of dry ground. His appliance to the tailoring business is almost a mystery to himself, and intuitive to the natural order of things.

He began this pursuit very peculiar to the regular way in which boys come into possession of trades. It was like this : One day while his mother was away, Mr. McHenry, who, at that time in Mr. Howell's early days, was acting as a machine agent, came to Mr. Howell's house to sell a machine. His mother being absent, McHenry saw by talking to young Mr. Howell that if he could get him interested in the machine, he might count on the machine being sold. This Mr. McHenry was very successful in doing. Mr. Howell was so delighted with what he had learned about the machine that he was now determined to do all he could to induce his mother to purchase the machine. Accordingly, on her return the young man succeeded in his attempt, and the machine was purchased. Previous to buying the machine, the young Mr. Howell had been engaged in peddling in mint, rags and bones, and such things; but when the machine was purchased, he began trying to learn to sew, and in a very short time he accomplished his much craved desire. He now understood more about the machine than any one on the place. This led him to feel that he could use this knowledge to a little advantage to himself and all concerned; so he purchased some cloth and made aprons for the hotel boys and the bar tenders.

Succeeding in this very well, he went on a step farther in the business, and began making ladies' dresses and underwear of all kinds, classes and sorts. Becoming very efficient in this, he began to apply himself more directly to tailoring.

How this came about was that one Captain Cook, who was running a tailoring business in the city, employed young Mr. Howell to carry his dinner to him. While the young man was waiting for Mr. Cook to finish dinner, he would employ these moments in trying to cut and sew. Captain Cook saw his aptness on this line; he gave him the benefit of all he knew about sewing while he was employed as a dinner carrier. It was with this man that he got the idea of sewing, cutting, measuring, and to some extent making men's clothes. He learned how to press and clean clothing from Mr. John Williams, who was then working for the Watson dye house. In 1883, while attending the Atlanta University, he opened his first tailoring shop in the engine room at the Atlanta University. Here he cleaned and pressed the clothing of the students. Out of this little business he earned sufficient money to defray all his school expenses. The reader of this sketch will learn a lesson of perseverance, energy, thrift and industry and what boys may do if they would use what knowledge they have of doing any one thing. They will learn also that it is not the man or the boy that knows the most, nor that is often times surrounded with every advantage in life to fit him for the successful carrying out of any pursuit or profession which he may desire to follow in life, but the man or boy that uses the knowledge and opportunities of fitting for the profession which he wishes to follow. After leaving Mr. Cook, he went to work with Rev. William Finch, of this city, earning one dollar per day for his labor. We can see how that from the little knowledge he picked up here and there, he is able to make somewhat an independent living for himself, and also to aid a struggling

mother and father.   In 18— he gave up working for Mr.
Finch to attend the exposition at New Orleans for the
purpose of enlarging his knowledge in his line of business
while in that city, this trip giving him an opportunity to
look in upon other business of his kind, and to see how men
more skillful in his line of work manipulated and carried
it on.   Gathering the experience he desired, he returned
to the city of Atlanta, opened in a shoe shop with his
brother—his brother using one corner to make shoes and
he using the other part to carry on his work.   His business succeeded in such a marvelous way, Mr. Howell
was obliged to seek a larger place, where he might better accommodate his customers.   Accordingly, he moved
to one of the most desirable places in the city.   Here his
business grew so rapidly on account of his skill and cheap-
ness in making the finest gentleman wear, that where it
was his custom to employ two or three hands, he was
obliged to employ from sixteen to twenty men and women,
including drummers in the city and agents on the railroads.
His whole stock, previous to coming to this place, never
exceeded at any one time more than seven dollars.   His
stock at this place increased from four thousand dollars
to fifty-five hundred.   This flourishing business went on
until his pay-roll ran up from ten dollars per week to
three hundred and fifty, until he met with a disastrous
destruction by fire, and although this fire completely destroyed everything he had, did not discourage his business ambition.   However, he had some little insurance
which, after a little trouble and a process of law, he succeeded in gaining, which enabled him to again carry on
his business, but of course not on as large a scale as it
was at first.

According to Bradstreet's report, Mr. Howell carried
on the largest merchant tailoring business of any man of
his race this side of Mason and Dixon's line up to the

time the fire took place.   His business now is valued at from twelve hundred to two thousand dollars.

In 1890 he married a very refined and accomplished young lady of the city of Augusta, Miss Sophie Summerville.   In 1866 this young man, of whom this noble and inspiring record speaks; came into this world, poor and penniless, and by his natural genius, push and shove, together with indomitable will, made himself eminently great in the industrial world.

Let those who read this sketch catch his spirit and go forward. His work is done neatly and of the latest styles, and at prices that suit every man's pocket.

A PREACHER, A DYER,

A MERCHANT IN OLD CASTAWAY CLOTHING—A CLEANER AND REPAIRER OF CLOTHING.

Robert B. Brightwell, a merchant hustler in old clothing in this city, is one of the most thoroughgoing, enterprising, stirring men of the city.   The business that he carries on in this city is one of untold service and advantage to the public.   At his place of business old clothes can be made new, the soiled made clean, at a little cost.   His industry and thrift has made him popular and very influential among the people of this great city.   He was born at Maxie, Ga., on the 15th day of June, 1864, and came to Atlanta in 1876 and engaged in the grocery business, which he followed till 1884, when he opened the business above named, of dyeing and cleaning and repairing old clothing, which business he carries on up to the present time.   His path in his business has not always been smooth, as the success which he has had in carrying on this business would seem to show.   He has had some very serious drawbacks since his engagement in this business. Once disturbed by the falling in of the Norcross building on the corner of Marietta and Peachtree streets, by which destruction of the building all his ready and unmade stock and other work in repairing, dyeing and cleaning of his customers, were seriously injured by the breaking of the water pipes, which flooded his whole business, and from which he suffered great loss. In the month of August, of the same year of this first destruction, 1894, he met with a simliar misfortune, the loss in which amounted to about eight hundred dollars, by fire which broke out in the Gould building, which caused his second misfortune in the same way. In the same year he met with another disaster in business, which was caused by the invasion of an army of cock-roaches, which destroyed a great lot of his goods. And yet with all these disadvantages and cripplings which have come to him in his efforts to develop and establish this line of business, he has not abated in the least in his efforts, energy and courage to still go on.

In my opinion, if there is any definition of perseverance and energy, Mr. Brightwell is that.

The young men of to-day, and of generations to come, who may read this sketch, will do well to take Mr. Brightwell as an example in establishing a business and sticking to it under whatever disadvantages or adversities they may meet in carrying it to a success. Mr. Brightwell, aside from carrying on this business, has availed himself of the opportunity of obtaining a knowledge of books by attending the Atlanta Baptist Seminary. For several years he has carried on a course in theology in order that he might be better able to preach the gospel. He has taken other studies along with this course of normal, which have helped him much in conducting his business to a great financial success.

He is not a young man who has in his possession much
of this world's goods, but presuming from the energy,
push and shove, and qualities of the like, will become a
great benefactor in finance to his people and charitable
good of his race.

GATE CITY COLORED PUBLIC SCHOOL.

The above-named school, more popularly known as
the " Houston Street School," is situated on the corner
of Houston and Butler streets. This school was first
taught in the basement of Big Bethel A. M. E. church,
in 1879 or 1880. When the colored citizens of the
Fourth ward asked the city authorities for a public school
for the colored children of that ward, the authorities said
they had no suitable building, and could not give the
school on that account until grounds were secured and a
building erected. The officers and members of Big
Bethel, who were then allowing a private school to be
taught in the basement of that church, offered the basement to the city to be used as a public school. By this
means all excuses for delay were obviated.

During the year 1880 the city bought a lot and erected the building now situated on the corner of Houston
and Butler streets, to be used by the colored people in
that section of town as a public school building. The
building is large and spacious, containing eight large
rooms, neatly furnished, four up stairs and four rooms
down stairs. It also has a large hallway, which makes the
building very convenient for a school-house.

The seating capacity of the school is four hundred and
fifty, which afforded, at the time of erection, ample accommodation for all who applied for seats. The community surrounding the school has increased so rapidly

G. M. HOWELL.

THE FOURTH WARD GRAMMAR SCHOOL.

since its erection that from one to two hundred children
are turned away every year for the want of room.   This
being a public school, it is directly under the management of the city government.   All supplies for running the school are furnished by the city, the teachers are
appointed by the city through the Board of Education.

Professor R. H. Carter, a graduate of the Atlanta University, and a teacher of some experience, was elected
by the Board of Education to the principalship of this
school in 1880.   Professor Carter had as his assistants
some of the best educators in the State among the Negro
race.   Notably among them were Mrs. M. A. Ford,
Mrs. Julia Turner, Miss G. B. Mitchell, Miss I. M. Clarke,
and other very faithful workers, whose names do not
now present themselves.   Professor Carter proved himself to be an efficient principal, giving very general satisfaction to the Board of Education and to his patrons.
He served them four years, after which he resigned to
take a position which paid better.

In 1885 Mr. A. Graves was elected principal of the
school, and held that responsible position for two years.
He proved himself to be an able man, a good disciplinarian, and an excellent teacher.   He managed the school
successfully, building it up as a useful factor for good in
the community.   As a man he strove to impress the law
of obedince upon his pupils.   If he understood the law
to be just, he would see to its being carried out to the
letter; but if he thought it wrong, or unjust, he wuld not
obey, neither would he make his children obey.   The
firmness of Professor Graves is illustrated by the following true story which occurred during his administration:
While he was principal of the school, the remains of the
late Jefferson Davis were removed from Mississippi to
Richmond, Virginia, by way of Atlanta.   The white citizens of Atlanta celebrated the occasion with a great dem-

onstration. In the line of march all the public schools were commanded to join, led by the principals. Mr. Graves thought that it was wrong to honor a man who had fought and died, as it were, to keep the teachers and pupils represented in the school in which he was teaching in slavery. He told the teachers and pupils the situation, and said to them that if they wanted they might go, but he would not.

The school made progress under the direction of Prof. Graves, who was assisted by an able corps of teachers.

During the summer of 1886 Professor L. M. Hershaw was elected principal of the Gate City Public school to succeed Mr. Graves, who had resigned. When he took charge of the school he found it in a progressive condition, having moved on so successfully since its beginning that it ranked as one of the leading grammar schools of the city.

Mr. Hershaw was principal of the school for four years, during which time the scholarship of the school was greatly promoted. The pupils from this school compared very favorably with the pupils of any school in the city in the entrance examinations to the preparatory course in the colleges and seminaries. He was a successful teacher and principal, having managed the school to the satsifaction of the Board of Education and the patrons.

In 1890 Professor Hershaw accepted a clerkship in the department at Washington, D. C., and Mr. W. B. Matthews was elected principal of the Gate City school. He found the school in a flourishing condition. Many of the teachers whom he found there had been with the school from its foundation. They were well experienced and knew the rules of the school and rendered great assistance to the new principal during his first week about the school.

Since 1890 the school has been growing in popularity. Many of the best citizens of the city have been attracted to the school under the management of Prof. Matthews.

The order of the school has improved very greatly, and the high scholarship reached under Professor Hershaw has been retained and improved.

During the last four years there has been less trouble between the parents and teachers than formerly. This school has competed with older and more favored schools located in the same community, thereby proving the solid work done by its teachers. Through the enengy and push of the present principal, the teachers and pupils have learned to regard their duty as a sacred trust. That the school is doing good in the community we do not think anybody has any doubts. That the money spent by the city government in support of this school is as seed sown in good soil, is very obvious. Let those who doubt come and see.

Many of the pupils who have gone through this grammar school have graduated from the colleges in our city and elsewhere, and are now very proficient teachers in the public schools of our city and State. Many of the young men are in business, holding government positions and filling other honorable callings in life.

The present corps of teachers who are doing good work in this school, are: W. B. Matthews, principal; Mrs Julia Turner, assistant principal; Miss A. D. Badger, seventh grade; Miss S. B. Pullen, sixth grade; Miss Aurora V. Peters, fifth grade; Miss M. P. Westmoreland, fourth grade; Miss L. E. Badger, third grade; Miss I. B. Pollard, second grade; Miss C. R. McGhee, first grade.

The patrons of the Gate City Colored Public School are proud of the work the school is doing for the elevation of the race. The school is under the immediate control of the city Board of Education, and that Board extends the same advantages to all of the schools in every respect save one—they do not pay white and colored teachers the same salary. This one fact makes a wide difference between the white and colored schools of Atlanta. The teachers of the colored schools see the unfairness in the manner of paying teachers here, but would not feel it so keenly if more accommodations were given to the colored citizens for the education of their children.

It is not a good idea to criticise anybody unjustly ; it is very poor policy to find fault with our friends, especially when they claim that they are doing the best they can for us; but it is never right to accept discrimination with sealed lips and silent pens.

The Negro citizens of Atlanta are thankful for what schools they have, but feel that they need more, and trust that the city, through its Board of Education, may soon provide more room for them.

MRS. OBEDIA CECILE BROWN CARTER.

BY MRS. M. A. McCURDY.

It is indeed interesting and amusing to watch with care an artist while he tries to transfer to his canvas the luster of a precious stone. After he has used his utmost skill, his picture proves to be dull, and in many instances valueless. The same can be said concerning the writing of a biographical sketch of a grand and Christlike woman, full of reason, love and godliness, that makes a whole crown of precious jewels; and all that one can do in the attempt, is to present a valueless opaque copy of her in the sketch.

The happy and beautiful name which heads this article belongs to one who was born May 10, 1858, in Athens, Ga., the "classic city of the South," yet with all its beauty and happiness, it fails to give us an idea of the remarkable energy and brave persistency of character of which Mrs. Obedia Cecile Brown Carter is the possessor. She is the daughter of Mr. John Wesley and Harriet Brown (deceased), of Athens, Ga., and granddaughter of the venerable Rev. Robert Brown, of Athens, Ga. Mrs. O. C. B. Carter was married at the age of eighteen, in the year, A. D. 1876, to Rev. E. R. Carter, now the pastor of Friendship Baptist Church, of Atlanta, Ga. At the time of her marriage, she knew not Christ as her Redeemer, but after being elected President of the West Atlanta Woman's Christian Temperance Union in 1888, she sought earnestly to know the Lord as her Redeemer, and was converted several days previous to the time she was to preside over that Christian body of women. She thereafter held the position of President for more than two years, much to the delight of her many admiring friends, and is now Vice-President of the same local union, as well as Superintendent of Prison and Jail work, assistant Superintendent of Evangelistic work, and has been Treasurer of the State Woman's Christian Temperance Union (subject to re-election) ever since 1892. Her value in this Christian work cannot be estimated, as she is and has ever been an untiring laborer, ever doing and saying such things as will eventually assist in the dethroning of the demon rum. She received her education at Knox's Institute in the city of Athens; said education has caused her to fill with honor and accuracy the many positions she now occupies, and when she is called from "labor to reward" it will be a difficult matter to find one to take her place. As a local missionary sent out by the church of which her husband is pastor, she is one of those Godly women who never tires in doing work for the advancement of the cause of Christ, going into the highways and hedges on errands of mercy, ever adminis-

tering to the sick, poor and needy. Just such things that
give life and strength to the soul and food and raiment
for the body, and thus making for herself a reputation as
a modern Dorcas, worthy of commendation and emula-
tion. As a member of her husband's church, she is
greatly beloved, especially by the juvenile members of
the church, as it is with them she labors most assidu·
ously, ever remembering that the future of our race depends very largely upon what the boys and girls of
to-day will prove to be in the to-morrows of the future,
when men and women will be wanted to fill the place of
those who are to-day making "foot-prints in the sands of
time," that cannot be erased and are "in the broad field
of battle," proving themselves to be heroes and heroines,
like the subject of our sketch, in this strife. She is also
the President of the "Woman's Fireside School" and
"Bible Band" of Friendship Baptist Church. The object of this band, which she is carrying out in a most
beautiful manner, is to cause, if possible, the reading of
the Bible in the homes of the members, at least once a day,
and bring about the much needed practice of praying in
the homes of many mothers, whose children know not
what it is to hear their parents pray. Last, but not least,
one of the most loveable and praiseworthy traits of this
grand woman, is her devotion to her husband and children.
As a wife and a mother, she is a model, one ever worthy
of commendation. When either one of the members of her
family are in pain or sorrow, she it is who ever adminis-
ters to their wants and necessities, with untiring care, during the wee small hours of the lonely night, and the heated
or cold hours of the day. Her trust, love and respect for
her husband is all that any one could wish, as she

> " Never doubts his fidelity,
> Never thinks his heart untrue,
> But, trusts him fully, trusts him freely,
> Even as he has trusted her."

MITCHELL ST. PUBLIC SCHOOL.

ALICE D. CARY, PRINCIPAL.

Early in the month of July, 1882, not far from the corner of Maple and Mitchell streets, the sound of nail and hammer was heard, which attracted the attention of the passersby and neighbors as well.

It was not very long ere it was generally known that there was to be erected on that spot a building to be used exclusively for the colored youth.

For two months the erection of this building was watched with much interest and anxiety by many, and when the appointed day for opening came, the first noon in September, 1882, the house was packed with children eager to get a seat in this new building.

Many parents came with their little ones, and each insisted that their children should be favored with a seat.

The parents' friends and children listened to an encouraging and pointed speech from the superintendent, Maj. W. F. Slaton, after which the work of seating and grading was done by the corps of teachers then employed for that year, viz.: Prof. H. L. Walker, Misses C. E. Jones, Helen Coles, E. M. Townsley, I. M. Clarke, L. Easley, Julia M. Tooke and E. M. Thomas.

It was not many days before the school was in good working order and continued throughout the year and at its close the teachers expressed themselves satisfied with the year's work, and showed an annual report of 493 pupils.

Mitchell Street School has been in session twelve years, has had eight principals, viz.: Prof. H. L. Walker, Rev. E. P. Johnson, Profs. E. A. Johnson, C. W. Hill, T. A. Johnson, P. A. Allen, Rev. F. G. Snelson and Mrs. Alice D.

Cary; with twenty-four assistant teachers; of this twenty-four two have crossed the river of death, Mrs. Katie (Short) Wright and Mrs. Ella M. (Townsley) Pitts; twelve of them have crossed the river of mantrimony and living in comfortable homes of their own; the remaining nine are still teachers.

You will observe that during these twelve years there have been almost a principal for each year. No school in the public schools of Atlanta has had so many; yet she has, despite the many changes and obstacles, braved the tide, and to-day we find her firm and sailing smoothly over them, and promises a still brighter future. Last year's enrollment was 450; per cent. of attendance, 96.8.

It is with much delight I recognize the fact that four of the teachers now teaching in the public schools were pupils of Mitchell Street School, and finished from that school with credit. Two of them, Misses A. Boswell and W. E. Keller, are now employed as teachers in the same building they were seated as pupils in 1882; of the other two, Misses R. Keiths, is teaching at Summer Hill school; Miss H. Studivant at Roach; and she hopes ere many more years have passed to have as many or more of her pupils employed as teachers in some one of the public schools.

I do not feel that a sketch of Mitchell Street School would be complete without the mentioning of our faithful janitor, Mr. Pat. Heard. He was with the school in its infancy, and performed his duties with faithfulness and credit, until sickness laid hands on him and bade him cease work and be nursed by its grim hands, but ere it had long held him, death relieved him and bade him go where there would be no more pain or death.

THE FIRST BAPTIST CHURCH—FRIENDSHIP.

BETHLEHEM BAPTIST CHURCH.

REV. EDWARD SMITH, PASTOR.

This little church is one of the most enterprising churches in the city. The people who compose it are a people of most untiring zeal ever gathered in any one place for the purpose of keeping house for God. They are in spirit and activity a perfect bee-hive—so earnestly are they about their Master's work.

There are a number of churches that have larger memberships and larger houses, and more embelished with the beauties of artistical paintings, in which to worship, but none more ardent and zealous for the advancement of the Master's kingdom than this grand little band of disciples.

They pride themselves in doing whatever the pastor, Rev. Edward Smith, assign to their hands to do. He only has to speak and it is done; to command, and his people go forward to carry out his orders.

At this point we will give a few names of some of the most faithful, active and eminent members of this church:

G. W. Person, Benjamin Pierson, Armus Weaver, Wm. Armps, Dora Norwood, Emma Fletcher, Lucy Brown, Sarah Beatle, Mary Arnold, Ida Thomas, Martha Weaver, Eliza Suttles, Nancy Dura, Josh Mathews, Julia Washington, and a host of others that this limited space would not allow us to name.

This church was organized March, 1879. The council was composed of Revs. G. W. Gwin, D.D., Jerry M. Jones, and Rev. Dorsey, with twenty-five members.

Since the day of its organization it has passed through many vicissitudes, but the Lord has heard their prayers

16

and they have accomplished great good since the day of their organization.

The church now has a beautiful set of working young men and women, who are always active in entertainments and mission bands, and thus aiding and keeping alive the church. They have had in a very short duration, eight pastors.

In 1889 the church extended a call to the present pastor, Rev. Edward Smith, and all that we have spoken of this church in the way of activity and work, is due entirely to the untiring zeal and energy of this noble man. Its membership has grown greatly under his care. At the time he accepted the call there were only about fifty in number; from that time up to the present, the church has increased on an average of seventy-five a year—the membership now being five hundred. On account of this rapid increase, this good people have been obliged to enlarge their house of worship. The value of the property has also increased under his ministry from five hundred to three thousand nine hundred dollars.

Rev. Smith is a bright, intelligent and able preacher—clear-headed, kind-hearted and generous. No man deserves more credit from this people than Rev. Edward Smith. He has done more in that part of the city for the Baptist cause and the kingdom of our Master than any other man could possibly have done.

They have given cheerfully to the mission and educational work whenever it was their duty to do so.

Be it said of this noble, generous-hearted preacher of the gospel, that he has done well.

FIRST COLORED BAPTIST CHURCH OF ATLANTA,

KNOWN AS THE FRIENDSHIP BAPTIST CHURCH.

There is no church in the city that is more worthy of the highest honor, praise and recognition among all the Baptist churches that are in the city, from the point of view that she has done more to inspire and to provoke the other churches to good works and to set up a standard of model preaching and worship. She has done more by the way of rendering her building to the educational service to the Negroes of Georgia than any other church in the city or State.

This church was organized by Rev. Frank Quarles, in 1868, and consisted at that time of twenty-five members.

In 1881, at the close of the eventful pastorate of Rev. Frank Quarles, it numbered about fifteen hundred. It had its beginning in a car-box, in the northeast part of the city, on Walton street, and after several changes as to location and house, a lot was finally bought on the corner of Haynes and Mitchell streets, where, under the leadership of Rev. Frank Quarles, a very large and commodious house of worship, 46 x 100 feet, was erected. But when the first pastor, Rev. Frank Quarles, died, a large debt of $3,000, created in the erection of the house, was still unprovided for. But when Rev. E. R. Carter took charge of the congregation the debt was soon paid, and interior improvements, costing about $2,500, were made to the church and paid promptly— making the property now worth $60,000.

Since the Rev. E. R. Carter accepted the pastorate of Friendship Baptist Church the growth in membership, strength and influence has been so marked that now this

is considered the second strongest, numerically and financially, of any colored Baptist church of organization in
the State.

To-day his membership numbers 2,500 souls, and is
increasing at the rate of nearly one hundred baptisms
annually, besides those received by letter and other
methods of Baptist usage.

The damp basement story of this church was the
birthplace of Spelman Seminary, which is now one of
the largest and most reputable schools on the continent.

The organization, growth and usefulness of this
church have been remarkable, evidencing most conclu-
sively the fact that God's guiding hand has directed its
course and blessed its labor.

While its first pastor was a devout Christian and devoted his life and energies to the interest of this church,
God again displayed the hand of a wise Providence
when Rev. E. R. Carter, although an obscure young
man, was called to fill the pulpit, so ably occupied by the
former pastor.

The present pastor, E. R. Carter, is one of the most
remarkable men (regardless of color) of the present
century. His native ability, present intellectual attainments, coupled with the great work he has accomplished
and the traveling he has done, makes him as a prodigy
in the estimation of those familiar with all the facts connected with his brief but eventful life of usefulness.

This church, under the wise leadership of Rev. Carter,
has given largely to educational and missionary work,
and secured and now maintains a home, where its old
and decrepit members can be and are cared for by the
gifts and appropriations made by a society known as the
" Ninety-and-Nine."

Rev. Carter was born in Athens, Ga., and while there
is no record as to the exact date of his birth, it is

thought that he is now about thirty-five years old. His was an uneventful life up to 1879, except the honest fight he made in ignorance and poverty, always hoping and longing for an opportunity and striving for means to educate himself.

He was married in early life, and an afflicted wife for five long years added to the obstacles in the way to education. But she was a true, patient woman, and when her health was restored, greatly aided him in his efforts to attain the great desired boon, an education.

In 1879 he entered the Atlanta Baptist Theological Seminary, from which institution he graduated after years of privation and battling with poverty. He actually did the washing for himself and family, and worked some each day in a shoe-shop, in order to make his way through college. His first call to the charge of a church was at Stone Mountain, at $8.00 per month, $32.00 of which is still unpaid and due him.

During his year of ministry at Stone Mountain twenty-five souls were converted, and from this number some promising preachers, missionaries and brag scholars of Spelman Seminary, have developed.

In addition to the great work he has done as a minister of the gospel and advocate of prohibition, he has found time to write a book, entitled "Our Pulpit," which was published in 1890. He has recently written a book entitled "Descriptive Scenes of Europe and the Orient," which is now ready for publication.

Rev. Carter has traveled very extensively, both in the Old and New World. He made his first trip to Europe in 1888. The object of this journey through the old country was to extend his information and render practical the extensive reading he has done.

The object of his second trip, in 1891, across the great waters was to familiarize himself with the historic

scenes recited in Biblical history, to better prepare himself for his life-work—that of teaching his race the way
of eternal life. While making these trips in the orient
he traveled in Egypt, Asia, Syria, Italy, France, Germany, Switzerland, Belgium, Ireland, England and Asia
Minor, thus having traveled extensively throughout the
Old as well as the New World, because he has visited
and labored in nearly every State in the Union and in
Canada. We doubt that such a record has ever been
made by any man living or dead, white or black, on this
continent, in so brief a time.

Nine years ago he could not write, but now he is a Greek,
French, Hebrew and English scholar, and has some practical knowledge of the Latin and German languages.

In addition to all the work and travel mentioned
above, he edited the colored Baptist paper of the State,
served as Grand Worthy Chief Templar of the State,
Vice-President of the Georgia State Baptist Sunday-
school Convention, and was a member of the Centennial Committee of the colored Baptists of the State of
Georgia.

He made himself a hero in two prohibition campaigns,
and has lectured in many prominent cities, on various
occasions and subjects.

Be it said to his credit, that all this has been accomplished in the last nine brief years. He is an orator
and theological student and scholar, linguist and author,
and a born leader of his race.

WHEAT STREET BAPTIST CHURCH.

The Wheat Street Baptist Church is one of the most
elegant and neatly arranged that is in the city. It has a
seating capacity of about one thousand. Its floor is that

of an incline plane, slanting from the door to the pulpit.
It has a splendid swinging or self-supporting gallery that
is most charmingly situated in the front entrance, a stair-
way going from the vestibule which leads into it. The
windows are of beautiful cathedral glass of variegated
colors, costing in the neighborhood of eight or nine hundred dollars. Its walls are covered with the most exquisite
and rarest kind of wall paper for church services. Its pulpit
is the model style and is situated in the rear end of the
house with just above a nicely and very beautifully arranged apartment, something like a small gallery, where
the choir sit. Up in this apartment is a splendid pipe
organ whose appearance and beauty add much to the embelished character of the house.

The choir ranks as equal to any in the city, and is
composed of the best class of people.

The church is beautifully lighted with the latest style
chandelier gas lamps. Its baptistary is conveniently
arranged underneath the pulpit. It is very agreeably
heated by a furnace having five registers, one in the front
of rostus and two on each side. It has a basement which
they use for society meetings, church conferences and
other secular meetings.

This church was organized on the South end of Fort
street, in 1870, by Rev. Andrew Jackson and a few of
Atlanta's most prominent citizens, who were at that time
members of the Friendship Baptist church, the number
being only six. The much esteemed Peter Eskridge was
one among the number. Rev. Andrew Jackson served
this church about four years, and then resigned and went
to Mississippi. The church was then without a pastor,
and the services of Rev. Henry Brewster were employed
until they could secure another pastor. During this time,
by some means not known to the writer, this church became acquainted with Rev. W. H. Tilman and extended

him a call.   The membership at this time was about two
hundred.   The house of worship, by the power and influence which this venerable minister of the gospel had
over the people who came to hear him, was crowded,
and the house which they were then using was too small
for the people who gathered.   The pastor and deacons
began to look about for a place more suitable on which
to erect a house that would give larger accommodation.
In 1880 the site on which the present house of worship
now stands, was purchased.

Deacon Thomas Goosby and Deacon S. Foster were
the two men who raised the first amount to purchase the
present house of worship.

Shortly after the purchase of this place, by these two
noble brethren, the erection of a far more commodious
building was seen going up.

The lot was valued at two hundred and forty dollars,
fronting about seventy feet on Wheat street (now Auburn Avenue) running back about two hundred on Fort
street.   On this piece of ground is the above described
house.   This piece of property is now worth from thirty
five hundred to forty hundred, all of which has been
paid for.

It numbers among its members some of the wealthiest
colored citizens of Atlanta, and also those of the highest
character and eminence of the citizens of Atlanta.   Among
them are Thomas Goosby, Peter Eskridge, S. Foster,
Willis Murphy, Joseph Johnson, W. T. Robinson, Lu-
cius Laster, Shadrack Laster, Crawford Austin, Thomas
Gray, Columbia King, Mrs. George Foster, Mrs. Mary
Goosby-Crumbley, Mrs. Emma Williams, Mrs. Effie
Brandon, Henry Dupree, Mrs. Adline Dupree, Mrs.
Georgia McGhee, Crawford McGhee, Elbert Roberts,
Mrs. Mary Smith, Martha Hayes, Hattie Eskridge, Mrs.
Caroline Badger, Mrs. Mary Gipson, Mr. J. S. Brandon.

INSIDE FIRST BAPTIST CHURCH.

WHEAT STREET BAPTIST CHURCH.

This list of names embraces some of the noblest citizens, in character, wealth and honor, in the city of Atlanta. Any church would be honored for having such a corps of citizens for its members.

The name was originally Mt. Pleasant which was then in a common wooden building and when moved to Wheat street they changed its name to Wheat Street Baptist Church, taking its name after the street, but since the existence of this beautiful building the name of the street has been changed to Auburn Avenue, so that the name of the church now stands as the Auburn Avenue Baptist Church. So well has this church succeeded under the grand leadership of its noble and much esteemed pastor, it has grown from two hundred to fourteen hundred in number.

This grand and noble man has done a great and noble work. Too much cannot be said of this great worker in Israel. He makes no pretention to scholarship. He has been moderator of the Ebenezer Baptist Association for eight years. He served as vice-president for some years of the Foreign Mission Baptist Convention for the State of Georgia.

The cost of this building erected by the present pastor, Rev. W. H. Tilman, is twenty thousand dollars. Within the pale of this church there are a number of live societies operating for the good of the church and its members. Among them are the Sisters or Love, the Rising Star, of which Mrs. Jennie Eskridge has been so faithful a president. There are also the Aiding Brothers of Love, the Woman's Mission, which does work both in city and State, This society has done much in the way of relieving widows and the poor little orphan children. Miss Hattie Eskridge, a most faithful and energetic woman, is its president. There is also the Sunday-school, of which

Mr. J. S. Brandon has been superintendent for the last six years.

Much of the success of this good and great church is due to its charitable spirit and its broad hearted pastor.

PAPERS READ

AT THE

TWELFTH ANNIVERSARY

OF THE

AUTHOR'S WORK AS PASTOR

OF

FRIENDSHIP BAPTIST CHURCH

ATLANTA, GA.

THE CALL.

BY MISS U. E. CRAWFORD, TEACHER IN FOURTH WARD
SCHOOL.

When the throne of England or any of the great
powers of foreign nations have been deprived of their
king or queen, their subjects are never at a loss to know
who will be their next ruler, as these offices are filled according to birth or hereditarily.

When the head of the American nation has been removed, either by death or expiration of term, the attention of every true American citizen is turned to the city
of executive power and the all important question of
the day then is, who shall take his place ? Who shall
stand at the head of this great nation?

The same question may be asked by each individual
State in reference to her Governor, the city in reference
to its mayor.

As in politics so it is with institutions of learning and
religion. For at the head of all these there must be
some one who shall feel the responsibility of all.

During the declining years of the venerable and much
beloved Father Quarles, when his feeble strength would
not permit him to fill his own stand, he would often be
seen wending his way to the plant bed of the Baptist pulpit, the Atlanta Baptist Seminary, and draw therefrom
a young man in whom he had implicit confidence as a
true Christian gentleman, Rev. E. R. Carter, to assist
him in his work. And while this young man was administering the gospel to his congregation, he would sit
at his back and invoke God's blessing upon him.

In the year 1881, after much pressing and hesitation,
he consented to go on a mission to the North for the pur-

pose of procuring funds for the erection of the now famous Spelman Seminary. He left Rev. Carter in charge of his church until he returned. But the allwise Father of all saw fit to call him from his well-harvested field of labor while away on his mission. And though the hearts of his sons and daughters were grieved at the sudden and unexpected death of their beloved father, friend and brother, the question was being asked by each one of them, who shall take his place? What man among us is there who is able to lead this people who have been from their earliest existence under the leadership of so great a man? In their grief and excitement it had not occurred to them the possibility of the man who was serving his apprenticeship, as assistant and supporter of their deceased father, was by divine injunction, under a course of preparation, the result of which would be his calling to the pastorate of the church he was then serving. And finally, after a brief consideration, he was unanimously elected pastor of Friendship Baptist church.

In appearance one may style him a very ordinary looking man. In character he is firm in his convictions, wide in his views, generous and sympathetic in nature, frank in his expressions, dares to speak his opinions and acts and moves according to the dictates of his own conscience.

His ability, while he makes no attempt at display, is well founded. He is a thorough scholar, a deep thinker, eloquent in expression, fluent in language, clear in his conceptions and arrives at conclusions from a logical standpoint.

He has written several books, among them the " Baptist Pulpit," "Scenes Abroad " and " The Black Side of Atlanta," each of which is a masterpiece of thought and ability.

Immediately after taking charge of the church, he was informed of the enormous debt of $1,500 which over-shadowed the church, the interest being one-third of the principal and if not paid would probably dispossess them of their home. He did not simply show them their sad plight, but immediately began to devise plans and ways by which the indebtedness of the church could be met ; and by his skillful management the debt was soon canceled, and the hearts of his people rejoiced that they could once more worship under their own vine and fig tree.

Hardly had this object been accomplished when he inspired them to remodel and beautify the home for which they had paid so dearly. And as usual they took hold with a will. The result of that effort can be seen in the beautiful and delicate designs which adorn these walls ; The displacing of the old pews for the present ones not only gives comfort but adds beauty and capacity; the removal of the breakable and often smoking lamps, for the beautiful and illuminating gas lights ; the large pipe organ which peals forth its sweet strains of music and often causes the congregation to forget church etti-quette in looking back to see from whence the sound came, takes the place of a much inferior one ; and last, but not least, the many souls which have been added to the cause of Christ since his calling.

The work accomplished up to this time covers the short period of six years, in which time the church has been raised to a higher standard financially, intellectually and religiously.

In 1891, to show their gratitude and high appreciation for his valuable services and the great work which he had accomplished in so short a time, his congregation extended him an invitation of a tour to the old country, at their expense ; at which time he traveled extensively through the old world, and visited many points of interest and institutions of learning, where he gained much information of the manners, customs, fashions and religions of the inhabitants of those countries.

That his mind is ever active and that the interest of his people is always at heart was seen when he showed them the importance of the church becoming the possessor of the valuable piece of property which adjoins them; for had it remained in the hands of some one who perhaps not regarding the absolute necessity of quietude in or near the house of worship, possibly may have erected a beer factory, a coffin factory, or some other establishment which might have been detrimental both to the comfort and value of the church. But instead of any of these objectionable features, there now stands the home of the old saints, where they rest from their labor and the church supports them.

When we notice the active and ever restless spirit of this man, to move onward and upward, we can but join the poet in saying:

"Tell me not in mournful numbers,
    Life is but an empty dream,
For the soul is dead that slumbers,
    And things are not what they seem."

Coming to his last great step of which we have any knowledge, of lifting up fallen humanity and furthering the cause of Christ, is the organization of the Missionary Society of a few days ago, in this church, and at the head of which stands one of our noblest and most earnest Christian young women, Miss Agnes Boswell.

An attempt to explain the good which has been accomplished by this band of Christian workers, would be but to fail. It is enough to say that many a hungry soul has been fed, the naked clothed, and the word of God read to all.

Too many good things cannot be said of one who is worthy of having a great many good things said of him. But I would not have you understand that while Rev. Carter possesses so many beautiful traits of character, eloquence and ability, that he is without any of the shortcomings which generally befall mankind. It may be true that his demonstrations upon people and things of this life may have been based upon false premises, from which the true results could not be deduced, yet be it said to his honor that in not one single act of his life was he ever known to degrade, to drag down or to crush his fellow-man; but rather to lift up, to elevate, and to encourage some sad heart.

Like Daniel he has often stood almost alone in protecting the unprotected woman. When the beast in human form would seek to crush out her life, he has come to her rescue, and in words of force and command say to him: "If you are not guilty, if you can establish your own innocence, cast the first stone." And in nine cases out of ten the casting of stones have been few and far between.

The W. A. W. C. T. U. tender you their congratulation for the many years you have led this people and the valuable service given them, and especially for the noble stand which you took in the prohibition campaign in saving our sons and daughters from the demon alcohol, and for God and home and native land.

May these twelve brief years in which so much work has been crowded, inspire us to do something to make the world better for having lived in it. And though we may not be called to preach, and though we cannot make a speech, we can tell the love of Jesus, we can say he died for all.

17

BY REV. J. B. DAVIS, PASTOR OF CENTRAL AFRICAN
BAPTIST CHURCH.

SIR—I greatly appreciate the compliment which I am
this day enjoying in having the pleasure of meeting with
you on this occasion.   High, however, as is the honor, I
cannot for one moment lose sight of the fact that, in accepting your invitation to speak at this hour, I am likewise assuming a responsibility which I shall seek to discharge with all fairness and earnestness, trusting that the
time will come, if not now, in your own life when you
shall see that the words which I am about to speak have
been verified by your own experience.   And the topic
which I wish to speak about is "Natural Ability as a
Preacher."

Rev. E. R. Carter, like the Apostle Paul, the great
preacher, avails himself of every opportunity to illustrate
the truth which he seeks to impress upon the minds of
those to whom he preaches or lectures.   The Apostle
found material which served to illustrate the great truth
of the Bible in the Greek games, in the military service,
and even the anatomy of the human body furnished him
with abundant opportunity to explain his thoughts.   He
never hesitates for a moment to employ them, casting
aside an idea of criticism and scorning all thought of
censure.

If he wished to speak of the Christian warfare he
dressed his thought in the form and garb of the Roman
soldier, helmeted and attired in full armor, with weap-
ons at hand and shield for defense.   So with Rev. E. R.
Carter, an educated gentleman, an eminent minister of
the gospel, a devoted pastor and a profound, practical
thinker.

From his youth he has been a close observer of everything around him, and his audiences have, in his lectures
and sermons delivered from this rostrum from time to

time, the result of accumulated years of observation from many standpoints of life—on the farm, in the schoolroom, in business circles, from the pulpit, and in the rounds of pastoral visitations—extensive knowledge of the Holy Land. His keen perceptives have caught and made a moral diagnosis of every idiosyncrasy and peculiarity of character passing before him, and with his wonderful ability and scalpel of caricaturing art, he has dissected them before the world.

If any one should enjoy the distinction of being original in the pulpit, it ought to be Rev. E. R. Carter, D.D. His sermons are full of practical every-day life, an d with that God-given endowment he moulds from the habits and customs of men a moral and a religious truth. His manner in the pulpit is unique, and attractive to the listener, whether young or old.

The genius for natural speaking or preaching is inborn and ineradicable with some persons. It is God-given and, like every other natural endowment, it is bestowed for a good purpose. And accompanying his natural ability is wit, of which one has truly said : "Wit is the ally of truth."

Bishop H. M. Turner, introducing Rev. E. R. Carter to some gentlemen, said : " Sir, he is as sarcastical as the devil and as complimentary as an angel." Many of the greatest preachers possess wit and humor in a high degree. The sparkling and caustic wit of Robert South has brought down his sermons from the seventeenth century to this day. He was the master of polished sarcasm, impaling an absurdity on the point of an antithesis with a skill never surpassed. Spurgeon's wit is no small element of the popularity which makes him the first preacher of his generation. Beecher's wit was irrepressible and brilliant, and did much toward making the Ply-

mouth pulpit in Brooklyn so irresistibly attractive to
crowded and cultured audiences for so many decades.

The same quality is found in Carter, in connection with
his astonishing powers as a word painter and theological
preacher. It was the natural ability and wit of Carter's
that has so indescribably shaken one side of these United
States during the recent prohibition campaign. One of
the daily papers published in Indianapolis, October 3,
1889, speaking of the ability of Rev. Carter, said: "Rev.
E. R. Carter, who preached on a recent Lord's day at
the North church, is pastor of a colored Baptist church
in Atlanta, numbering twenty-five hundred members. He
was at the time in attendance here upon the national
meeting of our colored Baptists."

He is a preacher of ability and a graduate of our Home
Mission Seminary at Atlanta. He is clear-headed, manly,
of bright intellect, and has had the advantage of traveling
very extensively in Europe.

During the late prohibition campaign in this State,
Rev. Carter received an invitation to come forthwith to
Monroe, Ga., to deliver a prohibition speech. After
many of Georgia's eminent sons had spoken, he was
called upon, and, after a brilliant ray of words in illustration of the suffering and misery derived from the use of
accursed traffic in liquor, the infernal fire-water, that
burns and scorches out all that is noble and grand in
humanity. After he had concluded his speech, the gentleman who had invited him there to speak, rose up
and said, that "there never was such a speech made in
this court house since Monroe has been a Monroe "

Dr. Geo. A. Lofton, of Alabama, in referring to the
defeat sustained by the Prohibition party in the last Prohibition campaign, held in this magnificent city, said :
"What more could have been done to save the city than
was done. There is Hawthorne, Grady, Hillyer and

Carter, Atlanta's true sons, have done their duty." I see a sketch of his life written by Dr. J. W. Lee, of this city, in which he said: "Rev. E. R. Carter commands the highest respect and admiration, not only of his own church and denomination, but of all churches and all classes of our people." He is original and unique. His wit and humor are of the freshest and most irresistible kind. His way of putting this is peculiarly striking and entertaining. Perhaps he has most prominently come before the people outside of his own denomination in connection with his work for the cause of Prohibition. When his natural ability became so conspicuous in 1885, during the first great uprising on the subject of Prohibition, in which he so valliantly fought, he was invited to Richmond, Va., Mississippi, South Carolina, Alabama and Indiana. His speech in Richmond, Va., excited a great deal of attention. Bishop Turner said that while it was being delivered, he thought he caught sight of the very pit as Carter uncovered the meanness of the whisky traffic.

So Dr. Lee says there was something however, about the man that went deeper than his speeches. It was his life and bearing. He was threatened, he was persecuted ; the pressure brought to bear upon him to weaken his purpose, was heavy. This only seemed to furnish strength to his zeal and determination. Perhaps it will be universally conceded that if an election was taken in this city as to who was the greatest hero in the prohibition campaign of 1887, E. R. Carter would receive almost the unanimous vote. No man among us met more, overcame more *than he did*. Hon. Pringle, the representative of the Georgia Legislature, has these words in the *Augusta Chronicle* :

"Among the gentlemen who spoke here to-day I would be guilty of gross injustice were I to rate Rev. E. R.

Carter, pastor of Friendship Baptist church, second to
any. At times he dived down into the purest African
dialect and showed ability without education; ere he had
done this, he soared to the loftiest heights of purest eloquence and diction. Few men have the *power as this man.*"

Rising from the mechanic's bench, and as much as St.
Paul the master of a trade, he respected labor and laborers
first salutes him with honors. He speaks to them and
for them, and they are proud of him. If he exaltes their
destiny, he does not refrain from exposing their faults
If they are intemperate, he denounces not them, but intemperance. If they are idlesome he set them an example of unflagging industry. If they are illiterate, he
shows how some knowledge had been gained by the
evening blaze of tallow candles and by the light which
breaks through the crevices of the early morning.

In his sermons he never has been betrayed into any
ambitious use of language, and seldom decorated anything with borrowed scraps. Pilate and Herod struck
hands, but the brave heart of Carter, strong from con-
tinous struggle, flinches in no wise from the task self-im-
posed and self-sustained.

God grant that you might live to see the dead carcass
of the great wrong of intemperance buried forever out of
the sight of man, and the once blackened besom of the
great Christiandom, pure again from that ancient sin.
May you live to do more in this spiritual struggle, amel-
iorating the condition of humanity, both temporally, in-
terlectually and morally.

Sin, the enemy of equity, justice and right, is as the
colossal forces that shook our broad land, and made its
earth-fast foundation tremble with the steps of uncounted
hosts.

Sir, this world needs men like yourself who can get the
great truths out of the Bible, and give it in child-like
simplicity to a dying world

AS I HAVE SEEN HIM.

BY PROF. W. E. HOLMES, A.M.

Rev. Edward R. Carter was called to the pastorate of Friendship Baptist church April 11, 1882, where he has served with acceptance these twelve years.

FINANCIAL WORK.

On coming into the work he was greatly surprised to learn that a debt of two thousand dollars rested upon the building, this amount having been borrowed from the American Baptist Home Mission Society of New York City to aid in erecting this place of worship.

Besides this, there were several obligations of smaller sums here and there to be met in the city.

The members were told the condition of affairs, and they went to work cheerfully and promptly to lift from their shoulders this load of debt which had been incurred in providing them with a church home and in operating it after completion.

Appeal after appeal was made with the most gratifying results. Collection after collection in a remarkably short time liquidated all the debts, and the church stood free and untrammeled to advance the cause of Christ.

With a view to encouraging the people and to congratulate them upon the success of their efforts, a large and enthusiastic meeting was held, before which an interesting programme of speech and song was carried out to the delight of the entire audience.

The building was decorated, and in a conspicuous place was displayed the legend, " *Free From Debt.*" Thus discharged of all its obligations, the church has since been prosperous in an eminent degree in everything it has undertaken.

MATERIAL PROGRESS.

Having an eye for the beautiful as well as the useful, under the direction of the pastor the building has been beautified within and improved without.

To enable everybody to see what is going on in front, the floor has been elevated at the doors and lowered at the rear; the pulpit has been enlarged, and on the arch above it, in prominent characters, is the statement from Scripture: "He that believeth and is baptized shall be saved." Beautiful cathedral windows take the place of the plain, unpretentious sash, and frescoed walls give evidence of cultivated taste, while from afar a roof of slate glitters in the summer sun.

Desiring to lengthen her cords and strengthen her stakes, the church has undertaken, on property of her own, representing an outlay of fifteen hundred dollars, to provide for her worthy, indigent poor. And now, while we speak, a number there are beneficiaries of her charity.

RELATIONS BETWEEN PASTOR AND PEOPLE.

No where can beneficial results be reached without hearty co-operation, concert of action and the closest cordial relations. And eminently true is this of the relations between pastor and people. In Friendship this has been repeatedly illustrated.

From the day Mr. Carter was elected to this pastorate to this hour, there has always been the " *Faithful Few* " to confer with their pastor concerning the interests of the church, to unite with him in furthering the success of Zion, and to strengthen his hands and encourage his heart all the time and everywhere.

Nor have they been slow to give liberally of their means to enhance his happiness and promote his welfare.

At the suggestion of one of his sincerest friends, they

have several times sent him North to spend vacation, and twice they have sent him abroad to revel in the beauties of other lands and to gather information for increased usefulness at home. So far as known, they took the initiative in this worthy, generous step.

SPIRITUAL RESULTS.

So much for material results and general success. But the noblest, the most enduring, and by far the most signal success, has been in the realm of grace.

Anxious to add to the excellent work already begun and so ably carried forward, the new pastor began at once to labor for souls for the Master, and in this line of endeavor he has brought much to pass. Ninety persons every year—eleven hundred the entire time—have come into the church as the result of his earnest labors.

And what more shall I say? The crown of his rejoicing is bright, shining as the sun, and when in the presence of our Redeemer, where are joys forever more, he shall be called to receive it; he will be welcomed with the salutation: "Well done, thou faithful servant; enter thou into the joys of thy Lord."

HIS ABILITY AS A HERO IN THE TEMPERANCE CAUSE.

BY LEWIS COX.

There has been much said as to the cause of temperance reigning in this section of this country. There have been a good many plans on foot to oust intemperance; many speeches have been made by our best citizens, who have lost many a sleepless night planning and arranging as to how we shall take advantage of this monster.

Among some of our most eloquent was the Hon. H. W. Grady, who now sleeps beneath the clods awaiting the final judgment, when the Lord shall say unto those who have done good unto the resurrection, " Come ye blessed of my Father;" Hon. George Hillyer, the Hammonds, Sam Jones, Sam Small, Dr. Morrison, Dr. J. B. Hawthorne, Captain Milledge, Captain Harry Jackson, Alex Smith and D. L. Moody.

Thus we see one among the Anglo-Saxon race who maneuvered the campaign fields and could always locate the enemy, was Mr. H. W. Grady, who seemed to be first and foremost in planning for his people. Many laurels he has won for his race, and yet to remember him the people of Atlanta have set up a monument in a street of Atlanta that all who pass by that way may be reminded of the great hero who once lived and did so much for the elevating of his race.

And last, but not least among the great men of our race who did what they could in promoting the cause was Rev. E. R. Carter, Bishop Gaines, Bishop Turner John W. Young, who now sleeps beneath the clods, and Granderson, Price, the great negro historian who by his eloquence won for himself and race many honors. Both white and black pronounce him an orator, but the Lord has taken this great man away through his providence to live with the just men made perfect.

Among the many speakers among our people there seems to be one distinguished from the rest, whose motive in life is to make a mark that unborn generation who shall come after him will see his foot prints on the sands of time, and will know from reading history that the great temperance hero lived. This great hero is in the person of our distinguished pastor and orator, Rev. E. R. Carter, whose aim in life is to promote his race, and whose greatest ambition is to see his people prosper and to do

everything in his power to elevate them to a higher standard in life. In fact, he is a model preacher, who has
studied extensively and knows exactly what good thing
to give his people. As a maneuverer in the gospel ministry he has no equal. A man for this day, has written
extensively.

First, " Our Pulpit Illustrated," a book worthy to be
in any house; second, a book known as the " Black Side
of Atlanta," that is now in the press, and still another
called "Descriptive Scenes of Europe and the Orient."

Thus you see the time he has spent in preparing good
literature and money too cannot be compared with the
glory that shall be revealed e'er he's gone.

Let us as young and old ones too throw our arms
around such a man and show him that we as a race ex-
pect to stick up to our race and honor them to whom
honor is due, then we can say as one has said, United we
stand, but divided we fall.

So powerful and influential was the speeches that they
were stereotyped and sent all over this State and other
States in the Union as a standard and temperance com-
paign document. Thus by the power of the press his
speeches on this great subject has gone nearly the round
of America, into nearly every family, and has done much
to shape and mold the great and powerful sentiment of
temperance in this great nation. From the compliments
and eulogies which the papers of this country have paid to
our pastor, I think I can be warranted to say that there
is no man, living or dead, that has undergone more to
glorify the temperance cause and to battle down the
strong hold of the traffic in liquor, than the man whose
twelfth anniversary we meet here to-day from all over
this beautiful city to celebrate.

We may, reviewing things as we do of the past,
truthfully and rightfully entitle him, as the Dow of
the Negro race in the temperance cause.

And may God grant that from the heroism that has
been displayed in our pastor from this pulpit and nearly
every rostrum and platform and stump in this State and
other States, so inspire and enthuse and mold and form in
every man and woman that here is to-day to catch on fire
from this hero and rise to that eminence that will make
them a blessing to home, to God and native land.

A PURPOSE AND WILL.

BY MISS SARAH DOZIER, TEACHER IN THIRD WARD
SCHOOL.

There may be somewhere on the globe, men who have
made themselves conspicuous to the world's eye as men
of prominence, of interest and wealth who started out
without a *Purpose and Will* in life, men who have rowed
their life-boat at random, men who have truly reached
the top, but how few men have climbed the ladder of
fame and prosperity, beginning with the round that
rested upon the ground to the one that leans against the
highest summit of human ambition, were men who had
marked out for themselves in life this motto, " *A Purpose
and Will.*"

A purpose and will means nothing more than a fixed
destination. This all men should have, for it gives one more
zeal, makes him courageous, makes him indeed a warrior
for the fixed purpose, and like the eagle which seeks to
rise above the mighty thunder storm, struggles, battles
and wrestles with the mighty winds (all the while with his
head upturned as if desirious of fixing his eye on the
goal), and screams only when he has proven to himself
at least that he had a " purpose and will," when he can
calmly spread his pinions and sail above the storm.

Not that the same person may become successful in all occupations in life, but it is enough that *success* is achieved in a single occupation, proves much to that man. He deserves well of his fellowmen and may justly respect himself. He had in life mapped out a purpose and will and accomplished it.

This man, though young in years, recognizing the divine call, without a thought of self, and a heart full of love for God and mankind, has proved beyond a contradiction that He, without whose knowledge a sparrow cannot fall, takes care of His own. He seemed to have realized that the highest success is achieved by making the most of one's powers and opportunities. He works in accordance with the will of the Master, and when difficulties confront him, they vanish before him as do the mists from the morning sun. But to the limited advantage for intellectual improvement, he has accomplished infinitely more by force of his natural abilities than have many who have ample stores of useful information.

Out of the material furnished and in accomplishing the controlling purpose of life, he has placed himself where he now stands. He has been advanced from one position to another, in each of them showing himself capable of meeting the demands made upon him.

His aim is high, and to help him reach it, he has availed himself of all the help, in the way of learning that were accessible; he has read only to learn more emphatically that God made all men to be brethren and that Christ gave as the sum total of his doctrine, that they should love one another. Let us take a view of the past twelve years of his life, when he first became pastor of this church. Just think a church of fifteen hundred members, a pulpit left vacant by the death of its dearly beloved pastor, he stepped in as a son taking up the great work, has labored under many disadvantages to lead his people to the desired haven. Notice the path through which he is passing. It is one of obstacles and difficulties, but being a self-made man he has worked his way up from the base to its summit.

In preaching to his congregation he always bears in mind the old as well as the young. With these two forces he has struggled night and day and succeeded in finding words to please both, and to-day when he takes his stand in the pulpit, mother and daughter, father and son, witness together the glorious truths that falls from his lips.

His purpose is not to gather a band about self, but unite a company around the Savior. He has not only devoted his time and talent to his own church, but has also gone abroad to better the moral condition of his race. Take, for instance, the work he undertook in advocating the cause of prohibition. In this movement he has made himself famous. During the great struggle in this cause in 1885, he stood, as it were, almost alone and defended his cause. He made in this campaign a name that is a household word with prohibitionists of the South. Look, if you will, at the enemies on all sides in the form of friends—men who walked daily by his side with smiles and words enough to cause him to cry out: "Truly the victory *will* be ours!" But in the midst of the great combat he is often found alone, and with a purpose and will, conquers his foe.

Another instance in which he has experienced great difficulties, is in preaching to his people on the subject of emigration. He was threatened and the pressure brought to bear upon him to weaken his purpose was heavy. Has he faltered ? *No*, it has seemed only to furnish strength to his zeal and determination. He has lived, and the people have lived to see and experience that many of the things he preached to them are indeed truths.

It must have taken a man of purpose and will to stand under such difficulties, amidst opposition of such strength. In viewing his life from early boyhood to where he now stands, we can see supreme purposes which he has formed running through his whole career. He has a mark in view, and is pursuing it steadily. It requires purpose, will and oneness of aim and invincible determination, to succeed. He has experienced the great difference between men, between the great and the insignificant, *is* energy, invincible determination, an honest purpose once fixed, and then death or victory.

This quality will do anything in the world, and no talents, no circumstances, will make a creature a man without it. The very reputation of being strong-willed and indefatigable is of priceless value. Such purpose and will have enabled him to cower his enemies and dispel the opposition that was about to confront him. He started in life with a determination to reach a certain position, and adhered unwaveringly to his purpose, rejecting the advice of the over-cautious. Can such a man fail? No, he will not fail, but is continuing to work until he reaches goal for which he set out.

He is a man who sees but little impossibility in whatever he undertakes. If he waits and does nothing, the reason is that he wants an opportunity to carry out his purpose. He has formed in his mind a divine purpose ; it has governed his conduct, as the laws of nature govern the operation of physical forces. I dare say, had he not been a man of courage and full of the divine will-power, he could not and would not be standing where he is to-day.

For the success which he has enjoyed, and for the wide, extended influence which he has exerted, not only in his own State, but in other States, ought not the church to be proud of such a man?

I have not written in terms of fulsome flattery of one, nor would I convey the impression of invidious comparison, but because he merits it, I repeat and affirm all I have stated in the assertion, that of all the choice spirits who preach the Gospel of the Son God, he is one.

POSITIVENESS OF SPEECH.

BY MRS. A. BARSWELL,

Teacher in Fourth Ward School.

Many know when to speak and what to say, but do not know how to say it. Many know how to speak, but fail to do so. Such possessions as these are possessed either with selfishness, cowardice or hypocrisy. Then there are few, very few, who know how to speak, and do speak in the real way. When, by chance, we find one of this few we should confer upon him the greatest honors, for this plain, positive, open way of speaking is the best way to reach the minds of the people. No doubt this very reflection has been stamped upon the mind of Rev. Carter, and that is why he chose this simple way of imparting his knowledge. He considers the classes of people that he has to minister unto ; for they range from the old gray-haired fathers and mothers of the dark days of slavery to the young blooming child of the nineteenth century; from the most ignorant to the most learned. Yet, even though his mind is filled with a knowedge of the various languages; even though he can reason with philosophers and contest with the great men of the nation, he knows that this is not the time nor the place for it. So he places himself in an attitude to make the lowest understand. He does not come in with all the fine words of Webster, with his hyperbolical expressions and oracular speeches to crowd out and crush down the understanding of the unlearned. But he is one of the very few who know how to talk, and who talks in the real way. He comes with good common sense reasoning; not with a puff and a blow, but to give the truth in a plain way, so as to reach the hearts of the people. He has that quality of candor in him which is one of the first if not the foremost of all qualities a man can possess. He is the man with power and not show; and throughout the land you will find that the man who has power is rather to be preferred than the one who has show. Rev. Carter pours out his heart's blood into the channels of public prosperity, but he does it in a way open to all. His hearers are carried away with him; they follow him in all that he says, because they can understand even every change of feeling. He speaks without mingling his speeches with falsehood. If he has to speak that he will do it and do it candidly. If he is asked his honest opinion, that will he give in spite of all the foes that may rise against him. Once I heard him say, "that if he had to be a man's enemy because he spoke his opinions, why then he would be his enemy." That very expression, in my opinion, won for him the name of a man who is not afraid of the truth. Sometimes I think he is too plain and that if he were to withhold some things of his mind he might the more gain the favor of the public. But he does not regard public sentiment; he cares nothing for the thoughts of the world. Let them do what they may his thoughts are his own and he does not smother them when they should be known. He knows what he does know; he knows when to make it known, and he makes it known in a distinct way. I say now, as I said in the beginning, that if any man cannot

18

speak his mind because of fear then he is a coward; and
if any man will not speak his opinion because of friendship's sake he is a hypocrite.   Let us then reflect upon
this; let us imitate the example of Rev. Carter. For, to
say the least of it, is to say that it is simply honest. We
all know that any undertaking, clear, round dealing is
the best deal. We have been told that this winding way,
this twist, this turn about is the course of the serpent
that God has lowered. If any man takes this way he
lowers his character and covers himself with shame. Let
us walk in the straight path then; for sooner or later
it will gain for us the principal instruments for action
which are trust and belief. We will see that, as the poet
says:

> There's wit there, we'll get there,
> We'll find no other where.

WALTER H. LANDRUM,

MASTER OF CEREMONIES.

DEAR BROTHERS, SISTERS AND FRIENDS: We are
gathered this beautiful Sabbath to celebrate the twelfth
anniversary of the administration of the Rev. E. R. Carter's work with us in this our church.

A little over twelve years ago it pleased the omnipo-
tent and all-wise God to transfer the late Frank Quarles,
our much beloved pastor, from this world of woe and
misery to the celestial city above the sun, moon and stars.

My much beloved brothers and sisters, I know
you remember him well—yes, I know you do. Yes,
just as true as I am standing here, I believe I have living
witnesses to what I shall say.

At times away down in the souls of you who labored
with the Rev. Quarles, can't you hear him giving out

that favorite hymn of his? Yes, when the Rev. Quarles'
soul was kindled with the flames from on high, he would
rise up with the tears running down his cheeks—

> 1 Servant of God, well done,
>   Rest from thy loved employ;
>   The battle fought, the victory won,
>   Enter thou thy Master's joy.
>
> 2 The voice of midnight came,
>   He started up to hear;
>   A mortal arrow pierced his frame,
>   He fell, but felt no fear.
>
> 3 The pains of death are past,
>   Labor and sorrow cease,
>   And life-long warfare closed at last,
>   His soul is found in peace.
>
> 4 Soldier of Christ, well done,
>   Praise be thy new employ,
>   And while eternal ages run,
>   Rest in thy Savior's joy.

Now, to Father Tate, Father John Carter, James
Holmes, Rivers and Houston, you who labored with the
Rev. Quarles so long, at times in your bosoms you can
hear the very sounds of his lining, and the tinkling
music of his favorite hymn, of which I have just spoken,
ringing and shall continue to ring until God shall call you
hence. God will not let the work of his people die.

But let us go back to the subject of to-day—the
twelfth anniversary of the administration of the Rev.
E. R. Carter. Twelve years ago this church was without a leader. The eyes of the deacons were turned in
every direction, thinking what would be the best for the
church. The prayers of the sisters ascended on high.

The God that we serve being surrounded by a legion
of angels, making music both day and night; but in the
midst of all that magnificent music the prayers of Friendship church were heard. God sent forth a young man

by the name of Rev. E. R. Carter to lead his people onward and upward toward the celestial city. But stop!
Satan was not asleep. Some of the members began to
find fault, saying the young man Carter was too young;
others said the debt that hung over this church was too
great for a man of his age.

The young man Carter being a commissioned officer of
God, his papers all duly signed by the Supreme Hand of
the universe, took his little army here, much out in the
fields, delivering the church from the great debt and adding hundreds of souls to her list.

Thus we have gathered to return our sincere thanks to
our God for the twelve years' journey in the wilderness.

A LOOK BACK OVER THE PASTOR'S WORK.

BY MRS. MAMIE (JACKSON) TATE.

As we look back upon the silent ocean of the past
twelve years, of which our beloved pastor, Rev. E. R.
Carter, has been our leader, we find that they are marked
ones in the history of our community.

In the year 1882, he was called to preside over the
congregation of Friendship Baptist church, which at that
time was a very small number. As the years rolled on the
church grew in membership, financial strength, and influence, and is now considered the second strongest of
any Negro organization in the State of Georgia.

Under the philosophical leadership of Rev. Carter,
this church has been successful in all of its undertakings,
and has given largely to the educational and missionary
work. Its organization, growth and usefulness are most
remarkable. In the midst of the pastor's grand work,

which is his happiness, there has beat around him, not
once but repeatedly, storm after storm, and at times they
seemed as if they would carry him down; but he stood
undismayed in the midst of he temptest, while darkness
seemed to bar the way, sustained by strong faith through
which he saw a brighter day, for beyond that belt of
darkness, where the years will roll on as rippling and
caressing waves, around the green islands fragrant with
the breath of flowers that never wither and whose atmos-
phere is joy and peace, there alone is life. When the
great waves of sorrow or depression have come striking
at individuals, he has never failed to give them needed
consolation. Notwithstanding the many difficulties which
have surrounded him, he has thrown out the life line and
brought many safely to the shore.

Friends, can we be otherwise than grateful for such a
man as Rev. E. R. Carter? For I doubt if there has ever
been such a record of any man, living or dead, black or
white, on this continent *in so brief a time* as this one which
is being brought before us to-day.

Does not the world need such men? Yes, we want
more men like the one who stands at the head of Friendship church, which a time like this demands, men with
great hearts, strong minds, true faith and willing hands;
men whom the lust of office does not kill, men whom
the spoils of office can not buy, men who possess
opinions and a will, men who have honor, and men who
will *not lie.*

A GOOD SHEPHERD.

BY MAJOR S. W. EASLEY, JR.

I am to speak to you of a good shepherd as contra-
distinguished from "The Good Shepherd." The term
shepherd in this sense is applied to one who provides

spiritual food for his flock, in whom he takes pleasure in caring for and constantly holding before them the love of God, the cross on Calvary, the bleeding wounds of Him who died for mankind, a pleader of our cause before the Great I Am, a loving Savior, the Prince of peace and King of kings. He who does this is truly a good shepherd, as was exemplified on the plains of Bethlehem when the angelic choir appeared unto the shepherds, apprising them of the fact that the Emanuel was born. This that choir of choirs did with a song of such melody and sweetness that the sound thereof is still upon the wings of the wind, which causes the blood-washed souls to become enchanted at each recurring sound.

Does the shepherd of this mighty flock in whose behalf these exercises are being held to-day, come up to this standard ? Is he mindful of his flock, standing before them with an acquitted conscience of a duty well done ? From my observation of him I have gleaned the following:

It is always a difficult task to even fairly estimate the character and purposes of a man filling an exalted position. He is so far removed from the ordinary plane that his in-coming and out-going are a mystery to most of mankind. Few people know him well. The multitude must gather their knowledge of him through the mist of conjecture and take their view of his conduct from behind other people's spectacles.

Years of association with men of more or less importance have taught me many useful lessons in criticism. A man of prominence once said that you never really know a man until you have been with him in his bibulous as well as his graver moments. This is entirely true. The most difficult of all the work writers have to do is to make an estimate of a prominent man and his acts from the eminence upon which he stands. Criticism is

therefore often as unjust as applause is undeserved. In
this spirit and in this light I am viewing Rev. E. R.
Carter, pastor of this church, whose broad personality is
worthy of careful consideration.

I have been led to make this attempt at an estimate of
the character of the most accomplished and scholarly
Baptist minister in Georgia, and is therefore rightly
called a good shepherd.

The doings and sayings of men in high places are oft-
times magnified or dwarfed by those whose self-interest
intrudes eulogy or defamation upon those who have not
the opportunity of seeing and hearing for themselves.
There is an old and true adage that "No man is a hero
to his valet," yet he may be a hero to the many who cannot reach him. There is no one so great in this world
that he is not an ordinary individual to some one.

The character under revision to-day by this congregation is known to you as one possessing lofty traits of
Christian virtues, a personification of the lowly Nazarine,
the embodiment of a true and faithful shepherd.

Those of us who cast our eyes heavenward at night
and as we behold the bright planets that adorn the skies
with their radiance of light and splendor, we observe
the satalites around which cluster the smaller ones. So
it is with us to-day clustering around a servant of God
commissioned by Him to preach Christ to a dying world,
and how well he has done so, the records of this house
of God is an answer for that.

We are asked to-day to stop and celebrate the twelfth
anniversary of the installation of the pastor of this
church. To me it is both a pleasure and a pride to be
permitted to add my feeble and humble testimony to the
intellectual, moral and Christian worth of our friend and
brother.

LINES,

BY LITTLE MISS PEARL SCHELL,

At the Author's Twelfth Anniversary of his work as Pastor of
Friendship Baptist Church.

1 The man I came to speak of to-day
Is one of whom the people say
Is a mighty speaker in every way.

2 He was born in Athens, they say,
A city not far away,
In the year of fifty-six—
The day of the month not accurately fixed.

3 He came to Atlanta in seventy-nine,
And in the people's hearts he began to entwine,
For he always was a fellow not to be left behind.

4 He drove the peg with hammer of shoemaker's kind,
That he might stay in school and prepare himself for the
task of the times.

5 In eighteen hundred and eighty-four,
He finished college and went no more,
For the Master's work called him to go.

SUMMER HILL GRAMMAR SCHOOL.

ABSTRACT OF AN ADDRESS.

By WM. E. HOLMES,

Delivered before the white teachers at Gainesville, Ga., June, 1894.

Besides the teachers there were present members of the Board of Education, Hall county, the expert in charge of the white teachers' institute, lawyers, the colored teachers of Gainesville and the county, and the colored pastors.

The address delivered at the request of Hon. John T. Wilson, Sr., Commissioner of Education, Hall county, was as follows:

LADIES AND GENTLEMEN: I am glad this opportunity presents itself. I shall improve it to the extent of my ability in the brief space of time allotted me to speak to you. I am always glad to address an audience of this kind. Two years ago before one of the largest and most representative gatherings ever assembled in the historic old First Church of the Baptist denomination in Philadelphia I was invited to speak. To that body I spoke of the Negro, and to you I shall speak of the same subject, because everywhere there is misapprehension, misunderstanding on this subject. And the cause of all this in the South is, that for thirty years—the life of a generation— you have not known anything of the Negro; you stand aloof from him; you have no adequate conception of the progress he has made since '65; nor do you know what he is reading, what he is thinking, or what he is doing.

In that elder day when he sustained the relation of slave to you, and you master to him, you saw more of him in your houses. You visited his cabin and his more pretentious dwelling place. He worshiped in your meeting houses and at your firesides, but with freedom came mistrust, alienation, and the withdrawal of your assistance and kindly advice.

Thus left alone, ignorant and irresponsible, to become
an easy prey to the demagogue who sought power and
preferment at his hands, and the South herself is responsible for the condition of affairs which followed
emancipation.

But here let me not rest. The Negro is misrepresented whenever he asks the worth of his money. On
railway lines and river steamers he asks not that you be
his associate, but that instead of crowding him into third-
rate compartments where the air is vitiated with the
smoke of the white man's cigar, and the water cups
are used to drink whisky from, you provide him with
accommodations commensurate with the expense his
travel involves.

Why charge him first-class rates, and in return give
him such fare ?   At present it is neither safe nor comfortable for our women to travel any considerable distance
alone on common carriers in most Southern States.   And
yet when we ask that this condition of things be changed,
the cry of " social equality " is raised, when, in truth,
there is not a sober, sensible Negro on the American continent who desires or seeks admission to your social circles.
This whole thing of social equality is a bugbear, and exists only in the minds of those who harp upon it.

The Negro is the best peasantry in the world.   You
talk about filling up the South with the hordes of immigrants who by the half million every year crowd our
shores.   You are talking and planning to introduce people here who are out of harmony with the genius and
spirit of our government ; people prepared to create a
reign of terror of which the Negro never dreams.   You
are planning to have enacted here such scenes as those

through which our fellow-countrymen passed recently at
Chicago, Boston, New York, and other places.

Let the white people of the South but make the over-
tures to the Negro they are making to the anarchists, to
the communists, to the socialists, and every old red hill
would be crowned with plenty and every neglected valley
would smile with the products of his labor.

Why should not the Negro be trusted ?   From day to
day, patient and uncomplaining, he goes to his task under
conditions no other people would endure.

Why should not the Negro be trusted now ?   When
the permanence and stability of this union was at stake,
and you of the South, at Bull Run, Shiloh, and Gettysburg,
contended for what you believed to be right, behind you
were your wives and your little ones, left to the keeping
of the faithful Negro about whose limbs you were forg-
ing more tightly the chains of slavery, and during that
entire struggle there was not one black hand uplifted to
to strike down the least of those committed to his care.

The Negro is an American citizen, and he is concerned
for the welfare of American institutions and the perpe-
tuity of American government.   And here let me state
that, however good and law-abiding may have been the
parents of the present generation of Negroes, their sons
and successors are no less so.

Here and there among them is found the vicious, shift-
less, lawless element—and where is it not found?—but
I deny that education has unfitted these people for residence in the land that gave them birth.   It has helped
them; it has not hurt them; it has done them good; it
has not done them harm; it has lifted them up; it has not
cast them down.

In conclusion, I would say Northern institutions for the
higher education of the Negro have not, as some have
claimed, made the Negro the enemy of his Southern

white neighbor. On the contrary, these schools have opened the eyes of the Negro to his duty to himself and to his fellow-men. If you and all the other white people of these Southern States knew what these schools are doing for the South in giving it a more desirable class of citizens, in preparing them to develop its resources, and so become powerful factors in its material advancement, you all would commend the public spirited philanthropists of the North for furnishing the means to reach such results.

I declare there cannot be found anywhere within the limits of the old Confederacy better or more effectual agencies at work making law-abiding, useful citizens of the Negro than the seminaries of learning everywhere in the South, which stand as monuments to the patriotism and humanity of Northern benefactors.

I invoke God's blessing upon these benefactors, and I pray that the light of his countenance may shine upon the institutions they have founded for the education of this race. And may they continue to be what they have thus far proved to be, powers for good to the latest generation of man.

Hoping what I have said may lead you to think more favorably of the race I represent, and thanking you, ladies and gentlemen, for your patient and polite attention, I have done what I regard a very pleasant duty.

LET US PLAY THE MAN.

Sketch of a sermon preached before the Second Battalion of the Governor's Volunteers (Ga.) on the fourth Sunday in July, 1894, by the Author.

We are living in one of the grandest countries on the face of the globe ; none like it anywhere. Whatever we may think of it, because of our attitude and situation in it, of course, protection of life, property, liberty, friends, and all other civil rights are of the first and highest importance with the people of the government; and if these things are neglected in reference to any part of its citizens, the country where that part of its citizens live will be taught by such treatment to seek a panacea for their ills, and will regard the local district and geographical line that encircles the spot of their habitation as the whole country, and that the meanest and most unrighteous spot upon the globe, but this will not blot out the fact of its grandeur in all.

There are other countries that may have some features that accord with our idea as to how a country ought to deal in equity with all of its subjects, and this idea may create dissatisfaction in the ill-treated part of that government, and with the love of liberty that burns in their bosom, may stir them to seek another clime, and as they go, shake the dust off their feet as a testimony against it. But on arriving at this goodly land, we come in contact with a more formidable foe, and may be called eternally to the battle-field to protect our property, religion, liberty and family. Worse than all, swim through a sea of blood to maintain them, so far as the right to own property in this country. We can own all we can pay for. So far as religious liberty, no man dare to molest us; so far as civil liberty, we may walk, stand, and act where we please. So far as our standing, walking, and acting are in the bounds of the law, and when I say this, I am not blind to nor ignorant of the troubles, drawbacks, hindrances and mighty resistances which, as a part of this grand republic, we have to encounter.

But, my fellow-brethren, we are not the only creatures of God's great creation that have to meet and encounter and struggle for the place they would occupy on this mighty, prolific, and progressive globe. All things have to struggle with all their might and main for the point of eminence for which they are striving to reach. The mighty king of day, as he rises out of the womb of the morning, has to struggle against the darkness of a preceding night with a mighty burning torch of light to gain his reign; the silvery lights that aid the way-worn traveler have to struggle through air and cloud, and a thousand other forces to give its light to earth's inhabitants; the little stream that comes tumbling down the crags of a mighty Alpine peak through valley and plain, pushing and shoving and dividing its way around curves, being repelled and tossed backward and forward before it reaches the mighty ocean. It seems to be the order of nature and the plan of Providence to develop and improve a nation of people through this method of discipline, and its subjects have only to wait for the fruits of its operation. "The bud may have a bitter taste, but sweet will be the flower."

It has just been a few centuries since the Jew was hated, persecuted, and brutally treated in Europe. And these very same people by wise conduct have arisen from this abject state to the best society and position that is within the gift of the United Kingdom. I have only need to refer to the Rothschilds, the monarchial gold-bugs; their moneys are loaned in every part of the world. Benjamin Disraeli is another mighty power that has arisen of the Jewish nation in the United Kingdom. He was despised and rejected of men. How bitter these words are, especially to the despised man; it weighs on his ambition like a millstone around his neck. So felt Benjamin Disraeli, the Jew. To be a Jew was to be out of the pale of English society, eligible to no office, ground down by special taxes. After working earnestly for many years, he was at last rejoiced to see the "Emancipation of the Jews" act passed by the

English Parliament, and he was elected by a small borough as its representative in the British House of Commons. When he made his first speech there, he became so confused and embarrassed that, amidst the jeers and laughter of the other members, he sank back silent into his seat. The ridicule so stung him, that he jumped up again and said, "You laugh at me now, but the time will come when you will laugh with me." By patient industry, at last, he was acknowledged to be the first rhetorician in the house, and when Disraeli rose in his seat, the empty benches became filled as if by magic, and the morning newspapers everywhere were filled with his great speeches. The words of this Jew moved the emperors and kings of other countries, and he became the exponent of English ideas to the powers of the earth everywhere. He became the most trusted minister of Queen Victoria, until at last, for his great services to her and the English nation, she said, "You are no longer plain Mr. Benjamin Disraeli, the Jew, but you shall be called "The Right Honorable Earl of Beaconsfield, a peer and nobleman of England, and the leader of the House of Lords, and second only to a prince of the blood royal."

At the close of the Russian-Turkish war, Russia dictated peace to Turkey, but the other European powers objected to the San Stefano treaty, and demanded that a conference should be held. The result was a meeting of the representatives of all the great powers in Berlin, Germany. Lord Beaconsfield was sent to represent Great Britain, and among all the great ones of these great countries, Lord Beaconsfield was elected chairman of that conference, to which the destiny of nations was intrusted, and the peace of the world involved. When he returned to England, the enthusiam of the people was beyond description when he stood up in his place near the throne and said, "He had brought back from Berlin to London peace with honor."

At last, full of years and honor, he lay down to his last sleep amid the wail of a grief-stricken nation. Around the grave stood the great ones of the earth, princes, kings, and emperors, none too great to do him reverence. He lives to-day, as no other statesman does, in the hearts of his countrymen. He alone has had dedicated and set apart a special day to commemorate his memory. On the anniversary of his death, his favorite flower, the primrose, will be seen decorating the homes and persons of high and low, rich and poor, in England, and if you ask its meaning, the people will say, "This is primrose day, kept in honor of Benjamin Disraeli, the despised Jew."

And now what do I mean by telling this bit of history of a despised race but to show you what is true of one race may be true of another, especially when its men will do their whole duty, and have for their sole object the elevation of the people. Benjamin Disraeli did not come to honor by incendiary speeches and teaching his despised race anarchy and rebellion, but by being a loyal citizen himself, and teaching his people the same, and playing the man for them. What we want are men.

> God give us men! A time like this demands
> Great hearts, strong minds, true faith, and willing hands.
> Men whom the lust of office does not kill;
> Men whom the spoils of office cannot buy;
> Men who possess opinions and a will;
> Men who have honor, men who will not lie;
> For while the rabble, with their thumb-worn creeds,
> Their large professions and their little deeds,
> Wrangle in selfish strife—lo! Freedom weeps,
> Wrong rules the land, and waiting Justice sleeps.
> —*Oliver Wendell Holmes.*

This was not in the land where they were recognized as men, and allowed every proper representation, but where they were ridiculously treated, sneered at, rebuked, and de-

ROACH STREET GRAMMAR SCHOOL.

spised that they have arisen to so great a height of eminence
and altitude of power and recognition. And what is true
of this people, is true of any nation or race of people who
will adopt the wisest and best method of producing peace
with the race among whom they are living, and follow it.
Know this that there is no place teeming with such opportunities and advantages for aiding a people to the
highest plane of civilization. We often charge bad government with most of the wrongs that we have received,
and then seek to check them by changing the government by political measures; and so we say that if the
Wilson bill goes overboard the country will be better. If
the Force bill goes into effect old things will pass away,
and behold all things will become new. If we had some
change in the government that would give all subjects
fair recognition and representation, then this would be a
grand country; but these remedies have been applied in
part, and still we are in want of a panacea. What
then? We see what we want, we feel what we want, but
where is the statesman that ever stood in Congress, in the
Senate, that ever formed the law or constructed a mode
of government that ever met the approval of all people.
God himself has never yet done it, and man need not ex-
pect it from sinful and erring man. The thing for us to
do as a part of this grand republic, is to view the state
of affairs as respecting us in the clearest light, and seek
in the most peaceful way, with the race which we are living and bound to live, the wisest and best method of adjusting them. Hot-headedness and incendiary speeches
never bring peace, but will sink deeeper and deeper the
prejudice and envy that now exist between the two
races, into irreconcilable depth. There is no other way
for us to live with another race but to seek mutual confidence and pursue it. We have tried politics long enough;

19

we have looked forward to the results of political measures in hope of a resurrection from all our ills, and still
we are in our graves without hope of ever living again.
The main thing for us to do is to become reconciled with
our opponents. All the wrongs done us in the South are
not from a natural pesonal hatred or personal envy which
they have against us as a people, but from the relation
which we sustain to the Republican party, and the Republican party to us. The Republican party, in its incip-
iency, guarantees so many things contrary and inherent
to the Democratic principles, and we being in such away
allied to the Republican party, we are ever made subjects
of their hatred and victims of their spleen. If both par-
ties had left off many harsh measures, which have been
used for adjusting the things relative to our condition, we
no doubt long since would have been enjoying the same
features of recognition and representation that any other
unliked element, in the form of people dwelling in the
midst of this great nation, has enjoyed; but however
dark and cloudy may seem the state of affairs, I candidly
believe that there is a turning point for our good, but not
in partyism, nor in political reformation, because all political reforms of to-day are nothing but tricks, and whatever danger and destruction and hurtful results that are
in these reforms, the pcor and ignorant part of the government are the sole victims. See the state of affairs
that is now in our midst; the people of the country, in
wild confusion, snatched the government with their ballot
from the wisest statesman that the nation ever witnessed,
thinking that a new reform would better the condition of the country. Alas! ere they had cleared the polls
and the grand old ship of State had been launched for a
glorious voyage on the sea of Democracy, she sprung a
leak in the lower deck of tariff reform, and she went down
into the gulf of bankruptcy, carrying with her almost

every conceivable form of industry; and as I watched her sinking into the deep, I saw the poor and ignorant class perish with her, while a few of the crew, such as the gold-bugs, leaped from the upper deck upon a little plank that floated upon the rough sea. The Wilson bill tried to save their lives, and all who looked on thought that they would finally be lost, and the plank on which they floated only left a sign of where they went down. Viewing these things as we have, and seeing that we have not as yet obtained any permanent and abiding benefit, let us not grow despondent, nor become discouraged and give up the ship, for things are not even now what they used to be. Many changes have taken place are taking place every day for our good, and as slow as they may seem to come, the day is breaking, and the skies of our political condition are already reddening with a beautiful and glorious sunlight of a charming day of recognition. Only let us do our part well in all the trusts that are vouchedsafed to us by the government, the people, and the nation, and take the advice of the Mighty General of the armies of Isreal, "Be of good courage, and play the men for our people, and for the cities of our God and the Lord, do that that seemeth good to them."

THE NEGRO IN ORATORY.

Delivered before the Teachers' Association of Georgia, June, 1894, at Augusta, Ga.

Mr. President and the Teachers of Georgia assembled:

I esteem the opportunity that has been given me to speak to you to-day as a great privilege, and the sense of the honor conferred by the distinguished presiding officer of this department is so profoundly fraught with your estimation of my ability to speak to you upon this subject that I find it exceedingly difficult to select words to express my feelings of the honor conferred.

The negro, in general, has shown himself fully susceptible of the fullest development in all the arts and sciences that have been discovered in this nineteenth century. As a historian, Johnson has fully shown competency, on the part of the negro, to write the story of facts in details. While he may not have had the time and experience and hereditary associations drawn about him that many of the brightest stars in this sphere of literary sky, yet he has arisen so high in the midst of the mighty constellation, that its brilliancy can be recognized by the most cultured, acute minds in such a powerful way that it compliments the race, not with that narrow circumscribed appellation as the best historian of the Negro race, but as a historian that is equal to any, and unrivaled by many of the Caucasians who have taken their rank in the mighty stellar system of the historians of the world. As a philosopher, I have only to refer to Bishop Henry McNeal Turner, J. W. E. Bowen, E. W. Blyden, and the irresistible and potent reasoner, J. H. Garnett, D.D. If we glance at the inventor's fields, I have only need to ask your investigation of the patent hall of the capitol of the nation, and there you will find ocular demonstration sufficient to evince the genius and ability of the Negro to produce almost anything in the ruder and finer arts that any other being that has a soul can produce. I speak in reference to these things and in the face of the most gorgon prejudice unlimited and uncompromising.

Some may judge me extravagant, but I shall never own it. And now, as I proceed directly upon the subject assigned me for this occasion, I come with no less words of limitation, with no less compromising words for the

Negro in the oratorical field. The Negro is not like the Caucasian race on this line, who have to be drilled and mechanically trained in order to become powerful in the art of speaking, but it is innate and ineradicable in the Negro. He can speak as powerfully and as eloquently, with a very limited vocabulary, as can many of the brightest stars in the oratorical skies, with all their literary attainments. I have heard the greatest speakers of the world. I have sat under the mild and dew-like falling tones of the matchless pulpit orator, Charles H. Spurgeon, the preacher of the nineteenth century; I have heard the brilliant and eloquent Parker of the city of London; I have heard the only Gladstone in the world; the enthusiastic, sensational, and bombastic DeWitt Talmage, Parkhurst, Stors, of Brooklyn, and Gordon of Boston, and Grady of Atlanta. But all their literary attainments, coupled with centuries of hereditary culture, when compared to the natural ability of the Negro, is like the blowing of fog horns in the midst of the mighty peals of a thunderstorm at sea. I do not mean by this that the volume of the Negro's voice is all fuss, but along with this thundering and earthquaking power in oratory comes inspiration that creates men into lions, or fashions them into lambs.. The Negro's power to speak is as charming as the mound-like waters of the Ontario, and as awfully grand as the dizzy heights of the altitude peeks of the Alps of Italy, and as electrifying as the beautiful powers in the forces of nature, and as eloquent as the heavens. This is due in a measure to the clearness and beauty of the Negro's voice.

The voice, in my opinion, and the power to use it, is the most important element in oratory, and this the Negro has without measure. I admit that rhetoric grammar and some elocutionary training play an important part in the art of speaking, but these without a good voice, clear as the ringing of a silver bell, would be as so much ammunition set apart to be used in a great battle without cannon or gun through which to give them force and power for which they are to be used.

The Negro has both the ammunition and the instrument through which to make it powerful. And with this mighty voice of his, with the appliance of these other elements, he has driven the guilty sinner into awe and lifted the Christian into ecstasy; with it he has charmed congress and the chambers of the senate; he has set the legislature into as great a rage as the Euroclydon ever stirred the sea. It has gone over sea and land that the Negro is an orator.

In proof of these strong utterances which I give upon the Negro in oratory, let us call your attention to some of the Negro orators of the past days, such as Toussaint L'Ouverture. It was at a time when the freedom of San Domingo was about to be overthrown, and when this man saw the fleets coming into the waters of the island, he exclaimed, "All France is coming to enslave Sandomingo! We perish!" and turning to his people he said, "Burn the cities; destroy the harvest; tear up the roads with cannon, and poison the wells. Show the white man the hell he comes to make." And at another time his little soul was fired with indignation, and he gave vent to it in these words: "I took up arms for the freedom of my color. France proclaimed it, and she has no right to nullify it. Our liberty is no longer in her hands; it is in our own. We will defend it or perish." The next to be noticed of the past days are the late Revs. Andrew Marshall, Henry Watts, and T. M. Robinson.

It is said that Rev. Andrew Marshall was such a wonderful speaker that the legislature of Georgia at one time gave him a hearing in an entire body. William Cathcart, in speaking o fhim, says his voice was so deep, sonorous, and tender, that its capacity for the expression of pathos was unsurpassed ; and then adds that he was endowed with ready argument and would have been a leader in any age or country. The late Dr. Joseph T. Roberts said that the eloquence of Andrew Marshall in speech could not be told from the most refined and cultured white man. Rev. Henry Watts, of this city, is another factor to be used in demonstrating that the Negro is an orator. This little, slender, wiry-framed man had a voice as clear as a sea of glass and as effective as the eloquence of Pericles, and as powerful as the sudden cracks of thunders of the heavens. It is said at times he soared to the loftiest heights of charming eloquence. So wonderful at times was his description of the city above that his people, and many of those who were of the other race, were forced to exclaim, What a man! Rev. T. M. Robinson, of Macon, is a man that few have power to speak as he, the wonderfulness in humor, wit, and the ready flow of it, clothed with such eloquence and earnestness that few men may be regarded as his equal as a speaker. These men were mighty men, mighty because they were natural men, mighty because they spoke as they knew, and not as others. I am one of those men that believe in the development of men, as we do nature.

There is some part of nature that can be developed, and some part, if touched by human art, becomes as ugly as hell and as ridiculous as an army of mosquitoes, dressed in soldiers' uniform. I have seen men attempt the improvement of springs, of natural scenes in the forest, and the attempt in nearly every case has only proven to be the destruction of their beauty and naturalness. What hand can make more beautiful and attractive Manhattan Island, the exquisite grandeur of the verdant-covered Alps of Switzerland, of Niagara, and of the grand Pyrenees system. Nature has done her work too well for man in his imperfection to improve. The ax has been applied to the tree, the knife to the flower, the hammer and drill to the spring, for their fuller development, to array them with more beauty; but in nearly every case the tree has died, the flower withered, the spring has dried up. How true is this when applied to the natural endowed ability of the speaker. Many a powerful speaker among us has been made weak by the ax of conventionalism, by the artificial knife and mechanical art in speaking. The first men never knew it; they spoke from the heart to the heart, unconscious of the key or pitch of voice. Men may be taught to move their hands and head, and they may use them on some occasions when they are merely formal, but when men are fired from danger of country, liberty, and property by the hostility of some invaders, the natural man forgets artificial and conventional speaking, and leaves it for less dangerous moments. Oratory is natural, and the proof of it is found in the men of the Negro race, who have not passed under the polishing stone of the elocutionist. The Negro, as an orator, speaks with his mouth open, with his eyes open, his hands open, and it is not long before all that hear him are in the same condition. This was the character of Andrew Marshall, Henry Watts, and is the manner of T. M. Robinson. Do not mistake me—I believe in trained speakers, but not out of their element. If the rock is more attractive and beautiful in the rough, do not destroy the beauty by attempting to improve it. And these men I have mentioned are and were more beautiful in the rough than they could have possibly been if polished. And now, as I proceed to speak of men of broader erudition and training in the art of speaking, the same principle, so far as the naturalness of the orator is concerned, must be applied to them as to the former, if they would be powerful and natural speakers. What has given Robert El-

liott, Richard R. Wright, J. B. Davis, J. C. Price, Crogman, Ellis of Savannah, William E. Holmes, Dr. C. T.
Walker, W. G. Johnson, Silas X. Floyd, W. J. White,
Douglas, Bruce, Walter H. Brooks, Langston, Booker
Washington, Grandison, Cyrus Wilkins, Vann, Lucy
Laney, Ida B. Wells—I say, what has given these men
and women their position in the grand stellary host of
the brilliant orators of to-day, but the same energy,
earnestness, and eloquence that is found in Robinson,
Watts, and Marshall.   Now, in conclusion, hear a few
extracts from these men's speeches.

Dr. Walker on the *Sunset at Sea:*

" We saw the sun set, and as night put on her sable
robe, his light went down in the west, its beautiful rays
lingering and irradiating the heavens for quite awhile.
Soon after sunset the new moon came out in her silvery
sheen and stationed herself nearly over our steamer, and
smiled upon the sea.   The stars then came out one by
one, taking their places in their diamond sockets, and
gave us the benefit of their effulgent brightness, while
the mountain, on the other side, were covered with snow."

Professor William E. Holmes on the *Negro Problem:*

" There are three steps.   The first is to make solid,
moral progress.   I want our people to recognize the fact
that there is rottenness and evil in society, and to remm-
ber that until this is remedied we must keep our mouths
shut.   The second step is to make common social progress, as we are too free and familiar, though not wishing to underrate the kindly hospitality, not wishing that
we should be social icebergs, yet dignity is to be cultivated.   Much that is called politeness is downright vul-
garity.   The third step is to make sound, mental progress.
We must have men of learning that are broad and deep."

Robert Elliott, in the house of Congress, speaking of
the much-honored Alexander Stephens, said :

"I meet him only as an adversary, nor shall age or any other consideration restrain me from saying that he now offers this government, which he has done his utmost to destroy, a very poor return for its magnanimous treatment, to come here to seek to continue, by the assertion of doctrines obnoxious to the true principles of our government, the burdens and oppressions which rests upon five millions of his countrymen, who never failed to lift their earnest prayers for the success of this government, when the gentleman was seeking to break up the union of the States, and to blot the American Republic from the galaxy of nations."

And as I leave off these recitations I wish to make a suggestion to the teachers assembled in this beautiful city, that they resolve from this time on to exhume these dead heroes, patriarchs, and their speeches, and see to it that hereafter the declamations of the boys and girls under us in school shall have their speeches and declamations made up of some one of the noble heroes, patriarchs, and orators of this race. Let Cicero and Demosthenes sleep in their almost mystical graves. Bring about a resurrection of Toussaint, Elliott, and let white robes and crowns and palms of victory be given to them, and the God of Heaven will break upon us the mighty literary millennium of the Negro race. wherein will dwell the beauty and grandeur of a cultured race. And old things will have passed away; all things will have become new.

THE TO-DAY AND TO-MORROW OF THE COLORED MAN.

By REV. SAMUEL GRAVES, D.D.,

Professor of Theology in Atlanta Baptist Seminary.

"Though ye have lain among the pots, yet shall ye be as the wings of a dove, covered with silver, and her feathers with yellow gold.'' —Psalm 68: 13.

The imagery of the text is highly poetical and expressive. It denotes restoration to beauty ; exaltation to honor ; out of degradation and vileness. The Psalmist sees a bedraggled dove, defiled by the soot and filth of an Eastern inn, hid away among the cooking utensils. This dove is to be sought out by a loving and gentle hand, and restored to the beauty and freedom native to her, and which have made the dove in all ages a symbol of purity, fleetness, and peace.

So God had brought his people Israel again and again out of the oppressions and defilement of the heathen, among whom they had often been carried, and had set them in honor and made them glorious among the nations with the beauty of the Lord their God upon them.

He had rescued them from Egyptian bondage, from Midianite and Philistine oppression, from the captivity in Babylon. And the text looks forward, as many believe, to yet unfilled promises, when Israel shall be again gathered and restored to the land which God gave in covenant to Abraham, Isaac, and Jacob.

And since the Word of God, " as we read," is of no private interpretation, the promises herein written may be claimed by all—whether individuals, nations, or races who come into similar relations to God, which those stood in to whom the promises were originally given.

How applicable this language is to every true believer; born as we all have been of a corrupt seed, with a damaged moral nature, by which we were children of wrath, how like the dove in the text, soiled and despoiled of grace and beauty, but as redeemed and saved by the grace of God, made glorious in the righteousness of Christ.

So too, of this lost world in its alienation from God, debauched and defiled by sin, yet redeemed by Christ, and yet to become the abode of righteousness when the new heavens and the new earth shall emerge from the ruin of sin.

I wish, however, as already suggested, to apply these words as in some sense prophetic of what, in his providence, God will yet do, indeed has already begun so signally to do, for the colored people of this country, and through them, of what he will ultimately do for Africa. The text very graphically expresses their former condition. They have "lain among the pots."

Africa has well been called " The Dark Continent."

For 250 years her wretched sons and daughters had been despoiled of the right of manhood and the virtue of womanhood; bought and sold and worked like cattle, under a——————of servitude, at——————cast-off as an enormity. ——————————————within these few years Africa has been opened to the light of the gospel and Christian civilization, and the nations of Europe are parceling it out among themselves to conquer and to colonize. In the exaltation of manhood which this century has brought about, the colored man has been lifted out of chattlehood, and in civil rights set beside his white brother—a citizen, a property holder, a voter—an integral part of our national life and unity; an element in our Christian civilization. He is here, and here to remain, for weal or for woe to himself and to us. His destiny is bound up with the destiny of the republic. What is good for him is good for the nation; and what is ill for him is ill for the nation.

When emancipation was first talked of, the question which sprung to thousands of anxious lips was, "What shall we do with the Negro?" But the spirit of Christ in its breadth and helpfulness, changed the question, and we asked, "What shall we do for the Negro?" The practical answer and outcome of this question has been, by our own denomination, the founding of a score of schools for the education of both male and female pupils, with equal opportunities and accommodation for both; 216 teachers, 4,861 pupils, an endowment fund of $750,-000, and an expenditure since the war of $2,300,000. Of the pupils in those schools last year, 416 were preparing for the Christian ministry, an increased number for mission work in districts and scattered through the darkest places in our own country, and others who are preparing to go to Africa; 1,756 were preparing to teach, others for various purposes, or in their own language, "to make men and women of themselves."

In these schools, I suppose, between 20,000 and 30,-000 have received an education which has fitted them very well for the business and duties of life.

The South itself, though at first it looked with disfavor upon this work, has become certainly the most liberal minded to appreciate the value of these schools, and has been stimulated to make larger provisions for the colored people in the public schools of the South.

The effect of this has already been, and in the course of a generation will be, of incalculable benefit. It is inspiring the colored man with self-respect, it is fitting him as nothing else can, for citizenship in this land where the citizen is the sovereign. Neither the Emancipation Proclamation nor the amendments to the Constitution could do this. They only furnished the opportunity. Christian training, patiently, lovingly pursued through the years, alone can bring these things to perfection.

Now, we justify what has been done for the colored people, and urge that it be continued and enlarged for the following reasons, viz.: Because, 1. It is but paying a debt which we owe. We have had the well-nigh unrequited toil of the colored man for seven generations. The wealth of the country, especially of the South, before the war was largely due to him. The rice, the cotton, the corn, the sugar were products of his hand, for which in return he received little but the coarsest food and clothing and rudest shelter. " And the hire of the laborer who had reaped our fields, which by us was kept back, cried and still cries in our ears and in the ears of the Lord God Sabaoth " for a full satisfaction. God is sometimes slow in settling his accounts, but in time they are squared with interest. And this debt we are paying as best we can by what we are doing for our creditors by these Christian schools.

2. We owe it to him because slavery starved his intellect, kept his moral nature in degradation, shut up the Bible and made the teachings of it to him a crime. True, he came here, or rather he was captured and brought here a pagan; but it was our Christian duty to him as our weaker brother, to teach him and enlighten him for whom Christ died, as he did for us.

We owe it to him because we robbed him of the most precious boon of life—all that the dear old Saxon word "home" can mean. For neither his wife nor his children were his own, marriage itself, the oldest, most sacred, and essential institution which God has established for the welfare of the race, slavery degraded into a concubinage which darkened and damned the life of the colored man; we are therefore in these things indebted to this race, and common honesty requires us to pay these debts in full, and with interest. God, who requires that which is past, yet holds us responsible.

3. We owe it to them as Baptists. One-third of our more than three millions of Baptists in this conntry are among the colored people. In their simplicity and sincerity, as in the days of slavery, they heard the Bible read and their warm and ardent natures were touched and renewed by the spirit of God. The way of obedience was plain. They did not know enough, as some seem to have, when they heard the Bible read, to be anything else but Baptists. And as they become better educated and can read the Bible for themselves, it only makes them firmer and more intelligent Baptists.

In Georgia alone there are reported 188,000 members, compressing into 1,400 churches. The pastors have, for the most part, been godly men who knew Christ and the way of salvation, though with scarcely any culture, who yet have believed and taught for doctrine many absurd things. But the schools which have been planted and so vigorously worked among them all through the South since the war, have made the demand for a very different order of men as pastors and teachers—men and women who can feed the open intellect of the people and guide them into right ways of thinking.

And we are sending out from our schools every year hundreds of young men who are tolerably well fitted to preach the gospel intelligently and to guide the affairs of the church discreetly in receiving members, in receiving and training the young. We send them out staunch temperance men, and they are doing a most needed work among their people in this line.

And with these are going out hundreds of Christian young women, many of whom become the wives of these pastors, who work faithfully with their husbands, and set the example of the cultured Christian family in the community where they settle. And this is of the very first importance. The family is God's institution. It is the oldest. It was meant to be an agency even higher than the church for the training of the race in higher and nobler living. No race can rise higher than its families. Pure, virtuous, intellectual families are the bed-rock and bulwark of a nation's safety, and the most inspiring and assured hope of all its prosperities. They are the electric lights to be kindled all over these yet dark regions in the South. Christian homes, Christian churches, Christian schools, which shall be fed from these Christian seminaries, as from electric plants goes forth the subtle fluid that flashes thousands of lights over our cities.

4. We owe it to them on the ground of the great commission, "Go ye into all the world, and preach the gospel to every creature." We have just been reviewing a century of foreign mission work, and it is the grandest record of the ages. There is scarcely a nation, race or tribe, save in the depths of Africa, to which the gospel has not been sent. God be praised! But here right at home, in darkest America, in what is known as the Black Belt, and bordering on the Gulf of Mexico, are thousands of colored families in which scarce a ray of light from these Christian schools has shone, as ignorant and superstitious and vicious, and in circumstances even more appalling than when Lincoln's proclamation brought hope and freedom to the race.

We know how hard it is to lift men and women out of such a state; how impossible it is to grow virtue in such a soil; to build the granite columns of manhood, the delicate shafts of pure, chaste womanhood, on such a morass as this. How discouraging, how impossible. But there is a subsoil, we believe, even underneath such bogs as these, which, concreted with the gospel and the grace of God, will make bed-rock, and we are going to find it, deep down as it lies, and build on it the kingdom of God and the beautiful and abiding structure of Christian homes, with the integrities that strengthen and the virtues that adorn life.

Again, we owe it to ourselves, as a safeguard to the nation. The Negro problem was not solved by the war. The war, for the time, only complicated it. Lincoln's proclamation and the fourteenth amendment have not settled it. It still confronts us with the face of a sphinx.

This problem has, in the providence of God, been put upon us to solve. Have we the wisdom, the patience, the patriotism, the perseverance, the large-minded Christian helpfulness, to find and work out the solution? This is one and not the least of these great issues that confront us to-day. The labor, the drink, and the race questions, how are we going to meet them?

In the ignorance and the vices which the colored man brought out of slavery, we have a perpetual menace to our free institutions which we know have their bottom safety, not in the wealth and enterprise of our people— to which such magnificent temples are being built, as the gods of this nation—but in the intelligence and virtue and godliness of the citizen; not of a class, but of the people as a whole.

The danger which threatens us to-day, as every thinking man knows, is an ignorant, irresponsible ballot, and the unprincipled recklessness with which it is used, coupled with the congested wealth of our rapidly increasing millionaires.

We have not yet passed the experimental period of our free institutions. Can they bear, without breaking down, these enormous strains?

20

What labor and capital have alike most to fear are the ignorance and vice and cupidity that can be marshalled by demagogues at the polls, to annul the will of the upright, intelligent citizens of the land.

And no use of money can be more judiciously or remuneratively made in this generation than that which will carry intelligence and virtue, and the thrift, contentment and safety which these beget, into the homes of ignorance and vice, and there build up true, responsible, self-respecting, self-directing man and womanhood.

Again, a solid *white* South against a solid *black* South, which the late Mr. Grady and his followers would bring about, has in it the germs of a *race war*, as do also the obstructions put in the way of colored voters, the threats and actual violence used to prevent their voting—which tend to the same end. And yet it is true that large numbers of colored voters are not competent to cast an intelligent vote as are thousands of ignorant foreigners in the North who are rushed into citizenship. It might greatly help to solve this race problem if some change could be effected in politics that would divide the white and the colored voters into something like equality. But that may be long in coming. Now our schools are fitting the colored man, as nothing else can, for intelligent citizenship. The pupil is taught not only his rights—he knows them already—but patience and self-restraint, and to deserve his rights, though for the present he be deprived of them. He is taught economy, thrift, to acquire property, to get homes; a better mode of living; these homely but necessary virtues. Piety, intelligence, thrift, are the trinity which is to lift them to the level of true man and womanhood. And so our work is rounding out our pupils, if we can keep them long enough, in all these best qualities of citizenship.

Let this work go on, as it has for the last twenty years,

and the colored vote may yet save the country from the anarchy which socialism and communism, allied to vice and ignorance and discontent, are to-day threatening us with, and which come largely also from our foreign population.

There is another danger which many far-sighted among us apprehend, and of which now and then we may see the danger signal, and what recent and very adroit but suspicious movement too plainly indicated, viz.: *Romanism*, as a combined political power. Those who have studied the matter know very well that Rome has always carried her religion into her politics. Her old-time dogma, from which she has never receded since the days of Hilderbrand, that the civil power is subject to the spiritual; that the Pope of right shall dominate kingdoms and cabinets and presidents; and that all she calls *heresy* must be put down where she bears rule. And Rome counts nothing so great and dangerous a heresy as *free religious thought.*

If some issue which wily Jesuitism may yet bring upon us, the *colored vote*, I believe, would be a unit against it. You cannot well make a Roman Catholic of the Negro. He does not want any priest or proxy to come between him and Christ. He wants to go himself to headquarters. And who knows but God is raising up in the South among these despised men of color, whose fathers and mothers we are to-day teaching, a *power* by which he will yet save this nation from perils, even greater than that of the rebellion, out of which, as a civil power, they have come. And whose prayers, from lowly cabins and forest glens, did as much in the great hour of our country's need to save it as did the statesmanship of Lincoln or the canons of Grant ; nay, were rather the backlying forces which, in the providence of God, gave efficiency to all these. And so it seems to me that God may be providing a reserve force to meet any such like

emergency that may hereafter rise in the unfoldings of
our national life.

The colored man is American born ; his home is here,
and he loves it.   He is tractable and responsive to the
highest and best influences.   He is naturally religious.
According to the last census, one in three of every colored citizen is a church member.   He is loyal, as was so
remarkably seen in his fidelity to his master's family during the war.   Any other race would have mutinied under
a like crisis.   He has in him the quality of true courage,
as was seen when our colored troops met with such heroism the shock of battle.

And one may see in these traits, when redeemed and
rectified from the harms of slavery, a justification for the
hopes I have spoken of, both for himself and for the
country.

Never in the history of civilization has a race so long
in servitude made such strides in all direction of progress
as the colored people in these last thirty years.   It is the
wonder of the world, and will so be recorded by the pen
of history.   It was four hundred years after the exodus
from Egypt before the Israelites had established a permanent government.   Have not the wings of the soiled dove
been growing *white* like silver, and her feathers like as
pure gold?

The work, therefore, which we are doing in the South,
by the aid so largely of Northen sympathies and help, is
paying a debt which before God we sacredly owe the
colored man; is averting, I believe, a great peril; is building, I seem to see, a bulwark for the nation against dangers which threaten its highest well-being, if not its very
existence, when times of coming peril may hereafter
arise.   It is caring, as we are bound to do, for our own
denomination.   While we are building such universities
as Chicago in the North for our people, we are not for-

getting the wants that appeal to us from the South. And
finally, but more important, it may be, than all, we are
doing in these Christian schools in the South what will
have a direct and vital bearing upon the redemption and
Christian civilization of the continent of Africa.

The belief grows upon me that in the providence of
God the colored people in this country are the agents
which he has chosen and is preparing for this great and
final missionary work. What agency seems so fitted by
nature to do this work? The colored man is of the same
race, and race affinities are very strong. He will encounter no such prejudices as the white man. He can
endure the climate, and his sympathies draw him to the
"fatherland." In this view may we not see the hand of
God in this matter? And it is always safe, nay, more
than safe, always sure of successi—ndeed, success is won
in no other way than along the line in which God's providence moves. Find these, follow these, and you cannot
fail, whatever obstacle you may encounter.

I do not pose as a pɪ ɪphet, but I believe with all my
heart there are possibilities in the colored race which God
means to develop and use in giving to the world a better
type of civilization than we, the Anglo-Saxons, have
wrought out.

There is a skeptical drift in the Anglo-Saxon mind
which needs to be corrected by a deeper and more earnest faith, a faith which seems native to the colored race,
in order to give to our common Christianity, and the civilization based upon it, their best and fullest development.
Christianity, while world-wide in its adaptations, is yet
Eastern in its origin, and peculiarly adapted to the Eastern mind and modes of thought; and the colored races
are natives of the East. And further, there is a rough,
overbearing, domineering quality in the white races that
we have inherited from our old Saxon ancestors, which

has done service through the past ages in conquering the savagery of nature and bringing its forces into the service of man. This needs to be toned down and rendered more amiable and catholic and kingly before we shall realize that condition of society which the gospel of Christ points to, and for which the best aspirations of the human heart yearn; I mean the *brotherhood* of man.

And so I believe. I hope in "the good time coming," when these prejudices against the colored man will pass away with his ignorance and vices; when the white man and his black brother—the Saxon and the Negro, the Aryan and mongrel--will stand side by side, each bringing of his own peculiar gifts of heart and brain, to work in loving rivalries towards the realization of the kingdom of God on earth.

But we must be patient and remember that "one day is with the Lord as a thousand years. Nations are of slow growth. It took five hundred years after the bondage in Egypt to rear a Jew of Solomon's time, and as long to rear a Greek of Pericles' time; seven hundred years to make a Roman of the Augustine age, and a thousand years to build an Englishman, an Anglo-American of to-day. And what may five hundred, nay, half that time do, when the world is moving so much faster than of old, for the colored man and the black races of the East, if they but have the chance, and we but do our duty toward them, and whose day seems to be dawning, or perhaps returning after a cycle of four thousand years, when Egypt taught Greece her letters and was the leader of the world's thought.

And this confidence is strengthened in my own mind by such a series of manifest providences of God as are circling around and centering upon him. Mark you, God suffered the violence and cupidity of the slave-dealer to bring him to this land. Two hundred and fifty years of slavery, with its crimes against humanity and heaven, was, after all, an uplift from the savagery of Africa. He learned of the true God, the way of salvation; and crude as his notions were, the light of these truths took hold of his deeply religious nature, while the wrongs he suffered drove him more and more to God as the hope and refuge of the oppressed. This rough discipline was God's school in which he learned the *alphabet* of trust and the rudiments of something higher.

And then, when Livingstone was finishing his sacrificial work for Africa, and was dying on his knees by her great lakes, and our own Stanley was making ready for the bold adventures which brought Africa into the sympapathies of other nations, and laid bare the arteries of her great central valley, with its five thousand miles of navigable rivers, God snapped, by the bolt of war, the fetters of the black man and made him a free citizen of this, the most Christian nation on earth.

And then what? In line with the same providence, God moved the heart of the great North to found and furnish these Christian schools, and by a marvelous enthusiasm to bring thousands and tens of thousands of colored youth into them, where, under able and godly teachers, they are being trained for leadership among their people here at home. And more, is calling some of the noblest of them to go back to the fatherland with the Gospel which builds civilization and saves men. Does not this look like God's work? What else, pray, can it be?

And what can be plainer in the light of these providences, and in the direction in which they have been moving for the last thirty years, than that God intends—and has been ripening events for it—that the colored Christians of America should become the regenerators of Africa, and carry their own English tongue, born of the Bible, as no other speech on earth has been, and to plant

there very largely the Christian faith and church as we
Baptists hold them, in their New Testament simplicity
and spirituality, and so make Africa largely a Baptist
continent?

The spirit of mission to Africa is in our schools in the
South. Already a number have gone there, and are
doing excellent service. Choice young men and women
from Africa are being sent by our missionaries there to
be educated in this country and to return.

Who knows but that in the rapidity with which the
world is now moving, there may be, by the close of the
twentieth century, a civilization on the banks of the Congo
which shall command the respect of the world, and em-
body the best elements of that upon the Thames and the
Potomac? It is like God to work in just this way.
"Though thou hast lain with the pots, yet shall ye be as
the wings of a dove."

And now further to show what the to-day of the colored man promises for his to-morrow, let me quote a passage from a recent number of the *North American Review*.

A Southern man, writing on the Negro Question, has
used these words, which the reviewer takes for his text:
"The Negro has made no progress since the emancipation, not because he was a siave, but because he has not
the faculty to rise above slavery. Twenty-seven years
have gone since the war, and the Negro is the barber, the
boot-black, the hotel waiter. Here and there a lawyer,
now and then a doctor. There used to be good mechanics
among them in slavery times. Where are they now?"

In reply to this, says the reviewer: "Twenty-seven
years ago, forbidden by law to read, without a school;
to-day, 25,530 schools. Then, not a child in school; now,
2,250,000 have learned to read, and most of them to
write; while according to the census of 1890, there are
now in colored schools 238,229 pupils. Twenty-seven

years ago a negro school-teacher would have been a
curiosity; to-day, by the grace of God and their own grit,
there are 20,000. Twenty-seven years ago it was thought
that the colored man was incapable of higher education;
to-day they have 150 schools of advanced education.
Among these are seven colleges, presided over by colored men, three of whom were slaves twenty-seven years
ago. And what was the colored ministry? Now there
are 1,000 college-bred Negro pastors in the land. Twenty-
seven years ago there were two newspapers edited by
colored men; to-day, 154. Then there were two negro
attorneys; now, 160. Then, three doctors; now, 749
And mark, 247 colored students in the universities of
Europe."

Look now at the question of accumulating property.
Twenty-seven years ago the entire taxable property of
the Negro was $12,000; to-day it is $264,000,000. And
a change like this has taken place in twenty-seven years,
and very largely by *our schools* which have so stimulated
the aptitudes and energies and economies of the colored
people. Now, in view of these showings, have not the
wings of the soiled and bedraggled dove "grown white
with silver and her feathers yellow with gold?"

These are the things I preach to our friends in the
North, and I bring them to you, young men and women,
for your encouragement and inspiration in your noble purpose to make the most of yourselves, and to look faithfully to the same end among your people. Be true to
youselves by becoming Christians, for unless you do, you
will still lack the best and highest qualities of manhood
and womanhood; and then consecrate all you have and
are to the service of God and your fellowmen.

"ALL THINGS WORK TOGETHER FOR GOOD."

By DEACON NICK HOLMES,

At the Pastor's Twelfth Anniversary of Friendship Baptist Church·

From the shoemaker's trade to the pulpit, with which trade he supported his mother and other children for a number of years, their father being dead.

When converted he joined Hill's Baptist Church at Athens, Ga., and felt that he was called to the ministry. He was licensed and served the above named church as a deacon.

Seeing that he could not prosecute work without an education he decided to make the sacrifice to come to Atlanta and attend the Atlanta Baptist Seminary. Without visible means of support, he entered school almost without any money at all. In 1882 he was called to the pastorate of Friendship Baptist Church. Here he found a debt against the church of $2,500, and a number of minor debts too numerous to be mentioned. The debts were canceled in about eighteen months. Then came the remodeling of the church, floor raised, new pews, gas fixtures, reslating of the house, which cost about $3,000. When all this was paid we had a jubilee meeting, rejoicing over the great victory that we had achieved.

In 1885 came the great prohibition fight against the great monster alcohol, to which he rose in the scales of eminence as a speaker second to none in the campaign, and thus he continued. At different places in the State he was called to speak against the monster king alcohol, and in Virginia and other places as a speaker and pulpit orator.

There are few that are able to compete with him. Some men are born for great things, and some are born for small things. And it is not written why some men are born at all, but " all things work together for good."

R. B. FERRELL,

CONTRACTOR, MECHANIC, HOUSE BUILDER.

Few men in the city of Atlanta, on account of their skill in the line of professions which they follow, demand more respect and credit than Mr. Ferrell.

His sober habits and promptness, and the manner in which he turns off all the work which he contracts to do, together with the great satisfaction which his work gives, has brought to him eminence in his business and a wide and lucrative field in which to labor. Doubtless no young man among the colored citizens of Atlanta has overcome more, gone through more to gain recognition in the city than Mr. Ferrell. He is one of those young men who believes that "if the will not is removed, the cannots will slip loose like a bowknot." In other words, Mr. Ferrell is one of those men that does not wait for something to "turn up," but is constantly turning something up.

On many of the beautiful hills and planes of this great city stands many a beautiful cottage spun from the architectural plans drawn and prosecuted by himself, which is a lasting illustration and recommendation to him as a mechanic.

Mr. Ferrell, like the most of the young men of his race, being surrounded with many hardships and privations of life, had but little opportunity for obtaining an education. He entered Storr's school when he was at the age of fourteen, and remained until he was seventeen. He was, on account of the poverty of his father, compelled to stop school. His father, being a carpenter by trade, took him in the shop with him, where he learned his first lessons in house-building. By his aptness he was soon made an acceptable workman.

In 1891 he married Miss Minnie Strong, a very pleasant, genial, and economical woman, to whom he attributes the success that he has made in life.

Mr. Ferrell owns some very valuable property in the city, from which he gathers a very satisfactory income, besides a very beautiful cottage home, neatly furnished with those things which make a home comfortable, pleasant, and cosy, of which his affable wife is queen.

Mr. Robert Ferrell was born in Macon county, Ala., in the year 1850. Soon after his advent into this life his parents came to Atlanta, bringing their infant son with them, where he has resided ever since.

Since his coming here, the facts in this sketch are the fruits of his labor. Mr. Ferrell is a man of strong Christian character, great charity, warm-hearted, and of a pleasing and generous impulse. It might be said of him that he allows no opportunity to escape for doing good.

REV. JOSEPH CONYERS.

A PREACHER—FIRST-CLASS BRICKMASON.

This character springs into life in Carroll county, of Georgia, at Sandhill postoffice, in 1852. At four years of age he was carried by his mother to Haralson county, where he remained until emancipation. He then returned to Carrollton and worked on the railroad for some considerable time.

Feeling the roughness which came to him in this class of labor, he was determined to find something that was more elevating, and in 1868 he went to Macon, Georgia, where he engaged in a small business, such as young men make for themselves with a small capital.

It was at this place that he was converted and made a profession in Christ, and was baptized by Rev. William Plant.

In 1870 he came to the city of Atlanta without anything. On arriving here he became acquainted with Mr. Felix Sours, who was a brickmason, under whom he went to work as an apprentice for the brickmason trade. Being very apt and industrious, he soon became very efficient. His treatment by Mr. Sours was so bad, and he now being able to pilot his own way, he leaves Mr Sours, who was paying him seventy-five cents a day, and establishes a business of his own. He had large contracts given to him, which were completed with satisfaction to those who granted them, and with credit to himself.

He was a poor boy, brought up without many of the advantages that other boys had for education, having the greater part of his juvenile life the responsibility of looking after the smaller brothers and sisters, who were in early life with himself, bereft of the care, love and tender instruction of a mother ; nevertheless, with whatever embarrassments or disadvantages, he was determined to push ahead and make the most of himself

In 1879 he was licensed to preach the gospel of the Son of God by Rev. Frank Quarles, the pastor of Friendship Baptist Church, in the city of Atlanta. At this period he began to feel more than ever the need of education. Accordingly in 1879 when the Atlanta Baptist Seminary was opened in the city of Atlanta, he enrolled himself as one of its pupils, and studied here for three or four years under Rev. Joseph T. Roberts, D.D., LL.D. Mr. Conyers had now come to better days in his life. His hardships, in a great meusure were, were now over, and he was able to live very pleasantly and comfortably In 1871 he was married to Miss Alice Collier, a very thoroughgoing, industrious, refined, and economical lady to whom Mr. Conyers, in the kindest words, attributes all that he has been able to accomplish.

He owns in the city of Atlanta some two or three lots with houses, to the amount of eight thousand dollars ($8,000.00), all of which he has accumulated and saved out of his hard labors.

In 1886 he was ordained to the gospel ministry by present pastor of Friendship Baptist Church, Rev. E. R. Carter, the author of this book. Since that day he has served the First Baptist Church, at Acworth, Ga., for three years, and was an active worker and teacher in his own church from which he received his ordination. In 1887 he moved to Chattanooga, Tenn., with his industrious wife. He has been able to accumulate a very pleasant amount of property at this place, working with the trowel and hammer in the week days and preaching the gospel on Sunday, when the B Street church was without a pastor, Rev. Conyers supplied the pulpit for three months. He was also pastor of the Pipeville Baptist Church, Tennessee, for two years.

We can see at this point of Mr. Conyers' life that through the varied scenes which he has passed, he has eaten no idle bread. Since the day that he arrived at Chattanooga he has been able to accumulate enough to purchase one of the finest lots in the city of Chattanooga, on which he has built a most elegant, commanding and stately building, which will compare favorably to any business house in the city. It lifts itself three stories, with four store rooms on the first floor and eighteen rooms on the second floor, and an elegant hall on the third floor.

This building is very tastefully trimmed with marble and is built of pressed brick, and is valued at five thousand dollars, making the property of Mr. Conyers in the city of Atlanta and Chattanooga all worth forty ($40,000) thousand dollars, all of which is contributed to the industry of Mr. and Mrs. Conyers' economical and saving characteristics. These two are a happy pair of noble Christians and generous-hearted citizens.

INDEX.